BANGLADESH

BANGLADESH
Writings on 1971, Across Borders

Edited by

Rakhshanda Jalil *and* Debjani Sengupta

Orient BlackSwan

BANGLADESH: WRITINGS ON 1971, ACROSS BORDERS

ORIENT BLACKSWAN PRIVATE LIMITED

Registered Office
3-6-752 Himayatnagar, Hyderabad 500 029, Telangana, India
e-mail: centraloffice@orientblackswan.com

Other Offices
Bengaluru, Chennai, Guwahati, Hyderabad, Kolkata,
Mumbai, New Delhi, Noida, Patna, Visakhapatnam

First published by Orient Blackswan Private Limited 2022

ISBN 978-93-5442-212-6

Typeset in
Adobe Jenson Pro 11.5/13.4 *by*
Le Studio Graphique, Gurgaon 122 007

Printed in India at
Akash Press, New Delhi 110 020

Published by
Orient Blackswan Private Limited
3-6-752 Himayatnagar, Hyderabad 500 029, Telangana, India
e-mail: info@orientblackswan.com

Contents

Publishers' Acknowledgements

For granting permission to reproduce copyrighted material used in this volume, the publishers would like to thank the following.

Kaiser Haq and *BDNews24*, for his essay 'With the Hamzapur Tigers', previously published in *BDNews24*, 16 December 2013, Dhaka. Reproduced by permission of the author and publishers.

Nandini Gupta and *Parabaas*, for her translation of the poem 'Shey Baro Shukher Shomay Noy, Shey Baro Anander Shomay Noy' by Shakti Chattopadhyay (1967), previously published as 'No Time for Cheer, Not a Happy Time This' in *Parabaas*, June 2020, Kolkata. Reproduced by permission of the translator and *Parabaas*.

Suraiya Elias and Andalib Elias, for permission to translate the story 'Raincoat' by Akhtaruzzaman Elias, included here as 'The Raincoat'.

Rakhshanda Jalil, for her translation of the story 'Neend' by Intizar Husain, previously published as 'Sleep'. Reproduced in arrangement with HarperCollins Publishers India Private Limited from the book *The Death of Sheherzad* by Intizar Husain, translated by Rakhshanda Jalil and first published by them. All rights reserved. Reproduced by permission of Seagull Books.

Selina Hossain, for permission to translate her story 'Amina O Madinar Golpo', included here as 'The Story of Amina and Madina'.

Bashir Mansoor, for the story 'Habeel aur Qabeel ke Darmiyan Ek Taweel Makaalma' by Rasheed Amjad, included here as 'A Long Conversation between Cain and Abel'.

Shehreen Ataur Khan, for her translation of the story 'Durba Ghash, Tiner Gher, O Alakananda' by Papree Rahman, previously published in *Lilies, Lanterns and Lullabies*, edited by Niaz Zaman (Dhaka: Writers.ink, 2014).

Khalid Hasan, for his translation of the story 'Apni Apni Sachaiyan' by Masood Ashar, previously published as 'Versions of Truth' in *Versions of Truth: Urdu Short Stories from Pakistan,* edited by Khalid Hasan and Faruq Hassan, copyright ©1983. Reproduced by permission of Jeffrey Hasan/Estate of Khalid Hasan.

Shabnam Nadiya and The University Press Limited, Bangladesh, for her translation of the story 'Gura Morich' by Shaheen Akhtar, previously published as 'She Knew the Use of Powdered Red Chillies' in *Fault Lines: Stories of 1971,* edited by Niaz Zaman and Asif Farrukhi, copyright © 2008 The University Press Limited, Bangladesh. Reproduced by permission of the author and publishers.

Massarrat Abid, for permission to translate the story 'Zabaan-e Khanjar' by Agha Sohail, included here as 'The Dagger's Tongue'.

Wasi Ahmed, for permission to translate his story 'Khancha O Acheen Pakhi', included here as 'The Odd Bird of the Cage'.

Sameena Nazeer, for permission to translate her story 'Paan Ka Beeda', included here as 'Betel Leaf'.

Trishna Basak, for permission to translate her story 'Shobuj Card', included here as 'Green Card'.

Tariq Rahman, for his story 'Bingo'.

Jhumur Panday, for permission to translate her story 'Jotawali', included here as 'The Woman with the Matted Locks'.

Raihana Hasan, for the extract from her novel *Sips from a Broken Teacup: Sketches from Life on an Assamese Tea Plantation* (Karachi: Ushba Publishing International, 2011), pp. 178–191.

Razia Fasih Ahmad, for the extracts from her novel *Breaking Links* (Pakistan: Oxford University Press, 2007).

Sorayya Khan, for the extract from her novel *Noor* (USA: University of North Carolina Wilmington, 2006), excerpted by permission of the author and publishers.

Yukta Publishers, Bangladesh, for the poem 'Proshnateet' by Alokeranjan Dasgupta, from *Nowalkishore Eseche Buker Toley,* copyright © 2013 Yukta Publishers, Bangladesh. Translated by

Subhoranjan Dasgupta and included here as 'Beyond Question', by permission of the publishers.

Mohammad Haikal Hashmi, for permission to translate the poem 'Mohenjodaro' by Naushad Noori.

Moushumi Bhowmik, for her song 'Joshor Road', which previously appeared in the booklet accompanying the album *Weaver of Words/Ekhono Golpo Lekho* by Tareque Masud, Catherine Masud and Moushumi Bhowmik (Dhaka, 1999).

Ali Madeeh Hashmi and Faiz Foundation Pakistan, for permission to translate 'Dhaka Se Wapsi Par' by Faiz Ahmad Faiz, included here as 'Upon Returning from Dhaka'.

Jharna Rahman, for permission to translate her poem 'Maanchitrer Pranpurush', included here as 'The Hero of Our Nation'.

Afzal Ahmad Syed, for permission to translate his poem 'Humey Bhool Jaana Chahiye', included here as 'We Should Forget'.

Minar Monsur, for permission to translate his poem 'Kobita Ki Jobab Debo', included here as 'What Answer Can I Give, Poetry?'

Zehra Nigah, for permission to translate her poem 'Bhejo Nabi ji Rehmatein', included here as 'Send Mercies Upon Us, O Prophet Ji'.

Bimal Guha, for permission to translate his poem 'Ekattorer Kobita', included here as 'The Poetry of 1971'.

Naseer Turabi, for permission to translate his poem 'Woh Hum-safar Thha Magar Uss Se Hum-navaii Na Thhii', included here as 'He was a Fellow-Traveller But He and I were Never Compatible'.

Javed Akhtar, for permission to translate the *nazm* 'Fateh Bangla' by Jan Nisar Akhtar, included here as 'The Bangla Victory'.

DAG, for permission to use the painting *Bangladesh War – 1971* by Chittaprosad Bhattacharya.

Salima Hashmi, for permission to use her painting (untitled).

Acknowledgements

I express my deepest thanks to my co-editor and collaborator Rakhshanda Jalil whose idea to have an anthology celebrating fifty years of Bangladesh's Independence set us off on a pursuit of authors and narratives that has resulted in this volume. My special thanks to all the authors who have made this possible: without them all our efforts would have remained sterile and fruitless. Their words have enriched this collection in ways impossible to enumerate, so I remain forever in their debt. I must however acknowledge their friendship and shared intellectual pursuits that have sustained me in spite of the vagaries of the borders: Selina Hossain, Wasi Ahmed, Shaheen Akhtar, Kaiser Haq, Papree Rahman continue to be ever generous in supporting and sustaining my work. In West Bengal, I am indebted to Manas Ray, Moushumi Bhowmik, Trishna Basak, and Shubhoranjan Dasgupta, who did not hesitate to answer my call to contribute. Jhumur Panday from Assam has always been unstintingly generous with her work. My special thanks go to Meher Ali for her moving piece on her grandfather. A special mention must be made of Anita Agnihotri, Asifa Sultana, Ahsan Ahsanuzzaman, Monobina Gupta and Ritwik Saha who helped out at a moment's notice and acted as excellent sounding boards. I want to acknowledge my deep and profound gratitude to the translators, who got down to a task they loved and did not hesitate to share the fruits of their labour. I would like to mention Subhoranjan Dasgupta, Rimi B. Chatterjee, Mainul Hasan Chowdhury, Shehreen Ataur Khan, Ali Ahmad, Shabnam Nadiya, Kamrul Hassan, Afsan Chowdhury and Kalyani Dutta in this context. A special word of thanks to Tapati Guha-Thakurta for her generous help; and to DAG for allowing us to use a great work of art on 1971 by Chittaprosad Bhattacharya for the cover of this book—I am deeply indebted. The publishers Orient BlackSwan have been greatly supportive and Vidya Rao continues to be a pillar of strength. I thank the editorial team, especially Nilanjana Majumdar and Moyna Mazumdar who steered this boatful of diverse beings and took us to shore.

This volume is dedicated to the people of Bangladesh, past and present, whose love for their land and language continues to inspire generations. And to the battle-weary dreamers who had dropped by the wayside in the years 1967 and beyond:

Tobu guro khwatey choyaye smritir beesh

Yet poison memory oozes from the deep open wound

Debjani Sengupta

Friendships are known to snap under the strain of joint authorships and shared academic work. Ours seems to have grown stronger with this—a hat-trick and our third co-edited volume, I am grateful to Debjani Sengupta for her constancy in friendship and solidarity.

Given that most of the background reading and research for this volume took place during the prolonged lockdown and the subsequent restrictions of the pandemic, one has missed the joys of browsing in libraries. However, friends and fellow-travellers have helped during this strange and difficult year. Virtual strangers have responded to e-mails and whatsapp messages, showing unexpected generosity and alacrity. I remember writing to Munir Pervaiz in Toronto in search of new writings in Pakistan on what was once East Pakistan and is now Bangladesh. Munir sahab, in turn, introduced me to Ameer Jaffrey, who very kindly emailed me the entire PDF of an incredible collection of short stories entitled *Zameen Zalim Hai* edited by Dr Bashir Mansoor. I am grateful for their help. I am also grateful to Haikal Hashmi, son of the legendary Urdu poet Naushad Noori whose poem 'Mohenjodaro' I have included here, for not merely granting permission to translate his father's poem but also sending me extracts from other Urdu poets from Bangladesh whose work was entirely unfamiliar to me.

I was unable to include those poems; nevertheless, they have helped me contextualise Urdu poetry in modern-day Bangladesh.

I am grateful to the following for allowing me to include their writings in this volume: Rasheed Amjad, Agha Sohail, Masood Ashar, Sameena Nazeer, Tariq Rahman, Raihana Hasan, Razia Fasih Ahmad, Sorayya Khan, Afzal Ahmad Syed, Zehra Nigah, and Naseer Turabi. I am grateful to the late Intizar Husain for granting permission to translate his stories; and to Javed Akhtar for permission to translate his father, Jan Nisar Akhtar's *nazm* here; and to Ali Madeeh Hashmi for allowing me to include and translate his grandfather, Faiz Ahmad Faiz's poem. Since this is essentially a work of translation as much as a literary history, I must acknowledge the assistance of the translators: the late Khalid Hasan, Tabinda Burney, Alvira Burney, Haider Shahbaz and Razia Fasih Ahmad.

When borders are closed, books become the first casualty and this is especially irksome for those of us in India who rely on Urdu books published in Pakistan to fill the gaps in our understanding of the subcontinent's literary history. Hoori Noorani, publisher Maktaba-e-Daniyal, has been most generous with her time and her wide network of contacts in the Urdu literary world. I have, time and again, pestered her—often late at night—for contacts, permissions, extracts. She has always responded with utmost generosity and swiftness. It is to Hoori that I wish to dedicate this volume.

Rakhshanda Jalil

Introduction I

Shono ekti Mujibarer theke
Lokkho Mujibarer konthoswarer dhwani-protidhwani
Akashe batashe othe roni
Bangladesh amar Bangladesh...

Listen, from one Mujibur
A thousand Mujib's voices rise
The sounds and echoes of those voices
Ring out through the wind and the sky
Bangladesh my Bangladesh...

—Lyrics by Gouriprasanna Majumdar,
sung by Anshuman Roy, 1971

In the historical memory of South Asia, 1971 is an year that is worth remembering for many reasons: the foremost being the birth of Bangladesh as an independent state, breaking its ties with Pakistan after months of war that can in hindsight be seen as a short but bitterly fought war in the recent history of the subcontinent. When the British left India in 1947, the two nations of India and Pakistan came into being as a result of months of negotiations to accommodate Hindu and Muslim nationalist interests and aspirations. Carved out of British India, Pakistan, comprising the two halves of West and East Pakistan, was an anomaly in geographical terms. The two parts formed non-contiguous segments of one nation separated by almost thousand miles of Indian territories. There were other ambiguities too. Although the two halves followed Islam, Eastern Bengal, before it became East Pakistan, had close cultural ties to West Bengal through language, literature and economic productions. The region looked at Kolkata rather than at Lahore or Karachi for education, employment and cultural affinities, expressed through the shared traditions of the Bengali language, food and attire. In many ways, even under colonial rule, the two Bengals had close bonds of kinship and political activism that had unitedly opposed the 1905 Partition of Bengal under Curzon and had succeeded in rescinding the order.[1] However, the British Divide and Rule policy was used in ways to complicate the electoral politics in the undivided province. Islamic nationalist objectives took definite shape from the 1910s onwards in the region. It was a way to define modernity in Muslim society that was seen as long suppressed by Hindu intellectual traditions and a hesitation to embrace Western education. If one explores Muslim identity formation in the years immediately before Partition, especially that which enunciated Purba/East Pakistani autonomy, we can find it in a literary cultural renaissance through journals and newspapers like *Azad, Mohammadi* and *Sowgat* in the early 1940s. The East Pakistan Renaissance Society, active through 1942–45, was a group that sought the promotion of *swatantrata* or difference in literature and culture of the Bengali Muslim, with a special emphasis on a free Pakistan in the Eastern part where a country would be established 'with many *jatis,* as India is a large federation of *jatis*.'[2] In this conception of the Bengali Muslim self-realisation, culture was to play a dominant part of self-fashioning and as a site of resistance to British and Hindu hegemonic national and social models. In 1942, a book named *Pakistan,* published by the Mohammadi Press, was the first articulation of a Bengali intellectual definition of Pakistan.[3] Bengali Muslim enunciation of the demand for Pakistan came out through various publications like Habibullah Bahar's 1941–42 essays on Pakistan and Nafis Ahmed's *The Basis of Pakistan* (1947). This debate had its detractors as well as supporters like the Communist Party member Gangadhar Adhikari's *Pakistan and National Unity* (1943) that saw the growing Muslim identity as an anti-imperialist consciousness of the Muslim masses. Similarly, Congressman Rezaul Karim's *Pakistan Examined* (1941) was a 'polemical response to the Pakistan demand' and was deeply critical of it as an ideology that articulated a communal viewpoint.[4]

In the months after 1947, the reactions to Independence were different in East Pakistan for obvious reasons. The newspapers and journals that supported a Muslim majority Pakistan were elated at being free from the hegemony of caste Hindus, and the creation of a new nation was greeted with euphoria. Journals like *Mohammadi* and *Mahe Nau* published articles passionately debating issues like language and cultural distinctiveness in the new nation state. The poet Golam Mostafa urged that a large part of Kazi Nazrul Islam's verses were incompatible with Pakistan's ideology, and therefore must be revised in the new Pakistani edition. Syed Ali Ahsan stated in an article that for national unity, the new nation state should be ready to discard, if necessary, even Rabindranath Tagore.[5] The Muslim elite's attempt to create a subcontinental Muslim culture and community was mainly shaped through a re-positioning of Urdu as a language that would bind the masses. However, inadvertently, this also alienated the Bengali Muslims who saw themselves as the inheritors of an Islam that had been regionally fashioned through the cultural practices and thought processes of a Bangla-speaking people for centuries past.

When Pakistan came into being, a large section of the people in East Bengal, now called East Pakistan, celebrated the birth of a new nation, seen as a just aspiration for the marginalised Muslim communities who had for years smarted under upper-caste Hindu economic and social domination. However, many others felt the pain as more and more Hindus left for India, leaving aside their homes and hearths, under a perception of threat and violence. The Noakhali and Tippera riots, the food shortages in the 1950s and the rising prices of essential commodities added to the feeling that East Pakistan could no longer be safe for Hindus who were now a minority. On both sides of the border there was a feeling of insecurity, anxiety and a sense of loss that underlay the experiences of Independence. Abdullah Abu Syed, remembering 14 August 1947, recollected:

> Even now, when I look back at 14 August 1947 I think that as we, the Muslims of Pakistan, were celebrating the Independence with the joyous abandon, at that very moment our neighbouring Hindu houses, behind their gaping front doors, were hiding a group of despairing, helpless and sad people standing speechless with the thought of an uncertain

> future. The same had happened in the lives of almost all the saddened and voiceless Muslim families across India.[6]

In 1947, in East Pakistan, the civil services were composed of West Pakistanis, 'optees' and refugees from India who were mostly Urdu-speaking. Within a year of Independence, in 1948, Jinnah visited Dhaka and announced that East Pakistanis must learn to speak and use Urdu.[7] In a land where 58.6 per cent people spoke Bangla, the imposition of Urdu by the Pakistan Government created large-scale resentment and anger. A Declaration on 26 January 1952 by the ruling Muslim League that Urdu would be the official language of all Pakistan brought things to an explosive head. The Bangla-speaking political leaders in East Pakistan declared 21 February as the State Language Day, and called for public protests and demonstrations all over the province. The new Pakistani state reacted with swift fury and the proposed province-wide *hartal* was banned. When students and teachers of Dhaka University defied the injunction and took out marches, the police attacked the unarmed procession with great brutality, leaving at least four people dead and many others injured. Hundreds of protestors were arrested. This day is celebrated in Bangladesh's national calendar as *Ekushey* (21st) that 'marked a turning point in the young nation's history and collective memory.'[8] *Ekushey* is now celebrated throughout Bangladesh as that defining moment that presaged the beginning of an inexorable march towards freedom and a new national identity that was based on ethnicity, language and regionalism:

> *Amar bhaiyer rokte rangano Ekushey February,*
> *Ami ki bhulitey pari?*
> Drenched in my brother's blood, *Ekushey* February,
> How can I forget that day?
>
> Abdul Gaffar Choudhury[9]

In 1949, Huseyn Shaheed Suhrawardy, Ataur Rahman, Maulana Bhashani, Shamsul Haq and Sheikh Mujibur Rahman founded a new political party, the Awami Muslim League that would represent the aspirations of East Pakistan's Bengali people. By the late 1950s, under the rumblings of the *bhasha andolan*, it changed to the Awami League and opened its doors to non-Muslims. In 1970, Pakistan held its first general elections in which the Awami League won 167 of 169 National Assembly seats. General Yahya Khan suspended the convening of the National Assembly. Martial law was declared and there was widespread disaffection. Sheikh Mujibur Rahman was arrested in Dhaka between 24 and 25 March 1971 and taken to a prison in Rawalpindi, while the Pakistani Army began Operation Searchlight to eliminate opposition to its rule. A large number of Dhaka University students and teachers as well as people on the streets were massacred ruthlessly.

The *Muktijuddho*, as the War of Liberation is called in Bangladesh, was unprecedented in the violence that the Pakistani Army unleashed upon the populace. The *muktijoddha* or the guerrilla warriors, up against the might of the Pakistani state, initially had to struggle to gain military ground. Hundreds of women were victims of rape and abductions (who were given an officially sanctioned term in independent Bangladesh, *birangana*). The Liberation War had an obvious leader, Sheikh Mujibur Rahman whose socialist, secular ideology gave a focus to the strife. In one of his famous speeches he reiterated:

> No country or nation has shed this much blood for independence. Our blood and our independence will become useless if we can't put smiles on the faces of the people of this country. If we want to build an exploitation-free society, we must build our country based on the principles of nationalism, democracy, socialism and secularism. I hope that the 75 million people of Bangladesh will take an oath that though we have become independent, we cannot enjoy our freedom unless we build an exploitation-free society. This is why our farmers, students, workers—all of us—must be united regardless of ethnicity, religion, party and opinions. Today, our vow must be that we must protect our independence with blood, the independence that we brought with our blood.[10]

Mujibur Rahman's speech touched upon issues that were ideologically and politically significant for the new nation. The

Bangladesh Liberation War was often termed *jonojuddho* (people's war) where ordinary people, irrespective of class or creed, had taken part. In a recent compilation of letters from 1971 we can see the extraordinary fervour and commitment to the cause that even the most ordinary of people had, especially women. In a letter written on 15 July 1971, an unknown *muktijoddha* writes from Mymensingha that the Pakistan Army had no war policy, and so the 'marginalised, unarmed peasant, labourer, students and teachers, children and women were being mowed down. This genocide has surpassed many My Lai of Vietnam.'[11] Anjali Lahiri in her memoir, *Smriti O Katha*, writes how after going to the Banshtala camp, 'the courage, discipline and energy' of the young fighters had moved her indescribably.[12]

Recent anthropological and historical studies and oral history projects in Bangladesh and elsewhere have tried to go back to this short but bitter history of violence. They have problematised the aspect of the male gaze on the *birangana* figure as latter-day testimonies unearthed their trauma and suffering just as they have tried to understand the nature of violence that was perpetuated on the masses, and vice versa. Sharmila Bose's book *Dead Reckoning* problematised the linear heroic narrative of Bangladesh's national struggle to bring in perspectives and interviews of Pakistani soldiers who had been engaged in the war to 'create a unique chronicling of the 1971 conflict that serves as a basis for non-partisan analysis.'[13] The war of 1971 continues to exert great cultural and political significance even on younger generations as on diasporic Bangladeshi writers like Tahmima Anam, who talks of her own complex understanding of it: 'The war was fundamental, a kind of birth, not just for the country but for all the too-young people who had willed the country into being.'[14] While the number of dead and wounded can never be fully ascertained, there is no doubt about the brutality of the nine months of warfare and the subsequent efforts at memorialisation inside Bangladesh.

However, the Liberation War also threw up other issues that have generated thorny debates. After Partition, a large number of Bihari Muslim refugees who came to settle in East Pakistan had supported the unity of Pakistan and taken part in the Pakistan Army-led genocides. Known as *razakars*, many of them who survived the war had to face harassment and social marginalisation in independent Bangladesh. The Biharis, left behind by the Pakistani Army and refused entry into Pakistan as refugees, had to remain as stateless people in free Bangladesh. Their camp in Dhaka, called the Geneva Camp, is a constant reminder of this unfinished business that has festered from 1971.[15] The national allegory of the Bengali people's struggle to free themselves has perpetuated a collective memory of Pakistan as oppressive and demonic.[16] In the initial years after the Liberation, retellings of this myth contained 'almost no mention of Indira Gandhi's government and military involvement in the war of liberation,'[17] although that has begun to change now under a new momentum of reappraisal of Bangladesh's Liberation War. Bangladesh's War Crimes Tribunal, set up in 2009, has tried to investigate and prosecute collaborators to the killings, while foreign nationals who had fought in the war or helped its cause have been felicitated, including Indira Gandhi who was honoured posthumously. Like the forgotten Biharis, the hundreds of Hindus who fled to India were initially urged by Sheikh Mujib to return, but few actually did; and the question of citizenship of the Hindus, especially those belonging to the Namashudra community who entered India in 1971 and thereafter, continues to be part of political wrangling in contemporary Indian politics, particularly in the states of Assam and West Bengal.[18] Similarly, the ethnic minorities that make up Bangladesh's population, like the Chakmas and the Santhals, have had little or no political representation and are outside the ideology of Bengali linguistic and cultural nationalism. Mujib's promise to Bangladesh's ethnic minority remained unfulfilled in the years following the birth of Bangladesh.[19] The years from 1950s onwards, in the backdrop to heightened social and political tension of the *bhasha andolan*, were also marked by the rising tensions among Hindus and Muslims in many districts of East Pakistan and resulted in large-scale communal upheavals. This strand of religious identity as constituting the nation's culture and politics has emerged in Bangladesh through the rise of Islamic factions like the Jama'at-i-Islami which see Bangladesh as part of a global Muslim culture with ties to the Middle East. The tussle between fundamentalist identity politics and secular socialist values on which Bangladesh was founded continues to this day.

Bangladesh's Liberation War had a great resonance in West Bengal. Artists, doctors and ordinary citizens lent all manner of support to the cause by setting up relief camps along the border to facilitate refugees and the *muktijoddha*, to tend to the wounded and give succour to the homeless. Following the Declaration of Independence on 10 April 1971, the Provisional Government of the People's Republic of Bangladesh was set up in Mujibnagar but the capital-in-exile was Kolkata. The Indian government, under Indira Gandhi, moved a resolution in Parliament expressing wholehearted support for the people of East Bengal. What was, however, one of history's ironies was that West Bengal's own political upheaval, the Naxalite movement of the late 1960s and '70s, had a different trajectory and in many of our memories, 1971 is a year to remember because of a juxtaposition of events and misfortunes. West Bengal, then ruled by a Congress government, had gone on to brutally suppress the Naxal upsurge, by then riddled with factionalism and internal contradictions. By 1971, a large number of students, labouring poor and political workers were killed or incarcerated in prisons.[20] At that very moment, across the border, Indira Gandhi's Congress government was aiding another group of Bangla-speaking people, mostly young, who were to wrest freedom from another nation. The dream of an equitable and just society, a revolution we may say, therefore had two different trajectories and two different outcomes within the same span of historical time. In so many ways, 1971 laid bare many contradictions and ironies of the processes of history.

The memories, events and nightmares of 1971 have had many inheritors. Like any historical moment that generated sweeping political aftershocks, it has also engendered contested accounts and remembrances: some vivid, others less so, marked by violence, nostalgia, pain and regret. Now, with the passage of time, many of the inheritors of loss and regret have had the time and space to look back to those times and have tried to assess their own culpability and investment in the ruminations about a nation's birth. The water has been muddied with accounts and counter accounts but in all these recriminations and eventual revaluations, the path to reconciliation and peace shines on. In the subcontinent's history, Bangladesh will always stand for hope, for her own people and for others elsewhere. Bangladesh's legacy remains in that originary moment of linguistic nationalism that overturned the religious fratricide of the 1947 Partition of India.

The Bangla Section

The Bangla stories and poems collected in this volume are varied in their understanding and responses to 1971. While some are explicitly nationalistic in tone, others explore the possibilities of a reappraisal of the past through themes of tracing what happened to erstwhile *muktijoddha* and *biranganas*. The poems of Jharna Rahman and Bimal Guha assert the national cause of liberation and the leader who lead that liberation (Sheikh Mujibur). Minar Monsur's poem is a nuanced understanding of the broken promises of 1971. Alokeranjan Dasgupta's short poem questions the literary and political legacy of *Ekushey* not just personally but for the entire subcontinent. A whole generation of poets in the 1960s and '70s writing in West Bengal were deeply affected by the events across the border, and we can see in their writings a re-look at 1947 and its legacy through the years culminating in 1971. Moushumi Bhowmik's song 'Joshor Road' is a piece of great power and pity that was first translated for *Ekhono Golpo Lekho*, an anthology published by Bhowmik, Tareque and Katherine Masud in 1999 from Dhaka.

In the selected Bangla stories that find space herein, the writers explore what the war has meant for generations of Bangladesh's people, especially those who fought in the war, and the gains and losses that nation-building entailed. Wasi Ahmed and Shaheen Akhtar's stories explore the profound sense of dislocation that a *muktijoddha* and a *birangana* have in the independent nation, while Selina Hossain's story is a celebration of the revolutionary ideal in the face of torture and rape. Papree Rahman's story, told through a child narrator, is a wonderful evocation of the quotidian experiences of war and what ephemeral losses can be accrued, while the two stories by Trishna Basak and Jhumur Panday look at the fallout of 1971 in geographical spaces located outside of Bangladesh.

The three essays in English, by Kaiser Haq, Manas Ray and Meher Ali, are very different from each other but can be termed memory texts. Haq, who participated in the Liberation War, writes a first-person account of the battle and its own internal contradictions. Ray looks at 1971 and its relationship to a turbulent Kolkata rocked by Naxalite upsurge, and traces the relationships between 1947 and 1971. Meher Ali's essay reflects on the intergenerational memories of her grandfather Nadir Ali, who was part of the Pakistani Army and whose reminiscences of his time in East Pakistan explore and dwell on the question of what 1971 had meant for him. In each of these texts, 1971 looms large not just as an event but as an ideology, a promise or a trauma. They try to go back to the past to make sense of a time that is now slipping out of the memories of people who took part in it.

This anthology is also a homage to all those who fought, on either side, and who lived through the aftermath, trying to shape modes of reconciliation and peace. The readers of this volume may take this in the spirit in which it has been created: to understand the past of this subcontinent, and to go forward by building on it.

Debjani Sengupta
New Delhi, 2021

Notes and References

1. The unities and dissention of this first partition (1905) is captured in Tagore's 1916 novel *Ghare Baire* (The Home and the World), translated by Surendranath Tagore.

2. Neilesh Bose, 'Purba Pakistan Zindabad: Bengali Visions of Pakistan, 1940–1947', *Modern Asian Studies* 48, No. 1 (January 2014), 7.

3. Ibid., 10.

4. Ibid., 20.

5. Syed Ali Ahsan, 'Purbo Pakistaner Bangla Sahityer Dhara', *Mahe Nau* 3, No. 5 (August 1951), 49–54.

6. Sanjida Akhtar, *Bangla Choto Golpey Deshbibhag, 1947-1970* (Dhaka Bangla Academy, 2002), 40, 71–86. Translation mine.

7. Sufia M. Uddin, *Constructing Bangladesh: Religion, Ethnicity and Language in an Islamic Nation* (New Delhi: Vistaar Publications, 2006), 120.

8. This song by Chowdhury became an iconic song in Bangladesh for celebrating the sacrifices and sufferings of 1971 just as the one sung by Anshuman Roy, quoted at the beginning, became hugely popular in West Bengal and Bangladesh. Songs have a special place in memorialising the past in both Bengals, especially if we recall that Bangladesh's national anthem 'Amar Shonar Bangla' is written by Tagore, who is also the composer of India's 'Jana Gana Mana.' For a discussion of 1971 commemorative cultural productions like songs and architecture, see op. cit. Sufia M. Uddin (2006), chapter 4.

9. Bangabandhu's speech to the nation in Dhaka on 15 February 1972, in *Omkarshamogra*, ed. Nirzhar Noishabdya (Dhaka: Oitijhya, 2017), 35–36. Translated by Ahmed Ahsanuzzaman.

10. *Ekattorer Chithi*, eds. Salahuddin Ahmed et al. (Dhaka: Prothoma Prokashon, 2009), 34. Translation mine.

11. Anjali Lahiri, *Smriti O Katha* (Dhaka: Ain O Salish Kendra [ASK], 1999), quoted in op. cit. *Ekattorer Chithi*, 32. Translation mine.

12. Sharmila Bose, *Dead Reckoning: Memories of the 1971 Bangladesh War* (Gurgaon: Hachette, 2011), 6.

13. 'Tahmima Anam: "I Have a Complicated Relationship with Bangladesh"', Interview by Claire Armitstead, *The Guardian*, 13 May 2016. Available at https://www.theguardian.com/books/2016/may/13/tahmima-anam-i-have-complicated-relationship-with-bangladesh-interview (accessed 15 March 2021).

14. See *This Side, That Side: Restorying Partition. Graphic Narratives from Pakistan, India, Bangladesh,* curated by Vishwajyoti Ghosh (Delhi: Yoda Press, 2013), 249.

15. Sharmila Bose, *Dead Reckoning,* 163–164.

16. Sufia M. Uddin, *Constructing Bangladesh,* 133.

17. The political mileage that the Liberation War continues to garner can be seen in recent times with the Indian Prime Minister's visit to Bangladesh in March 2021 to participate in the country's celebrations of fifty years of Independence. See Shuddhabrata Sengupta, 'A Satyagraha and Asatyagraha: Narendra Modi and the Liberation of Bangladesh', *The Wire,* 27 March 2021. Available at https://thewire.in/history/a-sataygrah-and-asatyagraha-narendra-modi-and-the-liberation-of-bangladesh (accessed 28 March 2021).

18. At a public meeting in Rangamati of the Chittagong Hill Tracts in 1975, Prime Minister Sheikh Mujibur Rahman implored the minority communities to embrace Bengali culture. See op. cit. Sufia M. Uddin, *Constructing Bangladesh,* 133.

19. The irony of this juxtaposition is caught in a 1970s' poem by Srijan Sen, titled 'The Mourners':

> The fire weeps for the oil,
> The flood, for the drought.
> And here weeps Jawaharlal Nehru's daughter
> For the outcasts, who sleep in the gutter.

20. *Thema Book of Naxalite Poetry,* ed. Sumanta Banerjee (Calcutta: Thema, 1987), 80.

Introduction II

Curled in the end lies a beginning and in every beginning lies the end of something old. Never is this truer than in the case of countries that are born after prolonged periods of parturition or when they are hived out of old nation states after much blood has been shed. Bangladesh has the unique distinction of having not one but three *partums*[1]: the first in 1905 when Bengal was spliced into East and West Bengal; then in 1947 when fresh borders were drawn on the Indian subcontinent[2] and the new wing of a new nation state called East Pakistan came into being; and the third in 1971 as Bangladesh was to be its final coming, an assertion of a proud new identity.

Our interest in this anthology is to probe the intersection of literature and history, to look at real historical events that lead to the creation of Bangladesh, to probe the ways in which the creative writer attempted—sometimes partially, sometimes well—to capture the moments and memories of those days and months. Our interest is also in those who attempt to look back with the benefit of hindsight and try to make sense of the madness and mayhem that took many by surprise. Some experienced it first-hand; others attempted to enter this great tragedy by way of empathy and imagination. And all of these experiences and, by extension, their expression in creative writing are valid and worthy of our interest in a collection such as this that attempts to put together as varied a set of responses as possible.

In the early years there was a small, almost minuscule, body of work by Pakistani writers on the disintegration of Pakistan. In Urdu especially, except for a handful of authors such as Intizar Husain and Masood Ashar, there was a tacit silence on the subject of what went wrong with the Two-Nation theory.[3] The poet Faiz Ahmad Faiz was another exception to the rule that said since people from West Pakistan heard no evil, saw no evil, they could not, therefore, claim to bear witness to the evil that had been festering in the hearts of men who were once brothers. Written in 1974, Faiz's now-iconic poem 'Dhaka Se Wapsi Par' (Upon Returning from Dhaka) is an acknowledgment of being a 'stranger amidst friends';[4] sung hauntingly by Nayyara, it is often disengaged from its essentially political mooring and, given its wording, often taken to be a purely romantic ghazal:[5]

> *Hum keh thehre ajnabi itni mudaraton ke baad*
> *Phir banenge aashna kitni mulaqaton ke baad*
>
> We who have remained strangers after so many hospitalities
> After how many meetings will we become acquaintances
>
> [p. 246, this volume]

While laudable, attempts such as these—few and far between though they were in Urdu—have merely alluded to that blood-stained legacy of shame; there was no serious attempt to flesh out the bare bones of that long-buried nightmare. Razia Fasih Ahmad made a brave attempt to do so through her novel *Sadiyon ki Zanjeer* (The Centuries-old Chain, 1986), but in the guise of a love story.[6] Reading it, I found its romantic content, slender to the point of anorexia, quite overshadowed by its feisty, robust political consciousness. In telling the story of Zari and Shams, both descendants of a Turkish soldier, one born in West Pakistan, the other in its watery twin separated by the vast Indian plain, Razia Fasih Ahmad has chronicled the disintegration of the two 'arms'. The first part, that deals with life in West Pakistan, especially its remote mountains and valleys in the Swat region, hurtles along at a breakneck speed, with events piling up one on top of the other. A huge cast of characters is introduced, adding to the sense of bemusement. By the time the action shifts to East Pakistan, you have stopped trying to figure out who is related to whom and how. The general idea seems to be to somehow follow the thread of dissolution in the tangled skein of several confusing sub-plots: the dissolution of a marriage and a country.

Sadiyon ki Zanjeer is important and deserves a detailed mention here because it is the first serious attempt to understand what, possibly, went wrong. It charts the history of the subcontinent through personal griefs and tragedies and records the birth of an independent nation. Interspersed with the depiction of everyday life are astute observations on the political state of affairs in West Pakistan:

> Conditions in the country were taking a new turn. The government had imposed Section 144 in every big city but people disregarded it. The police tear-gassed and lathi-charged, but it only resulted in more and more protests. The demonstrations were spreading like wildfire across the country, demanding blood money for the families of the martyrs, for the release of political leaders and for restoration of democracy.[7]

The observations become keener, the insight sharper and the commentary more unsparing when it comes to the state of affairs in East Pakistan:'…in a comparative study of the economic conditions of East and West Pakistan [there is] the glaring disparity in government jobs, particularly in the armed forces, the differences between the prices of commodities…'[8] Given the economics of 'integration', everything is cheaper in East Pakistan—be it arms or consumer goods. So, while the Westerners are contemptuous of the Easterners' demand for equality, they don't think twice before coming out East to shop—be it crockery, cutlery, cars, furniture or carpets. Everything is sent out by ship or aeroplane yet everything costs less in the East. These are things that never make it to the accounts prepared by professional historians; and it is precisely why, sometimes, literature offers a truer, more cruel, more stark, account of the way things were.

While there is mistrust and anger among East Pakistanis at this imbalance, their western compatriots are scornful of this desire for equality and parity: 'Everyone spoke Urdu till recently. Even the servants spoke beautiful Urdu. Now, all of a sudden, they want us to talk to them in Bangla,'[9] Razia Ahmad's unsparing narrative informs us. The East Pakistanis are acutely conscious of the contempt in which they are held: 'If we wear a lungi, or eat in stainless steel plates, it does not mean that we are barbaric or uncivilised. The bottom line is that people here are not going to bear (their) airs any longer. That's why the gulf between the two people has been widening.'[10] The fatal mistake West Pakistan made was that it thought it could browbeat the East Pakistanis and cow them into submission; it sent its army out, especially the infamous Rangers 'to chasten these black pygmies if they don't behave.'[11] The Rangers unleashed mayhem of the most barbaric kind and they were not merely dreaded but despised by the locals:

> They think all Bengalis are kafirs, and they have been sent to fight the kafirs and infidels…they are so ignorant that if they see someone saying his prayers or find a copy of the Holy Quran in a Bengali house, they are surprised. They think that Tagore must be a Muslim because he had a beard, so they leave his pictures and destroy Iqbal's because he is clean-shaven.[12]

Through the lives of Zari and Shams and their eclectic circle of friends and relatives, the novel depicts how the rallying cry for '*Amaar Shonar Bangla*' gains momentum: from hushed whispers to stray slogans to a single unequivocal demand that resounds across sylvan meadows and bustling cities, leaving no place for mutuality. Promoting any one must necessarily mean harming another—be it language, culture, even nationhood. With scorn and hatred tipping the scales on both sides, there can only be a cataclysmic, irrevocable upheaval, a sundering of limb from limb. In the end, there is the dilemma of people like Zari, ardent votaries of integration who don't just mouth platitudes but go to the extent of marrying the 'other' so the 'otherness' may be subsumed in 'oneness'. But every effort comes to nought, and Zari is left with a bleak prospect: 'If Bangladesh is right, then Pakistan is wrong.' And the even more heart wrenching: 'But we were told that the "truth" always wins. Were we wrong to insist on having one Pakistan?'[13]

And therein lies the nub of the debate: Was the Two-Nation theory wrong to begin with? Was Jinnah's announcement of One-Nation, One-People, One-Language fatally flawed from its very inception? Can countries break up only through 'conspiracy' theories, or is there not a groundswell of popular opinion to propel a people's movement? Can the silence adopted by many Pakistanis ever fully atone for the wrongs of their countrymen in what was then East Pakistan? And, for that matter, is silence ever healing? Why did the Urdu writers, so active, so voluble, so forthright on most political issues, write so frugally on Bangladesh? And even when they did, why did they adopt allusion and metaphors rather than the directness of a Saadat Hasan Manto or a Kishan Chandar who described the horrors of the Partition in all their grisly details?

It is these questions, and others, that we hope to address through the stories and poems chosen here.

Needless to say, editing this anthology required months of reading, of sifting the wheat from the chaff, of finding new voices and writers that were either forgotten over the decades or buried in old journals and periodicals many of which were not available to us in India. It took the kindness of virtual strangers, the generosity of friends across borders and the marvels of technology to find new resources. All along, our concern was to address the questions listed above that beset us as we delved into our reading and research. It is another matter that along the way, we found more questions, sometimes questions without adequate answers, and occasionally answers that were more disturbing than any of the questions we had set out with.

That language and ethnicity is a potent force has been borne out by events on the world arena more than once (Basque/Spain, Tamil/Sinhala, among others).[14] Pakistan has witnessed widespread ethnic clashes requiring military action against Baloch tribes in 1958, 1962–66 and 1973–76[15] as well as the disturbances in Sindh on the imposition of Urdu at the expense of Sindhi.[16] In India, we have had our share of language problems with the anti-Hindi riots in Tamil Nadu ensuring the amendment in 1967 of the Official Languages Act of 1963 that allowed the continued use of English as the official language.[17]

Social, economic and political reasons combine with issues of language and ethnicity to create an especially powerful cocktail of identity politics. The case of Bangladesh, and how it rose phoenix-like from the ashes of East Pakistan, is a perfect example. Given the centuries-old tradition of Urdu-speaking Muslims from Bihar, who identified themselves as the *ashraf* or the elites and held the Bangla speakers as inferior and low-caste rabble (*ajlaf*), there existed a volatile situation even before the advent of British colonialism. Long years of British rule crystallised these differences into intractable positions: those who spoke only Bangla occupied the lowest rung of the socio-economic ladder, were despised by the Urdu speakers and, in turn, despised them though secretly aspiring for upward mobility through the medium of language. With Bangla-speaking Hindus showing a greater propensity to acquire English-medium education, find employment in the colonial administration and generally better their lot compared to Muslims,[18] the *ashraf–ajlaf* divide deepened among the Muslims of East Bengal and subsequently East Pakistan.

As Pakistan's most-respected linguist Tariq Rahman, notes: 'When the fear of Hindu domination was removed after 1947, the Bengali-educated proto-elite opposed Urdu more openly and forcefully. As the rulers of East Bengal were the *ashraf* and the Muslim League administration in West Pakistan too considered Urdu a symbol of national integration…'[19] The brutal suppression of the Bangla language movement on 21 February 1952, the killing of activists and the firing on students unleashed a juggernaut which moved inexorably towards the defining moment of severance in 1971. In the interim, no efforts on the part of the Pakistani state to emphasise the Muslim identity of the Bengalis, by simultaneously de-emphasising their Bengali identity, bore fruit. In all such efforts, language and, by extension, culture bore the brunt of state scrutiny with 'native' dress, literature and culture seen as a display of affinity with Kolkata rather than Karachi. Proposals ranged from the radical—such as making Arabic the state language of Pakistan, as suggested by the Aga Khan on 9 February 1951—to changing the Bangla script to Arabic, to more practical ones such as excising Sanskrit words from Bangla and replacing them with Perso-Arabic ones. All such efforts further riled the Bengalis with the underlying assumption that their Bengali-ness was seen to be incompatible with both their Islamic and Pakistani identity.[20]

Just as Urdu didn't quite die in India in the face of an aggressive state-sponsored programme of popularising Hindi as the national language in the years following Independence, neither did Urdu disappear in East Pakistan. In the face of public opinion being vehemently against it, it survived but in ever-shrinking enclaves and became the language of lament and nostalgia, of cultural expression of a small but distinct minority. As university and college-level teaching of Urdu declined with fewer and fewer jobs available for Urdu students, its ties with employment weakened.[21] A complicated relationship existed between those who had come from India after 1947, opting for a new life in Pakistan and those who were 'native' Bangla speakers.

Desperate to retain links with a culture and way of life left behind in India, the new emigres from India sought refuge in the time-honoured 'high' classical tradition of the *masnavis* with their reliance on images and metaphors drawn from the Perso-Arabic literary tradition. Naushad Noori, educated in Patna and highly regarded as an influential Urdu poet, was an exception to this trend; despite his familiarity with the ghazal and the classical poetry of the 'high' tradition, he wrote a poem such as 'Mohenjodaro', urging people to hold on to their folk traditions. Written in 1952, this poem was published in *Afkaar* (Reflections) from Karachi and seems prescient, pointing towards the portents of disaster waiting to unfurl in the raging storm of language chauvinism:

> O people of my city
> Hold on to your *Geeta* and *Puthi*
> Your folk tales and fables
> Your songs and ballads
> Your letters of the alphabet
> Your languages and dialects
> Inscribe them on copper and iron
> And on leaves, stones, skin and papyrus
>
> [p. 242, this volume]

The creation of Bangladesh brought fresh perils for the Urdu-speakers who identified themselves as Bengali.[22] Some found themselves living in ghettoes and camps, such as the notorious

Geneva Camp in Dhaka, as refugees in their own land. Perceived as collaborators with the Pakistani state during the War of Liberation, shunned and despised by Bengalis who considered them traitors, many acquired an inferiority complex as a result of having to perforce live in a camp. Referred to disparagingly as 'Biharis' or 'stranded Pakistanis',[23] their writings, especially the Urdu poetry that came out of these camps, deserves to be studied for its complex skein of pragmatism and nostalgia, pathos and optimism, the pull of the past and the lure of the future.[24]

Others who chose to leave, especially those who were born from mixed marriages who chose to build new lives yet again in Pakistan, were met with a hostile reception in the new country and an 'othering' that was just as sharp as the one they had faced 'back home'. As Sameena Nazeer writes in her Urdu story 'Paan ka Beeda' (included in this volume as 'Betel Leaf'):

> 'Get lost, you Bengali!' The sentence kept replaying in his mind at night. He felt like he had murdered someone or committed some unforgivable crime. 'There, the Bengalis told us that we were Biharis...Here, everyone tells me, you are Bengali...Why can't I just be Pakistani?'
>
> [p. 172, this volume]

As mentioned earlier, it took a long while for the cloak of silence willfully worn by Urdu writers to slip somewhat. While in no way comparable with the voluminous writings on the Partition, enough fiction can now be located on what is, somewhat euphemistically, termed '*Saqoot-e Dhaka*' or the Fall of Dhaka. Bengali writers could well find this problematic and see it as yet another example of a majoritarian perspective that subverts history from the point of view of the oppressor rather than oppressed, for the word *saqoot* carries connotations of fall, elimination, defeat, capitulation; interestingly enough, it is also used for abortion or miscarriage!

Among the early literary responses, mention must be made of Brigadier Siddique Salik's 1977 memoir *Witness to Surrender*, published in its Urdu translation in 1986 as *Maine Dhaka ko Doobte Dekha* (I Saw Dhaka Drowning). Given his position as a public relations officer of the Pakistani Army in Dhaka in 1971, and the fact that he went on to enjoy the confidence of General Zial-ul Haq as his chief speech writer (even perishing in the ill-fated plane crash with him), the book cannot be considered an objective account. Among those Pakistani writings that address the East Pakistan issue with varying degrees of empathy, honesty and clarity, mention must be made of: the progressive Urdu writer A. Hameed's short story 'Ab Jaagte Rehna Hai' (We Must Stay Awake Now); Shahzad Manzar's short story collection *Nadia Kahan Hai Tera Des* (River, Where is Your Country); Jameel Usman's collection *Jilaa-vatan* (Exile); Tariq Mahmood's novel *Allah Megh De* (Allah, Send Me Clouds); Salma Awan's novel *Tanha* (Alone) and short story 'Sumita Didi'; Muhammad Hameed Shahid's novella *Mitti Aadam Khaati Hai* (The Earth Eats Humans); Mustansar Hussain Tarar's travelogue *Raakh* (Ash); Tariq Ismail Sagar's *Lahu ka Safar* (The Blood's Journey); and Altaf Fatima's novel *Chalta Musafir* (The Moving Traveller) published in 1981, and regarded as the first Pakistani Urdu novel whose theme was the fall of East Pakistan. From India, there's the Jnanpith award-winning Urdu writer Qurratulain Hyder's epic *Aakhir-e Shab ke Humsafar* (Travellers in the Last Watches of the Night) published in 1979, translated by Hyder herself as *Fireflies in the Mist*, which traces the history of East Bengal from the time of the nationalist movement against the British, to the creation of East Pakistan, and finally to Bangladeshi independence.

For various reasons, while all of the above were important and useful in providing a context and essential part of my background reading, they could not be included here. A collection entitled *Zameen Zalim Hai* (The Earth is Cruel), with the subtitle *Suqoot-e Dhaka ke Tanazur Mein Likhe Gaye Afsanon ka Majmua* (A Collection of Stories Written in the Scenario of the Fall of Dhaka), edited by Bashir Manzoor, and published as late as 2015, however did yield material that could be used here, such as the stories by Agha Sohail and Rasheed Amjad. Perhaps more than the contents, it was the dedication that moved me: 'To all those countless Pakistanis who even today languish in the jails of Bangladesh.'

It must be clarified that the stories, poems and extracts from novels chosen are all translated from Urdu, except for three which are in English, and all are by Pakistani writers with the exception of the *nazm* by Jan Nisar Akhar, the Indian progressive poet. Among the six poems I have chosen to translate from Urdu, there is of course Faiz's lament mentioned earlier with its note of deep sorrow and quiet regret; Zehra Nigah's moving depiction of a scene of pastoral domesticity that is rudely disrupted by an invasive presence referring to the large-scale atrocities committed against women by the armed forces; Afzal Ahmad Syed's traumatic experiences in 1971 limn his love for East Pakistan in 'Humey Bhool Jaana Chahiye' (We Should Forget); Naseer Turabi's dirge-like ghazal written immediately after the Fall of Dhaka has the knee-jerk Pakistani sorrow over a severed limb with no real acknowledgement of when and how the sepsis had set in; Akhtar's poem echoes all the popular Indian sentiments of solidarity, fellowship and big-brotherly affection; and Noori's poem has been referred to earlier.

The prose section carries many hidden surprises: Tariq Rahman's story 'Bingo', Sorayya Khan's novel *Noor*, and Raihana Hasan's elegant novel set in the tea estates are brutal in their honesty, unsparing in their apportioning of blame and responsibility. Intizar Husain's story 'Sleep' alludes to the immensity of the horrors witnessed by the more sensitive among West Pakistani men who were sent 'over there', an immensity that defies description. Rasheed Amjad and Agha Sohail resort to allusion, leaving unsaid and unspoken that which is, nevertheless, felt at a deeply personal level.

Rakhshanda Jalil
New Delhi, 2021

Notes and References

1. Rafiuddin Ahmad, *The Bengali Muslims 1871-1906: A Quest for Identity* (Delhi: Oxford University Press, 1981).
2. For a cogent analysis of the discussions that went into the division of Bengal, Jinnah's greed for a greater share of territory with

a Muslim-dominated population and the decision of the Boundary Commission, see Penderel Moon, *Divide and Quit* (New Delhi: Oxford University Press, 1998).

3. It was much later that enough writings by Urdu writers from West Pakistan on what took place in East Pakistan began to emerge for a collection of them to be put together in 2015.

4. For a contrarian view of Faiz's position on East Pakistan and his silence on the atrocities committed by the Pakistani military in East Pakistan, read https://cafedissensus.com/2015/05/15/faiz-ahmed-faiz-and-the-bangladesh-liberation-war-1971/ (accessed 1 October 2021).

5. There is also Faiz's other *nazm*, 'Hazar Karo Mere Tan Se...' (Stay Away From Me...), written on the Indo-Pak War of 1971.

6. http://www.raziafahmad.com/Zanjeer.htm (accessed 1 October 2021).

7. Razia Fasih Ahmad, *Breaking Links* (Pakistan: Oxford University Press, 2007).

8. Ibid.

9. Ibid.

10. Ibid.

11. Ibid.

12. Ibid.

13. Ibid.

14. Paul Brass, *Ethnicity and Nationalism* (New Delhi and London: Sage Publications, 1991).

15. Selig S. Harrison, *In Afghanistan's Shadow: Baluch Nationalism and Soviet Temptations* (New York and Washington: Carnegie Endowment for International Peace, 1981).

16. Feroze Ahmad, 'The Language Question in Sindh', in *Regional Imbalances and the Regional Question in Pakistan*, ed. Akbar S. Zaidi (Lahore: Vanguard Books, 1992).

17. Duncan B. Forrester, 'The Madras Anti-Hindi Imposition Agitation, 1965: Political Protest and its Effects on Language Policy in India', *Pacific Affairs* 39, Nos. 1/2 (1996), 19–36 (University of British Columbia).

18. W. W. Hunter, *The Indian Musalmans: Are They Bound in Conscience to Rebel Against the Queen?* (Lahore: Premier Book House, Reprint 1974 [1871]).

19. Tariq Rahman, 'Language and Ethnicity in Pakistan', in *Contemporary Issues in Pakistan Studies*, ed. Saeed Shafqat (Lahore: Azad Enterprises, 2000).

20. Tariq Rahman, *Language and Politics in Pakistan* (New Delhi: Orient Longman Pvt. Ltd, 2007), 88.

21. Rukhsana Rahim Chowdhury, 'A Search for the "Self": Trials and Tribulations of Urdu Writers in Bangladesh' (BRAC University, Dhaka). Available at https://www.academia.edu/27724254/A_Search_for_the_Self_Trials_and_Tribulations_of_Urdu_Writers_in_Bangladesh (accessed 24 November 2021).

22. An estimated 300,000 Biharis lived in Dhaka city, scattered in various localities namely Shahjahan Pur, Kamla Pur, Motijheel, Purana Pultan, Nawabpur Road, Nawab Bari, Thatheri Bazar, Moulvi Bazar, Armani Tola, Islam Pur, Azim Pur, Saddar Ghat, Eskatan, Dhanmandi, Dhakeshwari, Neel Khet. An eyewitness account of one such 'Bihari' can be found at https://www.dawn.com/news/1522385 (accessed 24 November 2021).

23. Since many wish to be repatriated to Pakistan but Pakistan refuses to acknowledge them as their citizens or assist in their relocation.

24. Jessica Mudditt, 'Breaking the Silence of the Camps—Urdu Speakers in Bangladesh', *The Independent*, June 2010. Available at https://jessicamudditt.com/2010/07/24/breaking-the-silence-of-the-camps-urdu-speakers-in-bangladesh/ (accessed 24 November 2021).

ESSAYS

Kaiser Haq
Manas Ray
Meher Ali

Overleaf photograph: Moyna Mazumdar

1 With the Hamzapur Tigers*

KAISER HAQ

In May 1971, I trekked across the border to join the Mukti Fauj and, by a curious concatenation of circumstances, fetched up at a Youth Camp outside Balurghat, the district headquarters of West Dinajpur, where I found myself among a boisterous half-dozen of my cronies from Dhaka, including my Gregorian schoolmate Tanna, the [then] Dhaka Club president, who left not long after to devote himself to giving Bangladesh a sporting side. The camp had a couple of thousand youths going through Boy Scout-like drills as they waited for their turn to be sent up to improvised military training schools offering three-week crash courses to shape them up into guerrillas who would operate in small squads in occupied territory.

Just then a recruiting team doing the rounds of various Mukti Fauj sectors to select young men for officers' training visited the camp, which was adjunct to the headquarters of Sector 7. My friends and I queued up for interviews before a three-member board headed by Lt. Colonel Kazi Nuruzzaman, aided by Colonel Shafayet Jamil and (Shaheed) Major Najmul Haque, the acting Sector 7 commander. Quayyum Khan, a Club member, and I were selected and in due course made our way to Murti, a military station amidst the picturesque forested hills and tea gardens close to the Bhutan border. Film buffs may be interested to know that the forest guest house where 'Mr and Mrs Iyer' hole up for a night is in Murti. (I have written about our training in 'Strike a

---

*This piece was previously published in *BDNews24*, 16 December 2013, Dhaka. It is reproduced here with minor edits with the kind permission of the author and *BDNews24*, Dhaka.

Heroic Pose', and will skip details). On 9 October our batch of 61 cadets were commissioned by the Bangladesh government in exile and within a week posted out. Sheikh Kamal went to Calcutta as Colonel Osmani's aide-de-camp (ADC), and 60 of us to the 11 sectors and units of the East Bengal regiment. In other words, the Bangladesh Liberation Forces (BLF) had 60 freshly-trained company commanders. We were ready to intensify so-called conventional operations.

Five of us were sent to Sector 7, now with Colonel Zaman in charge. As we entered the Colonel's tent we found a stocky, ebullient officer in olive green giving an exciting situation report. He was Captain Idris, one of the sub-sector commanders, whom Quayyum and I had passingly met while at Balurghat: one morning we trekked to his camp and found him briefing a rag-tag band that would go in for patrol duty inside Bangladesh. An engineer by training, he had briefly been a lieutenant in the Electrical, Mechanical and Engineering (EME) Corps of the Pakistan Army and had been court-martialled and cashiered after knocking out his Punjabi commanding officer (CO) for having used anti-Bengali racist slurs. He was employed in the Jaypurhat Sugar Mills when the independence war broke out. He organised a band of young volunteers, collected whatever arms he could lay hands on and began guerrilla operations. He was now commanding the Hamzapur sub-sector, so named after the border village where it had its headquarters. And he had something dramatic to report.

'Sir, we will take Dinajpur town within a week if you can arrange Indian artillery backing,' he told the Colonel as he pointed out on a map where his company had taken up position.

This was electrifying. The Colonel promised to try his utmost and assigned two of us, Amin and I, to Idris's command. In two jeeps laden with arms, ammunition and other supplies we drove that evening to Hamzapur. To our surprise—and Captain Idris's shock—the camp was teeming with people. The company had come under a surprise flanking attack while the Captain was on his way to Sector Headquarters (HQ), and an undignified *sauve-qui-peut*[1] followed. One had been killed, several wounded. Captain

Idris was livid with rage; expletives shot from his mouth like sten-gun bursts. He made one particularly pusillanimous ex-EPR NCO[2] pick up a heavy wooden chair and do knee-bends. Amin and I were crestfallen and morosely went to our assigned tent to sleep away the shock.

The next morning Captain Idris was in a far more equable mood. He was a battle-hardened commander who had gone through many ups and downs and knew how to pick himself up after a setback: a truly indomitable spirit. He ordered the entire company to get ready for patrolling. After breakfast we trundled out, platoon by platoon, including the 3-inch mortar detachment. This much-used weapon didn't have its sighting mechanism and had to be fired blind, like a 2-inch mortar, but such was the rapport between mortar-man Rahman and this lethal tube that it was as accurate as one could wish.

We crossed over to the western bank of the Punarbhaba river and headed towards the border, just a couple of kilometres away. To our sorrow, shock and dismay we found a fresh stream of refugees pouring out of Bangladesh. The Pakistanis had driven everyone out of the villages that Captain Idris had liberated, and then lost. We would have to start all over again. When we reached the sports field of Kamdebpur High School we came under small arms fire and some desultory shelling. We secured a base area and spent the day patrolling and probing and skirmishing. The dead body of the *shaheed* who fell in the retreat was recovered under cover of darkness and taken to Hamzapur for burial.

After a week or so with Captain Idris, I was recalled to Sector HQ and ordered to raise a new company with about 200 youths who had just finished the three-week guerrilla course. I was joined by Saifullah, who had escaped from the Pakistan Military Academy (PMA) with his friend, Bazlur Rashid. They joined our course, but rather too late in the day and were asked to stay on and pass out with the next batch; but they didn't want to miss out on the action and opted for field commissions in the Mukti Bahini.

We trained day and night and waited for our arms and equipment and marching orders. In the middle of all this the Colonel asked Saifullah and me to accompany him on a mission. We set off in the middle of the night and arrived at Hamzapur in the small hours; it turned out we'd be part of the Sector Commander's party at a set-piece battle. The objective: Khanpur Border Outpost (BOP), occupied by a Pakistani company. With headlights turned off we crept past camouflaged Indian artillery batteries, a squadron of tanks, and leaving the jeep, walked till we met up with scouts from the Hamzapur Company. We had brought along some light machine guns (LMGs), which we handed over to them.

The Colonel chose the tree-lined bank of a small pond for the observation post; a section of the Hamzapur boys were positioned nearby. All was quiet. Mist lay thick over fields and copses. It was Ramadan. In towns and cities one would expect sirens to go off suddenly to announce *sehri* time. Instead the air was rent by artillery shells as a whole regiment opened up. The enemy responded with all the small arms at their disposal. The continuous thunderclaps of artillery, the manic whine of hundreds of automatics, tracers winging overhead...we felt our bodies tingling with excitement. Saifullah and I joined the section that had been assigned the role of 'jitter party', to create distracting noise with small arms. But amidst the tremendous racket going on, the 'jitter party' was quite redundant. Presently we could hear the voices of attackers rushing through the paddy fields. My course-mate Amin was leading the assaulting troops. The shelling moved forward, the firing gradually retreated, then faded away. The darkness slowly dissipated and through the mist emerged columns of Indian soldiers of 4 Madras Regiment, moving forward to take up position beside the Hamzapur Company. We joined them with the Colonel and went up to the front line command post, where we found the 4 Madras CO and Captain Idris. An artillery duel with the retreating Pakistanis was in progress. Suddenly someone spotted a black uniform—used by the Armoured Corps—in the distance. Fearing there might be enemy tanks in the vicinity the Indian CO radioed for Cavalry backup and in minutes a troop of them appeared behind us. 'That should act as a deterrent,' the CO said. The war had entered a new phase. The time for concerted action by the Mukti Bahini and the Indian Army had arrived.

Not long after, Saifullah and I were ready with our company to move to the front: Hamzapur again, and in the area I had already seen briefly, west of the Purnabhaba. The battlefront scenario now was like this: east of the Purnabhaba were Captain Idris and Amin with the original Hamzapur Company and 4 Madras under Lt. Colonel Malhotra. West of the Purnabhaba were Saifullah and I and our newly raised company, which we called Alpha Company. The main Pakistani defensive position in the area centred on Ramsagar, the famous hillock that dominated the surrounding countryside right on the eastern bank of the river, about halfway between Dinajpur town and the border. The veterans of the sub-sector had by now given our new company a proud nickname, derived in true Bengali style from the king of the Sundarbans: the Hamzapur Tigers. It worked like magic. 'You are now members of the Hamzapur Tigers,' we told our raw recruits, and their chests puffed up.

The tactical situation was on our side. The western bank had changed since the last time I was there. After the retreat of Captain Idris's company the Pakistanis put up numerous bunkers in a network of fortified villages, from where they came out patrolling to maintain their control of the area. Straddling the border in southern Dinajpur is a *sal* forest that is home to a *Santal* community. The Pakistani bunkers stopped short of the horizontal line across the northern tip of the forest: I suppose they didn't want to make themselves vulnerable to guerrillas sneaking out of the woods to take pot shots and then vanish into them again. At this point, I'm afraid I'll have to stop short of a detailed account and sum up very briefly.

We set ourselves two tasks: to wrest control of the countryside from the Pakistanis and dislodge them from their bunkers. We laid siege to the fortified villages and intensively patrolled the countryside. It was a war of attrition. Though ill-equipped (bolt-action rifles, sten guns, LMGs, 2-inch mortars, one 81-mm mortar, grenades, but no rocket launchers; not even grenade-firing rifles:

Quayyum at Mohdipur, under Captain Jahangir, had some of these, though), we had the advantage in manpower, and the Pakistanis, to their disadvantage, were dispersed in penny packets over the whole countryside. The enemy tried a couple of desperate tricks, which failed. One morning they launched a flanking attack along the riverbank, and were beaten back. One night, intense firing erupted away to the west, where we had a section stationed at the tip of the *sal* forest. We remained on stand-to all night. The next morning I took out a patrol and found out what had happened. The Pakistani firing was so heavy that our section withdrew into the forest. Strangely enough the enemy's aim seemed to have been simply to scare away our boys. Suddenly one of our boys shouted and pointed to a few patches of loose earth on the mud track down which the enemy had come. I removed the top layer and saw a little bit of plastic sticking out. Very, very gingerly I removed more earth and uncovered a plastic anti-personnel mine; but it had been screwed on top of a larger thing: a whopping anti-tank mine. There were four such devices that I defused. One false move and, as my boys said with grim humour, I'd have become *keema* (mincemeat). Mines prove to be a big problem in every war. A trip-wire mine wounded several of our boys. After the war all the mines collected from the Dinajpur area were stocked in a school building in which Mukti Bahini boys were also billeted. At least one of them hadn't been defused. The whole building blew up and over 300 were killed. We could hear the explosion in distant Bogra, where we had by then been transferred. People came to our headquarters to ask what had happened; one of them said he had thought it was the US 7th Fleet, which had been making threatening moves.

4 Madras had a setback—a patrol was surprised by the enemy and an officer and a couple of jawans taken prisoner—and was replaced by 12 Garhwal Rifles. We now had a field telephone spanning the river, and once an artillery operator (OP) came over and went round with me taking shots at enemy bunkers. Early one morning we overran the southernmost of the network of bunkers and moved up. Another village we laid siege to was simply abandoned by the enemy without a fight. We were reinforced by

another new company raised from the guerrillas so we could go patrolling deeper up the countryside. In one village a boy came up crying and told us how both his mother and sister had been forced to become *biranganas*. I will never forget his tormented expression.

With two companies under us we split into two commands, so to speak. We now even had walkie-talkies for easy communication (they were particularly useful in directing mortar fire) and a couple of motorbikes on which we could go inspecting our positions. Saifullah was in one village with one company, I in the next village with the other company. Between us lay a stretch of farmland. Both companies faced an occupied village. Every morning Saifullah and I would get together to decide on the course of action for the day. One morning Saifullah decided to walk across the tip of the field to my side, counting on the mist to shelter him from the enemy's view. Suddenly there were gunshots and a boy ran to me shouting that Saifullah had been hit. I went and saw that he had almost made it across when a sniper got him. I ran and dragged him to the shelter offered by the trunk of a felled tree. The sniper kept shooting: every couple of seconds the tree trunk rang as a bullet hit. I shouted for an LMG to be handed to me, placed it to the right of the trunk, carefully aimed at a tree from where the bullets were coming and let loose a withering burst. The sniping stopped. We carried Saifullah to safety and packed him off to hospital; luckily the bullet had gone clean through his arm without hitting the bone.

But the hospital couldn't keep Saifullah confined for long. Brave to a fault, he absconded and was back at the front, smiling, with his arm in a sling. By now the war was in its final, hectic phase. Ramsagar was strafed by a couple of Hunters, and with one well-coordinated artillery-backed attack by 12 Garhwal and our Sector Troops we could have taken Dinajpur; but the strategic decision, as the Indian CO told me over field telephone, was to hold our horses. This didn't prevent us from keeping up the aggressive patrolling or Captain Idris from a last desperate campaign. With two of his platoons and two of ours, plus our mortar, and with Saifullah as his Second-in-Command he decided to advance on Birol, near the district's western border. On 14 December they ran into a trap:

Idris was wounded in the hip; he was later decorated with a *Bir Pratik,* though he was also unceremoniously and inexplicably discharged soon after the war was over. 14 December was also when Bir Shreshta Captain Jahangir fell in Mohdipur. The next day the enemy evacuated Dinajpur.

Let me end with a salute to the unsung heroes of 1971. They are the ordinary people of the country who risked everything (many becoming *shaheed*), to do their bit for the country. Among the boys in our two companies there were no university students. There was a 15-year-old student of Class 9, a cheerful lad as brave as any man; a few college students who were made platoon commanders, along with a very brave ex-EPR JCO;[3] the rest were simple village youths, peasants who dreamt that once it was liberated, the country would be peaceful and prosperous. I tried to tell them not to nurture unrealistic dreams; I don't think my words made any impression on them. They were eager to work to build a better land. The idea of a National Militia comprising volunteers from the freedom fighters who would work to rebuild the war-ravaged land was floated and then unceremoniously shelved. We were ordered to give 50 taka to each of our men and send them home. It left me with a lingering sense of sadness and guilt. I wanted to get back to my studies as soon as possible; I had to submit three applications before I was finally released at the end of June 1972. And yet, like all the boys in our companies, if I had to live all over again, I would make the same choice. I am proud to have been with the Hamzapur Tigers.

Notes

1. *Sauve-qui-peut,* literally 'save himself who can' in French, is a state of panic, disorder or complete rout where every man is for himself.
2. EPR was formerly East Pakistan Rifles, the border security force pre-Independence; NCO is a non-commissioned officer, for e.g. havildar or sergeant.
3. East Pakistan Rifles junior commissioned officer.

2 The Unputdownable 70s

Memory Matters*

MANAS RAY

My steps falter, my head swims, walls on walls, cornices on cornices,
Pavements change at midnight,
On my way home, houses within houses, feet within feet, heart within heart
Nothing more—(so much more?)—but well before that
My steps falter, my head swims, walls on walls, cornices on cornices,
Pavements change at midnight
On my way home, houses within houses, feet within feet, heart within heart
Nothing more.
'Hands up'—put up your hands—till someone picks you up
Black cars within black cars, and another black car inside.
Rows of windows, doors. Graveyards—skeletons topsy-turvy
White worms within bones, life within worms, death within life—hence
Death within death
Nothing more.
'Hands up'—put up your hands—till someone picks you up and
Flings you out of the car, but inside a different car,
Where someone always waits—like a banyan sapling clings to the plaster
Someone or the other, someone you do not know
Lies in wait, like a firm bud lurks behind leaves

---

*This essay, written for this volume, is dedicated to my college friend, Ranajay Gupta, who fell to COVID-19 and passed away in the summer of 2020, virtually unnursed and unsung.

With traps of golden cobwebs, ready to garland you—
You'll be wedded at midnight, when pavements change—
Steps falter, head swims
Walls in walls, cornices in cornices.
Imagine, the train still, stations rushing by, stars shining beside dimming light domes
Imagine, shoes walking, feet still—this, that, any poppycock
Imagine children carrying corpse-bearing palanquins to Nimtolla—
And beyond,
The old lined up for a wedding dance—
Not a time for comfort, not a happy time this.[1]
Just then,
My steps falter, my head swims, walls on walls, cornices on cornices,
Pavements change at midnight
On my way home, houses within houses, feet within feet, heart within heart
Nothing more.

—Shakti Chattopadhyay (1967),
translated from the Bangla by Nandini Gupta

As I jot down my thoughts, a discrete event comes to mind. It was not exactly an event, just a few utterings, and happened back in 2005. I had gone to Dhaka for the first time. A friend had lent me his car to visit the locality where my parents once lived. I had heard so much about it from childhood. As we, the driver and I, were meandering through the narrow lanes of Gandaria in old Dhaka, I told him, soliloquy-like, 'Do you know had the country not been partitioned, I would have grown up here?' Out came his sharp query, 'What?' I said, 'Partition.' 'What is that?' Baffled, I impatiently explained. He said, 'Now that you tell me, it reminds me that my mother had also said something similar. She used to say, at one point these places would be teeming with Hindus. So… why did you all leave?' Exasperated, I asked him whether he had heard of the war, the 1971 war. For the rest of the journey, his endless narration of the stories of the war he was brought up with accompanied our ride. He was a man in his mid-thirties. I realised that for the man on the street at least, the war had erased the Partition or perhaps the Partition resides within the war.

I

Nations have their own ways of dealing with memories of trauma. For the newly independent India, an endeavour of silence seemed necessary for the project of the nation-state. After the initial disoriented years, the Partition was assigned to near oblivion in the public arena. From my childhood memories of the early sixties, it seems to me that the Independence Day celebration referred more to the new nation than the severed nation. Of course, it would be wrong to say that the Partition died out from popular memory. Communal flare-ups are above all sore reminders of an unresolved past—till, of course, they became organised, calculated pogroms of contemporary India.

In recent years, the more untenable the national narrative of stability, growth, and statist secularism has proved, the keener has been the interest in the Partition, taking it, if not as the originary point, then at least as the dividing line of our national life, as if it holds the secret of much of our present misery. However, this is not to say that Partition became part of academic discourse only from the 1990s. Big fat tomes were being regularly churned out, probing into who was responsible, how could it have been possibly avoided, the big actors, the big story, the big picture of the big nation. The scholarship that emerged in the 1990s started asking *new kinds of questions*, questions that came with new epistemological assignments in history-writing, literary studies, and cultural anthropology: How did people undergo the experience of Partition—as a group, as a family, as an individual? How did Partition become part of our selves? What does it mean to suffer? What is it to witness? What does it mean to be violated and raped and then to have to live with those poisonous memories that cannot be shared even with very intimate relations? In short, the after-life of pain and trauma. This scholarship paralleled, tied up and at times drew intellectual sustenance from the emergence of a self-conscious discourse of memory in history-writing made possible by the Holocaust discourse, the emergence of cultural studies, and new trends in philosophy, loosely clubbed under the rubric of post-structuralism. Over the past three decades, this new scholarship on the Partition has grown in bulk as well as prestige, attracting some of the best writings in history, cultural studies, and cultural anthropology as well as other branches of social and human studies.

If history's project is an attempt to reduce an always already plural to sameness, the counter-posture of memory is to keep this plurality alive by considering that which cannot be thought of in history—hence, the interest in the marginalia of history. Memory thus is framed as a counter to the unifying mode of history. Hence also the interest in oral histories, of vernacular memories, counter-memories, all of which would capture the fragmented, interiorised experience that the normally practised protocols of history-writing misses out.

While the Punjab Partition produced literary and academic accounts concentrating on violence, trauma and living with agony, the Partition literature of Bengal began mostly as upper-caste Hindu Bengali nostalgia about lost land depicted as a pastoral idyll with a lingering sense of eternity—the lush green meadows of rural East Bengal, a bucolic plenitude of food, rivers and other waterways, the vibrant blue sky of autumn, quotidian religiosity with each solvent family having its family deity placed in a *thakur dalan*,[2] the numerous religious rituals, *bratakatha*,[3] the village fairs, *doljatra*,[4] *rashpurnima*[5] and such other joyous Hindu festivities.

A collective, popular recollection can unobtrusively become a national recollection. The numerous memoirs—written or oral—in recent times of refugees from erstwhile East Pakistan seem to have already acquired standard generic protocols: the villages of plenty where Hindus and Muslims lived harmoniously; the sudden eruption of the Partition due to the connivance of the British rulers and some misguided and opportunist leaders; the enormous hardship and bravery in the initial decades of resettlement aiding, paradoxically, the formation of a new solidarity among the refugees and; finally, the gradual upward journey on the economic and social curve.

Palpably biased, this story narrates only a part of the story of Bengal's Partition. For Bengali Muslims, the Partition of 1947 was half the victory. The other half would be enacted in East Pakistan and result in the liberation of Bangladesh from the clutches of West Pakistan in 1971. The struggle for the self-esteem of Bengali Muslims could not stop merely with ceasing to be part of united India but continued till the Urdu-speaking West Pakistanis were fully ousted from the land. 1947 and 1971 are part of the same conjoined processes of the historical search for self-esteem. Interestingly, the early 1970s was also the time when West Bengal witnessed an unprecedented political and social upheaval. Starting as a peasant rebellion in the foothills of the Himalayas in northern Bengal, the unrest spread like wildfire to other parts of Bengal, particularly Calcutta, where it took the shape of a full-fledged urban uprising when traditions were questioned, the bourgeoisie-landlord rule challenged, the continuation of colonial legacy attacked and prevailing cultural, ethical and sexual mores put under the scanner. Though written from the author's own experience in Calcutta, as a late-teen and as a young man in his early twenties, by taking a look down memory lane the present essay tries to show how the streams of events in Bangladesh and West Bengal had remarkable convergences. They were not merely coeval processes but shared larger historical truths.

II

I remember the date clearly, 7 May 1971. That was the day my school-leaving exam was to start had it not been indefinitely postponed due to the prevailing unrest in the city. Towards the evening, the postman delivered a letter, a postcard, by slipping it under the door of my father's room. Father asked me to get it for him. Reading the short note, he called out for my mother. As he essayed his legs down the cot and looked for his slippers while tying the knot of his *lungi*,[6] Ma came in. He handed the card to her. 'Who is it from?' Mother asked. He kept quiet for a few seconds and replied, 'Satish of Chattogram. He has come with his family and is staying at a refugee camp in Ranaghat.' It was not unexpected, though not expected either. The raging war across the border had already pushed millions of evacuees to Bengal and Assam.

'When did they come?'

'Apparently, more than a month now, he with his wife and two children. He earlier wrote to his two relatives; they did not reply.'

'Do you propose to go yourself to fetch them? Where will you find them in that mad crowd? Better to send a letter.'

'Letter? To which address? It just says Camp 7. Plus, he doesn't have a coin left.'

'Remember, during the 1964 riot, when they came over, you told Satish so many times to stay back in Calcutta and not to return. But he was too tied to their house there and his *sahib* company job!'

The next morning my father left early only to return late afternoon. Accompanying him was his boyhood friend Satish, his wife Lata, and their two children Tamal and Latika. My mother had seen Tamal and Latika, but that was a good seven years back, and Latika was only a small girl then. In the fading sun of late winter, my mother held Latika's face up and remarked, 'Whom has she taken after? She looks like Satishbabu.' To which Lata*kakima* was prompt to reply: 'You think so? People over there think she looks like me!' *Kakima*[7] looked quite at ease; there was hardly a trace of the travails they must have gone through in the preceding two months. Tamal was playful, but Latika carried a streak of sadness that did not seem merely circumstantial, unusual for a girl of sixteen or seventeen. Satish*kaka* was distinctly sad and disoriented.

The following day, Satish*kaka* went out to fetch his relatives and returned with one of them. Abanibabu was a jovial elderly man, and assured Satish*kaka* he would take him to a few places that might have some job openings.

I came to know later that Satish*kaka* had started his career as a steno-typist in a British firm dealing with tea export in Chattogram. He rose from an ordinary clerk to the post of floor manager and was quite content with his life there.

The search for a new job began in earnest from the next morning itself. But it was of very little use. Finally, on the fourth day, he managed to get a steno-typist's position in a Marwari concern in Park Street. They would pay him on a daily basis, thirty rupees for each of the five days of the week; Saturday and Sunday being holidays, he would receive no pay. The next Monday morning, *kaka* set off in a clean pair of trousers, the only decent one he had, and a blue terylene half-shirt with a pen tucked in the pocket. He looked like a regular office-goer. Very quickly, I thought, he had managed to put his recent turbulent past behind him. But luck was not on his side. He came back in the evening with a long face. Apparently, his Marwari boss had told him he would receive thirty rupees at the end of each day all right, but that one rupee-fifty paise would be deducted for every error. Since he was long out of touch with steno-typing, what he received at the day's end was barely ten rupees and fifty paise. I was quick to calculate the number of errors: thirteen! Father expressed a strong sense of disgust; mother said, 'মারওয়ারিরা কোনদিন কারো ভালো করসে নাকি! *Marwarira konodin karo bhalo korshe naki!* When did the Marwaris do anyone any good!'

On father's advice, Satish*kaka* didn't go back to that office again. Instead, taking some clues from father, he went to see some people at the city's office quarters, Dalhousie Square, which did not work out. But *kaka* got fascinated by the enormity of activities he saw there, so many thousands of people in so many different organisations and occupations. He started going there every morning and checking with private firms to find out whether a vacancy existed. In the evenings, he came back, sad as ever. In his absence, my parents had worried exchanges regarding his job prospects. But *kakima* looked the same contended lady. Tamal spent his days climbing trees and flying kites with the local boys, an activity I thought was a bit childish for his age. After all, he was three years my older and must by then be twenty. Latika sat mostly in our wide red verandah, either looking at the sky or at her fingernails.

A couple of days later, Abanibabu came for a visit again. He offered *kaka* some money. In course of the conversation, he suddenly hit upon an idea.

'Satish, wasn't K. M. Dutta your friend?'

'K. M. Dutta who?'

'The one who did law at Calcutta University when you were doing your B.A. and who stayed in the same boarding house?'

'Oh, you mean, Kamini? Kamini Mohan? What about him?'

'*Aare*! He is now a famous lawyer and runs a law firm in Dalhousie! Why don't you meet him? Meet him tomorrow itself!'

My father also remembered Kamini. After all, they were all in the same boarding house in Calcutta.

Satish*kaka*'s luck at long last smiled on him. K. M. Dutta and Sons was indeed a large firm, right in the heart of Dalhousie Square. Kamini apparently had remained the same good-hearted man, and he indeed had a place for Satish*kaka*, that too, a good one. The office administrator had died a month back and Mr Dutta was looking for a good replacement. Satish*kaka* fitted the bill perfectly. Mr Dutta was very relieved to find a person he knew with the right kind of experience. Satish*kaka*, needless to say, was relieved too.

K. M. Dutta and Sons offered *kaka* a resettlement allowance. A two-bedroom, ground floor flat on the other side of the main road was rented, not too far from our place. The necessary furniture was procured, including a dressing table with a long mirror at the behest of *kakima*. They soon moved to their new place. It was unbelievable that the drama would take less than a month to be over.

When Satish*kaka* came to see us after a month with sweets, he seemed to be a different person altogether. Gone was that unsure look; here was a seasoned alert man, settled in life. My parents were warm in their hospitality. They talked like age-old friends, mostly in the remembrance mode of their life together in the village and of my maternal grandfather, who was the political mentor of both my father and *kaka*.

We began to visit them occasionally. Father usually went on Sunday mornings, my mother and I on the weekdays in the late afternoons. One day, Lata*kakima* asked me to get five *rosogolla*s from a nearby sweetshop. It took me no time to return with the consignment. *Kakima* went to make tea. From the kitchen, she called to me and asked softly, 'Did you have one of the sweets on the way?' Taken by complete surprise, I shook my head with some effort and equally softly said, '*Na*.'

A few minutes earlier, I had noticed Tamal enter the house in a hurry, only to leave soon.

My mother could make out that some words were exchanged in the kitchen. When she inquired about it on our way back in the rickshaw, I merely said, 'I am not going back there again. From now on, you come alone.'

Satish*kaka*'s days of happiness were short-lived. It was clear soon that Tamal had become friendly with the local rough elements, some of them with Naxal links. After all, their rented house was not very far from Chanditala, a notorious Naxal hideout. Satish*kaka* was looking for a place in another locality, closer to the city. But before they could move out, one day Latika went missing. On sustained enquiry, it was found out that a Bangladeshi acquaintance of hers was sighted a few days back near their place. After a month or so, news reached us that Latika and her friend, Rana, Rana Mohammad Shahidullah, had crossed the border and had got married. Not only did Latika marry a Muslim, but a liberation fighter too. It took some effort for Satish*kaka* to relate the information to my parents. He looked terribly distrait. My father heaved a deep sigh and could only say, 'কি আর করবা, মাইনা নাও। *Ki aar korba, maina nao!* What else can you do but accept it?'

A deep silence fell on Satish*kaka*. He remained quiet for a long time. Father only said, 'ছেলেটা তো ভালও হইতে পারে! আগে তো বাইচা থাক দুই জনে—ভালো আর মন্দ! এই লতার আস্কারাতে কান্ডটা ঘটতে পারল! *Chheleta to bhalo-o hoite pare! Aage to baicha thak dui jane—bhalo ar manda! Ei Lata'r ashkarate kandota ghot-te parlo!* For all you know, the boy might be good! Let both be alive and well—for better or for worse! What is there to talk about. It is for Lata's indulgence that all this could happen!' Satish*kaka* left at some point. It was clear that the family had known Rana quite well. Ma told my father, 'Had Satish listened to you and stayed back the last time they came, nothing like this would have happened!'

They moved out to a relatively peaceful place, far from our house. The visits of the two families thinned out. Tamal went to a polytechnic for a diploma course. Satish*kaka* became the right-hand man of Kamini Dutta. Lata*kakima* was busy with matinee shows, reading film magazines and knitting.

About three years later, one afternoon, they all came to visit—Satish*kaka*, Lata*kakima*, Tamal, Latika and Rana. Latika carried their little daughter, Shukla, in her arms. Rana was a tall, quiet, impressive-looking man. The two touched my parents' feet and did *pranam*. The tips of my mother's forefingers, I think I saw, crawled back for a moment and straightened again. To touch or not to touch, when the context is a tradition of transmitting ritualistic practices from one generation to another, becomes more of an ideomotor reflex and not so much of a conscious act. My father started chatting with Rana and was happy to find that he had read his Tagore well. Rana, on his part, was pleasantly surprised to find an elderly man taking so much interest in *Shesher Kabita*, Tagore's romantic meditations on the mysteries of love.

Shukla in no time became the centre of attraction through her cries, babble and endless tantrums. She was a beautiful little girl of about two. They all left after lunch, save Satish*kaka*. He stayed for long that day. My father praised Rana and assured *kaka* that everything would be all right with time. After all, in God's universe there were no religions, only humanity mattered. I think I noticed a hint of happiness on Satish*kaka*'s face. He started talking of their days together in the college boarding on Raja Dinendra Street; and with my mother, recounting memories of their village home in Dhaka and of her parents. He was not reminiscing; he was clinging to a common blissful past to cope with the present.

III

In the final year of school, when I was not busy giving private lessons to students, who were at times as old as me, I started attending the secret classes of Swadhin*da*, the local contact for the CPI(ML) party. His dark, damp room added to the ambiance of what we were taught and asked to perform. I earned a great deal of notoriety for taking part, along with fellow comrades, in an evening raid of our school premises when the nose of Gandhi's statue was broken to pieces with a sledge hammer. It took a lot of persuasion on my parents' part for the local leaders of the CPI(M)[8] to allow me to return to the locality again.

The date for the Higher Secondary Exam (the school-leaving exam as we call it) was never to arrive, always arriving, always postponed. At one point I lost patience and started reading other things, storybooks mainly. Even if I had managed to remain attentive through the rollercoaster of its continuous postponement, it would not have helped much such were the kind of distractions, at times, life-threatening. Nights brought sounds of stealthy footfalls, brisk running, and sudden distant cries and screams for help that faded slowly in the dark. If a coconut fell at odd hours, we knew someone was hiding at the top of the tree. Heavy sounds of boots meant we closed the windows and allowed the armed policemen to go past. Finally, three days before the exams started, the secretary of the West Bengal Board of Secondary Examination gave a press statement asserting that there would be no more postponements. I got out my books and exercise books back on my desk and tried to regain my lost concentration. It was difficult.

Our exam centre was a school in another refugee colony, Bapuji Nagar, near Sulekha Glass Factory. On the morning of the first exam, my mother performed the usual ritual of touching sandalwood-smeared holy flower petals on my forehead and putting the stuff inside my shirt pocket. I touched her feet as well as my father's and set off for the exam centre in a bus, escorted by my sister. Halfway through, I noticed a large crowd assembled at a playground. As the bus slowed down, I tucked my head out of the window and saw four men lying with their throats slit. One seemed to be still alive. My entry into adulthood was hastened. I reached the centre, completely disoriented.

In the late afternoon, as I came out of the hall into the school courtyard, I found my sister waiting with a bag. She looked disturbed. I was told that a few hours earlier, the Central Reserve Police had cordoned off our locality and shot down five escaping men, all of whom I knew and save one, all of whom died on the spot. I was not to return home but was to stay at my maternal uncle's place in New Alipore. The bag apparently contained some books she thought would be useful for the rest of the exams.

My *mama*[9] was a senior manager of a rather reputed pharmaceutical company. Their airy three-bedroom flat was delightfully done up. My sister stayed back for him to return from office. After a brief chat with her, *mama* called me and asked how I proposed to go to the exam centre the next morning. I had no idea. He told me not to worry, he would drop me at Gariahat junction, though that meant making a long detour. From there I could catch a southbound bus. I nodded my head though it did not make matters any less confusing.

My sister did not bring any of my exercise books which contained all my notes, including some answers written out. It did not bother me as I had already developed a nonchalant attitude. At dinner, my uncle asked me if I still hobnobbed with my Naxal friends and added, joking: 'I hope they will not follow you here!' *Maima*[10] tried to smile to hide her anxiety. My cousin, then five or six, asked curiously who the Naxals were. My aunt replied: 'জানো না তো নকশাল কি! সব খেয়ে নাও, নাহলে কিন্তু নকশাল ধরে নিয়ে যাবে! *Jano na toh Naxal ki! Sab kheye nao, naholey kintu Naxal dhore niye jabe!* You don't know what Naxals are! Eat up everything, or else the Naxals will come and take you away!' The little girl looked strangely at me and for the rest of my stay, kept a safe distance.

The morning after the first exam, the vernacular daily carried a list of ten exam centres in Kolkata, where what was happening was not an exam but pure farce. Our centre came third in that list. The news consoled me for not having the relevant books and other study materials.

Exams over, I rang my father at the school where he was a headmaster and asked him to take me back the next morning.

Father came, and in no time, I packed my little bag and was ready to leave. *Maima* made tea for him; by then *mama* had gone off to work, and soon we were off too.

The next evening *mama* turned up at our place to take me back again since Netaji Nagar was no longer safe for a young lad like me. The gesture brought us closer. Gradually I started feeling part of his family. *Maima* would at times call me aloud to taste her curry, still on the oven, and check for salt and spices. *Mama,* on his way to office, would drop me near the British Council, where I spent the whole day browsing. I was provided with lunch—the same that was given to *mama*.

I didn't know which book to look for or how to look for a title on the racks, for I had no title in mind. I used to pick up one, mostly arbitrarily, from the pile of returned books, read a few pages and keep it back from where I had got it. In the course of my meandering search, one day I chanced on a book called *Industry and Empire*. The author's name, I found, was Eric Hobsbawm. Halfway through the book, as I read about the formation of the industrial working class in nineteenth-century Britain, I started dreaming of a land of distant church bells, rows of oak trees, stately buildings from a different era, a long tapestry of sonorous hums coming from somewhere I didn't know, of ponds and ducks and beautiful white children, young girls with small golden braids, a picture I suppose I drew in my mind from the few poems of Keats I had read at school. The discussion on class struggle would draw my attention later, never free though of a lulling pageant of peace and harmony of a far-off land.

I didn't expect to do well in my school-leaving exam, and I didn't. My marks were just about enough to secure my admission to a college run by Hindu missionaries and barely enough to be eligible for taking the entrance test at Presidency College, Kolkata. My tenure at the missionary college far south of the city was over in a week. By then I had received two warnings from the *maharaj,* the head priest. On the first occasion, my roommate Soumitra and I were caught smuggling cigarettes tucked inside a small packet of puffed rice. The next warning was soon to come. In desperate need of transgression, one early morning Soumitra and I landed up in the prayer hall wrapped in bare, red quilts. We were asked to wait outside the hall. The principal's call came soon after. Knowing that the final warning could not be far off, Soumitra waited for the admission test results of Jadavpur Engineering College, I for Presidency. We felt empty in the head and had nothing better to do than gazing at the white ceiling more intently.

One early morning, still not fully awake, I thought I saw my father and *didi*[11] enter the college gates and approach the hostel. I knew I must have made it to Presidency. And for the first time in my stay with the saffron missionaries, I felt excited and happy. It didn't matter that I didn't actually see my father and sister, that it was only an apparition—I just needed a thread to hang my hopes on.

Around nine that morning, they did land up. They were carrying the news of my admission to Presidency College, which was announced to me in concealed excitement. We, all three of us, proceeded towards the principal's room; by then I had already packed my luggage and put on my best apparel. The principal muttered in a moaning voice: 'এখানে অন্তত চরিত্রগঠনটা হতো! *Ekhane antata charitragathan-ta hoto!* Staying here would have at least helped in character-formation!'

IV

Leaving behind the project of character-formation that the missionary college might have on offer, I tried hard to be part of the Presidency crowd. The very first class was taken by Kajal Sengupta, everyone's Kajal*di*. She was lucid, loud and clear, and had a stunning appearance. Not very tall, she was comely; her sari, white with a large red border, sat tight on her, her eyes, sapphire bright, actually burning, and a grey patch weaving through her hair. I felt sad, for I knew I would take no time to fall for her. One day I confided it to a senior. He asked me not to worry: 'This is a ritual young men perform on entry to the college. You will be all right.' Very early in life, I experienced the erotic spell that an attractive woman of poise can create. The project of character-formation had by then retreated a long way off.

Presidency English Honours class those days was an elite bastion. Not only did I not have English, I lacked the practice of speaking in the standard Calcutta dialect of Bangla. Born in an unadulterated refugee colony, I could only speak in a mixed East Bengal dialect, with the Dhaka variety enjoying a clear hegemony. Soon the girls of my department took me to be an introvert, and I was happy to be left alone.

Presidency was my early adolescence dream. In retrospect, a magazine brought out by the radical students of the college during the fiery days of the early second part of the 1960s decided my fate. The cover contained a huge nib scribbling, bold and scrubby: 'এই নোংরা, পচা, গলা বুর্জোয়া সংস্কৃতি নিপাত যাক। *Ei nongra, pocha, gola bourgeois sanskriti nipat jaak*. Down with this dirty, rotten, festering bourgeois culture'. Inside were articles arguing how the bourgeoisie weaves a chimera of deception through its cultural artifacts, each piece a veritable cannonball. To date, I am yet to come across an ideological criticism so fierce, so targeted and so committed. One such pointed target was the film *Balika Bodhu*. It disturbed my secret bonhomie with the film's early adolescent romance. Nonetheless, I took the analysis to represent a higher realm of revolutionary truth, a sacred realm at whose altar I must sacrifice my boyish infatuations.

I continued giving private lessons—or 'tuition' as it was commonly called—to local lads and girls, but hiked my pay by five rupees. Some left, others continued, some new ones from the adjacent Ranikuthi Government Housing joined, who paid me more than what I expected. I gave my earnings to my mother, who in return gave me one rupee-fifty paise every morning. By the time I returned home at night, it was already ten, and I was half-dead with exhaustion, having spent the whole day on gallons of replenished tea at the college canteen and an occasional cup of coffee at the Coffee House, courtesy of Ranajay Gupta, my dearest college friend. Added to my intake was the standard refreshment offered at 'tuition places': a cup of tea with two Marie biscuits that, by the time it was served, had lost their edges to the spilled tea on the saucer. After dinner, I lay down for a while. When I started my day's study, it was past 11:30 at night. I worked till the early hours of the morning. Next day at eight, when I was dragged out of bed by one of my sisters, I proceeded straight to the shower, head soaked in sleep that my body rightfully demanded.

I took the 9:15 bus to Esplanade from the Gachtala bus stop adjacent to Netaji Nagar, where I lived. It was packed with locals and gave the feeling that the red double-decker was a moving Trojan Horse with refugee commandos who would soon invade the city centre. Kamal*da,* sitting in the front row on the upper deck, used to sing a Bhojpuri score: '*Ram chale aage-aage, Laxmanbhai peechhe…*' (Ram walks ahead, brother Laxman following behind) while a select few kept the tune. It was real fun.

One day, we were stopped at Azadgarh by Congress goons, among whom Kajal and Sajal, two brothers, had already acquired a great deal of notoriety. Their father, Santoshbabu, was from Dhaka where he lived near our village. The tall man carried a huge pile of brassware on his head and inevitably while passing by our house, stopped and had a chat with my *thakuma,*[12] mourning in the course of exchange of nostalgic tales those days of peace and plenty left behind. *Thakuma* served him a glass of water and a *batasha*[13] and offered him a paan which he chewed with great relish.

Kajal and Sajal, wearing dark glasses that day, their collars turned up, commanded everyone to come down. They were looking for their enemies at Netaji Nagar: 'Don't be scared. We know who we are looking for.' They meant CPI(M) activists. I don't know why they took me to be among the chosen ones. A hard palm held me by the collar and dragged me inside Azadgarh. I don't know who else they chose to keep me company. Soon I would be blindfolded and made to walk a distance. At one place, I was stopped and asked to turn around. I could make out that I was not the only catch of the day, since similar orders were given to at least one more person. There was a gunshot without much fuss, a fall and a withering cry. It all happened like the trailer of a crime movie. Then someone came up to me and asked, 'কি করিস?' 'প্রেসিডেন্সি-তে পড়ি।' 'বাঞ্চোদ।' '*Ki korish?*' '*Presidency-te pori.*' '*Banchod.*' 'What do you do?' 'Study at Presidency.' 'Sister-fucker.' A motionless stillness. I imagined a white wall running behind me, as I had read in the newspaper the morning after the Operation Steeple Chase in Baranagar, when young men were lined up next to a white wall by the Indian Army and shot dead.

Some whispers were eddying around me, then a voice that said, 'শোন, মারিস না, সিপিএম করে না। অর বাবা আমাগো হেডস্যার, ও অনিলবাবুর ছেলে। আমি অনিলবাবুর কোচিং-এ পড়সি, অরে আমি চিনি। পার্টি-টার্টি করে না। *Shon, marish na, CPM kore na. Or baba amago Head-Sir, o Anilbabur chhele. Ami Anilbabur coaching-e porshi, ore ami chini. Party-tarty kore na.* Listen, don't kill him, he's not a CPM fellow. His father is our Head-Sir, he is Anilbabu's son. I've been to Anilbabu's coaching, I know him. He's not into party-politics.' There was some more discussion in whispers, and then a man's footfalls approached me, the unfolding of the blindfold by rough hands, and I was set free. Someone said, 'ভাগ বোকাচোদা! *Bhag bokachoda!* Run, you fucking fool!' I walked down the lane to the bus-stop, my eyes and temples aching from the tight bind. Caught between fearlessness and paranoia, I thought I could not see, as if it was not necessary to see to keep walking. Years later, I read Raghav Bandyopadhyay's Naxal memoir, *Journal 70*. There, the writer-protagonist was similarly let off at the last moment by a firing squad of policemen on the realisation that he was the only son of a widow and a brahmin, that too a Bandyopadhyay (Banerjee). Killing him on a Tuesday evening would be a great *paap*, a sin. Such merciful acts happen once in a blue moon, but when they do happen, they are magically real.

That day after the third class, as I was approaching the college canteen, a waiter told me, 'Your father is looking for you.' I had not shared the morning episode with any of my college mates; it was too fresh, too close to me still. My father did not ask me anything. He took a taxi and following a different route, we reached home around four; he was silent and pensive throughout the journey. My mother too said nothing. At night, I was told that I would be taken to the college hostel next morning, where I would stay, not to come back home even for a casual visit unless specifically instructed.

V

A five-minute walk from College Street, in the old, long, red building with an imposing green iron gate that closed to an arch suspiciously tight, we ate mutton for dinner every night of our lives. I discovered a new world at the hostel. Like me, the other boarders too were not from Calcutta, many of them were from the districts. Like me, they also could not speak faultless English, had no idea of New Market, did not know about Nizam's kebabs or Flurys' cakes, neither were they used to the Italian flavours of Firpo's Restaurant. Some of them were wealthy farmers' scions and carried, on every return from home, a large bag full of puffed rice and molasses with a delicate sweet smell of coconut and date-palm. They were fiercely regular about their studies and pursued their goals—or 'aim in life' as it was called—breathlessly. Between them and their goals (which were mostly restricted to qualifying for the state civil service cadetship) were two obstructions: women and Naxals. They joined the college fully briefed and allowed no distraction. But one or two did slip out of such vows, with mostly miserable results.

One late afternoon as I returned to the hostel, I found a small crowd in the aisle leading to my room. They seemed to be enjoying the scene inside a particular room. I took a peep and realised that one of our mates had lost his sanity. Lying on the bed, he kept murmuring in a sing-song, wavering voice, 'চড়ুই পাখি, কুটুর-কুটুর... *Chorui pakhi, kutur-kutur*'. It did not mean anything, apart from suggesting that twittering sparrows were having fun. Apparently he was doing that for the past few hours; windows closed, the room was dark and damp. The secret travelled from one lip to another, and in no time, the entire hostel would be a party to that sight. We were told that the chap—a short, thin, quiet fellow from an interior village—had fallen in love with a college girl who wore sleeveless blouses and *bileti scent* (foreign perfume). No one questioned the inevitability of the fall.

Assuredly, he came back to his senses the next morning after being administered a healthy dose of sedative. He looked forlorn, his face shrunk and dry. He was sent back home that afternoon escorted by a fellow student. After a couple of months, the news reached us that his father had arranged a bride for him and he was going to get married and look after their land. This was the best his parents could do to rid their son of city-vices.

Of course, not everyone in the hostel was like this. There was another crowd, mostly from district schools or from the two sides of the Hooghly river, the industrial heartland of Bengal on the verge of rotting. They ranked very high in the school-leaving exams. Save a few who joined economics, they were mostly in the hard sciences—physics and chemistry. The IITs were yet to demand their pound of share, at least not on the first fifty toppers. These boys were a cheerful lot, widely read. I was introduced to Hemingway and to photography by one such boarder, who chose to, as an aberration, do physiology. Animesh and I went for long walks together after dinner, a path that took us at times to the city centre, Esplanade, where the movie theatres mostly ran English films. Stepping inside those theatres was itself an experience. The dimly lit halls with ladies and gentlemen seated neatly and talking in soft voices, the chairs that reclined on your wish, the thick spongy soft carpet (mostly red), the curtain that went to the two sides in tidy folds with the ringing of the bell, the huge spotless screen, the dim lights half tucked at the bottom of the walls and on the steps—all seemed so magical as if a somnambulist had cast a spell on the spectator. I was willing to believe everything I saw on the screen.

On one such occasion, we watched *Summer of 42*. The heroine's long shapely legs, her climb up the ladder to the attic as her young lover watched in erotic shiver left a deep impression on me. It inaugurated a chemistry I was not sure I understood, a world of fantasy that was for me still new. Like an addict, I watched the film perhaps half a dozen times without letting anyone know. The scene of the unknown pristine West with bells and church spires that I used to weave in the idle afternoons at British Council while reading Hobsbawm as if reached its adulthood, its fruition. I told myself, I too belonged, though I wasn't sure where or to what.

Certain evenings we went out for the night-show in a group, giving a shout from the gate, 'Jiban, this many late meals!' By the time we came back, it would be past midnight, and an old cat with its protégés had by then finished off two or three of the meals covered with thick brass *thalis*. We settled for the ones that appeared untouched—chapattis like dried hide and mutton as cold and taut as it could get. Occasionally we could hear a gargle-like sound coming from the open drinking water tank. We knew what it was and what we would see—a beautiful frog, green and golden with protruding eyes, looking wistfully at the world outside and seeking our mercy.

One day three of us had gone to watch a James Bond film. It was the summer of 1972. Halfway through the film, as Bond was about to push a villain from a high-rise, a bomb exploded at the gate, then another in the passageway to the exit of the theatre. A huge commotion erupted as men and women tried to leave the auditorium all at once. We were on the third floor, the area reserved for those with the cheapest tickets. We could do little better than stand where we were and breathe the air carrying sulfurous odour. It was quite some time before we could leave the place. By then, the police had come and were busy collecting the leaflets that our marauders had left for us. One of us managed to collect a couple of them. It was a roughly printed sheet of paper gone yellow. The write-up reminded us of the glorious revolution being carried out by our peasants in Debra and Gopiballavpur in the interiors parts of Midnapore (now Jhargram). The day was not far when the revolutionary peasants would surround the city of Calcutta and ask the middle class to pay for its total genuflection to the bourgeois-landlord state.

Suddenly we found three policemen running after a thin, tall figure. They caught hold of him near the main road, started kicking him straightaway and then threw him bodily inside the waiting van. We kept walking, for hiding would invite danger. We knew what awaited that chap. The van in all possibility would zoom deep into the Maidan, dark and soulless, the door would open and the man would be asked to flee. As he would get out and run, he would be shot from behind, ending one more episode of urban uprising.[14]

After ten, the mutton and chapatti dinner over, the whistling began from young men in wards one and two, those adjacent to the road and those, we told ourselves, who were from other colleges and not, by any means, from Presidency. They were looking for Sonali, a tallish young beggar woman who apparently squatted outside the hostel gate at night, her newborn child on the lap, her age no more than seventeen or eighteen, her voice husky, her complexion dusky, her unclad breasts shapely, enough to set fire to the arid lives of the undergraduates in their late teens or early twenties. Soon, as the gate would close and Shukheswarji, the hostel *darwan,*[15] start making his bed, the whistling would become intense: young men calling out from their rooms to someone they never saw, yet everyone was sure she was there. They wanted her to be let in, as the halogen lights on the adjacent street went dim and finally off. Their whistles and fervent calling out by the name echoed down the deep hollow street. From the second floor, I tried to follow the calls and the whistles, as if in a place far from home I have come to a pure land of adult despair and desire. The cries were make-believe, yet despairingly human and so real. Years later, I went back to the hostel one day and enquired with the present boarders about Sonali, the common source of inspiration in our times. It didn't amaze me that she was still being called out as she sat every night next to the hostel gate holding her newborn on her lap, dusky skinned, husky voiced. The whistles and calls still continued and reverberated in the hollow of the nightclad street, celebrating our common totem for years.

Looking back, those mirthful years at the Hindu Hostel seem a long dirge to death and decay in the midst of our youth, those ever-repeated, horribly male sex-jokes like the unresponsive flesh of a paralytic limb. Sonali, however, remains the bridge over the passage of time, our timekeeper of adolescent Eros.

VI

As days passed, the city Naxals became more and more an alienated lot, more and more cornered and finished off by the lethal state apparatus. The class factor, however, remained important. Some months earlier, the vice-chancellor of Jadavpur University was hacked to death by a group of students in the name of the revolution to come. They belonged to influential fathers who managed to soon parcel off their sons abroad. But Naxals from ordinary middle-class, mostly refugee, families were tortured, maimed or killed in droves. By the end of 1971, state oppression acquired some systematic formality to it.

One day while crossing the newly-built Dhakuria flyover in South Calcutta, probably in late 1972, I noticed a few words scribbled in a rough, hurried brush of tar on a hoarding displaying a cigarette brand: 'জনগণ শুয়ারের বাচ্চা, আমরা চললাম। *Janagan shuworer baccha, amra chollam*. People are a pack of swine, we bid adieu.' To my mind, this remains the most truthful testimony of the state of mind of the departing Naxals, exasperated as they were in body and soul and utterly loathful of the betrayal of the middle class. Years later, the hoarding will be used to display the arrival of a new rightwing newspaper, *Bartaman*, which announced: 'ভগবান ছাড়া আর কাউকে ভয় করে না। *Bhagaban chhara aar kauke bhoy koreyna. Bartaman* fears no one, save God.'

Not all was over, however. More than a year later, in the wee hours of one morning a van of armed policemen arrived at the gate of our hostel. They had a job to do and knew exactly where to go. In a room locked for ages, they discovered a whole armoury stacked in cupboards. It mostly consisted of choppers, knives of different shapes, and even swords. The whole collection was whisked off in another van, which arrived soon after. The work was done briskly, methodically, without fuss. We could make out they were acting on the information that some Naxal prisoner must have provided under torture.

VII

It was late 1973. For some time I had noticed Robin*da* frequenting ward number five of the hostel where I stayed. Like me, most boarders of this ward were from Presidency. Robin*da* was a tall, middle-aged man with a swaying potbelly in a striped khadi *kurta* and white pajamas. He carried a *jhola* that bulged at times. His hair was crew-cut, which allowed each strand to stand on its own independent of others. His spectacles were small and round in a metal frame that touched the tip of the nose as he bent his head to read something. He had a disarming, carefree smile, a bit Micawber-like. It took no time to realise that he was a man from a world of narrative who carried a large pile of anecdotes on his back.

His repertoire was huge—right from reading horoscopes to scientific methods of circumcision to the latest in soccer strategy devised in Germany, which he preferred to call, 'hit and run', borrowing a term, I suspect, from the Che Guevara quotes. He was mighty helpful, though his resources were nil. It took no time for me to become his *chela*,[16] willing to follow him to the end, as once did the children of Hamelin to the tune of a certain pied piper. And I was not alone. Robin*da* was particularly keen to make friends with Prasun, the true Naxal among us, though only in spirit. We, the rest of my friends and I, were merely post-Naxals, a less glamorous breed, confused and surely an ineffectual brand of revolutionaries. What saved us was our noncommittal attitude. But Prasun was different. He was thoughtful and looked at the world intently from the upper half of his spectacles as he thought, curling a patch of hair around one finger all the while, a *mudradosh* that he liked to preserve.[17] He was a strict moralist and loved his girlfriend Dalia more morally than, I suspect, erotically, a trait that would make him lose her to one of his dear friends, Amal, a fellow Naxal. (But Prasun also read Kafka's *Letters to Felice* and was passionate about the book). I soon noticed Prasun and Robin*da* talking quietly at times, Robin*da* looking this way and that as he talked. They changed the topic if we were anywhere near. It did not bother me, for I admired everything that Prasun did, and Robin*da* was so immensely lovable.

Robin*da* was a man full of ideas, quite often business ideas. Once he asked me, how about getting into the sari business and making a quick buck as the Puja approached near. The idea was to get saris from weavers in interior Bengal and sell them at a moderate price. As bonus, three months installment payment would be offered. But where to sell them, I asked. 'Hah-hah!' he laughed, 'At the gates of women's colleges.' It didn't strike me that it could make for risky business to sell saris in installments to a floating crowd. Surely the women would not leave their colleges to escape paying a paltry sum of money, Robin*da* reasoned.

The operation started the very next week as planned. After our initial success, Robin*da* told me that we should try selling to university graduate women students who had more say in the family. So we tried our luck at the Calcutta University Arts Building, just next door to our hostel. Emboldened, we started displaying our wares in the large, cemented courtyard of the campus. Women flocked in droves as we explained the distinction of each sari. When the excitement was at its peak, there appeared a stern old professor, thin and gaunt-faced. His voice was suitably dry and devoid of any positive emotion. He chastised us: 'Some limits ought be maintained. You guys have crossed all!' The assembled crowd quickly thinned. But by then we had dispersed a good number of saris on the promise of payment in three installments. The Puja vacation followed soon. After a despondent break, when we went back to the courtyard, and then to the lecture theatres, a few of the women could be traced but many were reported to have got married in the break or simply decided not to continue their studies anymore. Our dream of making a quick buck only left us in debt.

Robin*da* disappeared one fine day, never to return. I used to enquire after him with Prasun, who would put up a blank face. More than a year later, I came to know that the man we knew as Robin*da* was actually Altaf Latif. He was a Bangladeshi influenced by the ideas of Charu Majumdar and associated with Naxal groups in northern districts like Rangpur and Pabna. When the newly formed Bangladesh government took a hardened stance towards the splinter groups of Naxals, Altaf fled to West Bengal and was living 'underground'. He went back in early 1974 with the idea of getting together the disjointed groups. True to his mores, he was biting more than he could chew, and was soon arrested. In the skirmish that followed, apparently he was shot dead. I did not know how much of that story was to be believed and how much discarded. Either way, it did not solve the puzzle called Robin*da*. Was his half-baked idea of making a quick buck genuine or was it an act? Be that as it may, we both lost a sum of money, not meagre, given our diehard poverty.

VIII

Many years after the volatile '70s, in the early 1990s, I was then in Brisbane, my friend Renata and I decided on a day's outing to the famous Byron Bay in north Queensland. We left early and in about three hours reached the bay. The day was spent in vain, with our eyes glued to the binoculars, waiting for the whales to make their appearance. But we did catch sight of the dolphins jumping in wild mirth.

Halfway through the afternoon, we set back for home. We saw a village on our way back. By then, we must have been halfway through our journey. There was nothing special in seeing a village had it not been for a particular artifact that came to our notice. At the front of each house, there was a special kind of letterbox, a jerry can with a lid and a slit at the top end. We could make out this was a post-hippie village and smiled to ourselves. But what was written on the cans took the storyline some distance. For each name of the houses, on the cans were inscribed words like Ganga, Manali, Rishikesh, Tumbani, Chaibasha and such others. It did not take me time to fathom that this was not only a hippie colony but a colony of those who had at one point settled in different places in India. We could not help but pull up and walk around the place.

Seeing us, a man past middle age came out. Patrick was his name. He told me that the best years of his life were spent in my country. 'Why am I saying *your* country? India is also ours. It was in India that we could give up our elders' corrupting habits and outlook, the hangover that was passed on to us, to discover something much deeper, a mode of being close to the ways of the soul. ...Kindly spend the night with us.'

Patrick was from New South Wales, an engineer by profession; his wife, Sue, a self-taught artist. They made black bread, drew, and were into pottery. They took their ware every Saturday to a village fair. Their children went to the village community school and spent time mostly outdoors, in rain and sun. The bathroom had no roof but was instead covered with the foliage of a large, prosperous tree.

After dinner, it must have been past ten, we sat in the verandah and were chatting aimlessly and drinking green tea. At one point, Sue said matter-of-factly: 'After some time, a python will come down the tree and stretch out on the lawn. It loves soaking in the moonlight.'

That night, I lay wide awake under the stern watch of the moonlight.

IX

Decades have rolled past. I am in contact with my physiologist friend, Animesh, who switched to Life Sciences after his BSc and now lives in California where he heads a reputed computer lab engaged in understanding the fundamental biological basis of life. And also Prasun. He retired recently from a bank, a job he tried to run away from several times only to be lassoed back by his benevolent bosses each time. I remember spending the whole of the summer of 1983 at his place at Narayana in Delhi. The university was closed *sine die* due to student unrest. I had to complete writing my MPhil dissertation, and home was not the place to go back to, at least not for an MPhil student who was merely elongating (as per family wisdom) the unemployment channel.

On returning from office, Prasun spent an hour or so in the kitchen preparing the meal for the night. He would occasionally call out to me and wanted me to watch with a binocular the third floor of an adjacent house where, I was told, his dear friend Amal and his once-girlfriend Dalia were keeping a vigil on him. He was soon diagnosed as a schizophrenic. The unfulfilled dream of revolution had left a permanent scar on him. He still curls a patch of hair around a finger and looks askance at the world through the upper half of his glasses as he thinks. He goes to the Ram Krishna Mission Library in the heart of south Kolkata every morning and stays there till late, reading Vivekananda, Aurobindo, the Gita, and the Upanishads.

X

Let me get back to where I began: sightseeing in Dhaka in my friend's car. I had heard of Shankhari Bazar in old Dhaka from my mother. Actually it was a kind of a refrain in her Partition reminiscences: 'আমরা হিন্দুরা জানতাম, শাঁখারি বাজার যত দিন আছে, আমরা ঠিক আছি। যেদিন শাঁখারি বাজার পড়বো, বুঝুম এইবার যাইতে হইবো। *Amra Hindu-ra jantam, Shankhari Bazar joto din achhe, amra thik achhi. Je din Shankhari Bazar porbo, bujhum eibaar jaite hoibo.* We Hindus knew, as long as Shankhari Bazar existed, we were fine. The day Shankhari Bazar falls, we would know the time for our departure has come.'[18] I was eager to see Shankhari Bazar and its labyrinthine lanes. I stood at the entrance of one of those lanes and looked perhaps with eyes that had consumed many stories from ancestors. Suddenly I noticed an old man, wrapped in a white *thaan*,[19] with a long neat marking of white sandalwood on his forehead, staring at me. He said nothing, but came closer, step by step. When about twenty feet away, he said in a voice of quiet disapproval: 'আমাগোরে দেখনের কিছু নাই। বিপদে পড়ছেন বুইঝা নিজের মা রে ছাইড়া পালাইয়া গেছেন, যদি দেখনের থাকে, নিজেগো দেখেন। *Amagore dekhoner kichu nai. Bipadey porshen buijha nijer ma re chhaira palaiya gyachen, jadi dekhoner thhake, nijego dekhen.* There is nothing to look at us for. Knowing yourself in trouble, you abandoned your own mother and ran away. If you want to look, go look at yourself.'

That mortifying gaze kept looking at me. I left the place.

XI

Does the memory of a past land, a mode of living that once was real, ever die? Doesn't it get embedded in the body tissues and become part of the many fibres? On my way to the home of Chitra, my school-day fancy, there used to be a narrow bamboo bridge over a small rivulet. The bridge dipped every time one walked over it and touched the water. As a result, it was permanently wet. I enjoyed crossing it. The cool sensation on my feet seemed the right finale for all the warm throbbing and squeezing of heart I felt as I passed her house. The bamboo structure has long been replaced by a proper concrete bridge. After ages, the other day I took that lane again and crossed the bridge. Strangely, I could feel that wet sensation on my feet once again. Blood dries, yet leaves a wet feeling behind.

For those of us who spent their late teens and early twenties in the 1970s, that wasted, crumpled, scrawny part of life now looks like our fortune coin. I cannot discern through what alchemy the nefarious after-college hours, those memories without ancestry, now seem to be my primary link with the spiritual flow of life. Looking back, I wonder whether the 1970s' youth uprising had something more to it, a kind of geological existence, a veritable geological explosion. Otherwise, why did it find expression in every part of the globe, albeit in different forms? In Australia, it was time to cast asunder the long-held colonial cloak and turn to indigenous histories, to local flora and fauna; in Paris, Amsterdam, Berlin, Berkeley and New York, it took the form of celebrating sexuality in all its splendour and also fighting for change in gender roles; while in Africa and large parts of the colonised world, people engaged full-swing in decolonising movements. For Bangladesh, it was time to announce independence from the Pakistani rulers and also the sovereignty of the Bengali Muslim self, a process that started with the Partition of Bengal in 1947. In the western flank of Bengal, we dreamt of armed peasant insurgency on the borrowed philosophy of Chinese Maoism and of fighting all the fetters that held us back from the dreams of a fuller existence, often in the name of our great nineteenth-century achievements. We all were fighting our past, right, left and centre—action first, philosophy to follow.

In retrospect, I wonder whether one common underlying theme to these various forms of protest could be the liberation of our erotic lives from the shackles of tradition, and reminding ourselves never to forget that the middle of the road was a very dead end. Back in 2002, in my autobiographical essay *Growing Up Refugee*, I had observed:

> So often in our high school days, we had gushed out in a team ignoring the scornful looks of older teachers, shouting in unison slogans of gigantic simplicity: *Amar naam, tomar naam, Vietnam, Vietnam* (My name, your name, Vietnam, Vietnam). I didn't exactly know where Vietnam was in the map. It didn't matter, for Vietnam was everywhere, a libidinal expanse, a name-place where blood flowed to announce the death of a world order.[20]

Looking back, it seems it is this 'libidinal expanse' which brought the different uprisings of that period together, made us look for new ways of relating to the self, strive for new cartographies, sing songs, march in processions demanding new modes of belonging, a new communion with fellow humans and nature.

I am a rag-picker of the past, a collagist in the world of waste…

XII

Let me end the piece on a brighter note, or, what I prefer to call, life at reality's optimistic end. What I am witnessing at the present moment all around me in Kolkata in the Left mobilisation for the coming Assembly polls is a rejuvenation of the youth. I am witnessing a new enthusiasm among young men and women, both rural and urban, a chorus of youth, so to say. This trend cannot but lead us to a better future and will one day find an adequate replacement for the old guard. Let a hundred flowers bloom (in no cryptic sense). Let politics be the glasnost of the youth. Let young people sing freely in processions, not tied to some tired old scores of the old. I dream of witnessing a procession of young men and women passing by, singing Joan Baez's immortal, metonymic song: 'How long since I've spent a whole night in a twin bed with a stranger'. Let the 1970s come back again! Let us be talking of adequate procurement prices for peasants and equal citizenship rights for LGBTQ members of society in the same breath. Let revolutionaries be convinced that repression is the soul of reaction. This is particularly true for the era of neoliberal rights.[21]

> How long since I've spent a whole night in a twin bed with
> a stranger
> His warm arms all around me?
> ...
> All of your history has little to do with your face
> You're mainly a mystery with violins filling in space
>
> —Joan Baez

Notes and References

1. সে বড়ো সুখের সময় নয়, সে বড়ো আনন্দের সময় নয়

   Shey baro shukher shomay noy, shey baro anander shomay noy

   No time for cheer, not a happy time this

A 1967 poem by Shakti Chattopadhyay, translated from the original Bangla by Nandini Gupta. Available at https://www.parabaas.com/shakti/articles/shakti_notimeforcheer.shtml (accessed 25 March 2021). I have taken the liberty to change the above line in the translation to: 'Not a time for comfort, not a happy time this'.

2. A public courtyard, often with pillars and verandahs reflecting influences of European architecture. In keeping with tradition, the idols are placed on a single platform against a single semi-circular background (*chalchitra*). See, Uttara Gangopadhyay, 'Come to Kolkata to See How the Traditional, Aristocratic Houses Celebrate Maa Durga's Visit to Her Paternal Home', *Outlook Traveller*, 21 September 2017. Available at

https://www.outlookindia.com/outlooktraveller/explore/story/61216/top-10-bonedi-bari-durga-puja (accessed 30 March 2021). For more on this issue, see Tapati Guha-Thakurta, *In The Name of the Goddess: Durga Pujas of Contemporary Kolkata* (Delhi: Primus Books, 2015).

3. Stories of the lives of various Hindu gods and goddesses, narrated in a rhythmic fashion by the womenfolk of the house at a fixed time of the year. They are usually parables relating the powers of the deities and having a moral connotation.

4. *Doljatra,* also known as Holi, is a major festival of eastern India dedicated to Sri Krishna. On this auspicious day, an idol of Krishna and his beloved Radha, richly adorned and besmeared with coloured powder (*abir,* as it is called), is taken out in a procession in a swinging palanquin decorated with flowers, leaves, coloured cloths and paper. (See, https://en.wikipedia.org/wiki/Dol_Purnima [accessed 30 March 2021]).

5. Devotees of Krishna celebrate the frolics of the Lord with Radha along with her female companions (known as *gopinis*) on a full moon night of autumn (last day of the Bengali month of Kartik). A pious occasion for the Vaisnavs, the divine game or play (known as *lila*) has distinct erotic overtones, and is an occasion of mirth and festivity.

6. A type of sarong popular in the subcontinent.

7. *Kaka* is paternal uncle, father's younger brother; *kakima* is aunt, *kaka*'s wife.

8. Communist Party of India (Marxist); CPM is a popular abbreviation.

9. Maternal uncle, mother's brother.

10. Maternal aunt, *mama*'s wife.

11. Elder sister.

12. Grandma, father's mother.

13. Homemade sweet usually made from jaggery and looks like a thick yellow coin; those made of sugar are white.

14. Jawhar Sircar recounts those days of violence:

> But what happened in the autumn of 1971 has hardly been discussed in the public domain. Through that year, the military crackdown in East Pakistan and the genocide and mass-scale rapes there had infuriated people in West Bengal. People demanded a response and the sight of the army moving in large numbers through the city was a comforting indication that we were preparing to take on East Pakistan. We had no idea that S.S. Ray's government had decided to use some army regiments to assist civil police in 'exterminating the Naxalite menace'. As General J.F.R. Jacob of the Eastern Command confessed later

> on, sections of the army joined hands with the local police to hunt down Naxalites—in what was branded as Operation Steeple Chase.
>
> In Kolkata, the extremists were cornered and holed up in their last 'red bastions' like Baranagar and Chanditala. The commandos and armed police cordoned off entire areas with the help of antisocials, many of whom would become Congress leaders later on. The extremists were then shot in cold blood, often tied to lampposts, or at their very own doorsteps. Some were arrested and taken in police vans and many never seen ever again.

Jawhar Sircar, 'In a Calcutta Gripped With Naxal Violence and Police Brutality, People Lost Sons, Brothers and Friends', *The Wire*, 11 March 2021. Available at https://thewire.in/history/calcutta-naxal-violence-police-brutality-1971 (accessed 23 March 2021).

15. Gatekeeper; guard.

16. A guru's disciple who promises total loyalty, usually used sarcastically in Bangla.

17. Apart from meaning idiosyncrasy and mannerism, the Bangla word *mudradosh* also has a hint of ideomotor action, which *Webster's Dictionary* defines as: 'involuntary motor activity caused by an idea.'

18. *Shankha* is a bangle made of white conch shell that married Bengali Hindu women are traditionally supposed to wear. Shankhari Bazar derives its name from *shankhari*, the craftsmen who make these bangles.

19. Borderless white dhoti.

20. Manas Ray, 'Growing Up Refugee', *History Workshop Journal*, Issue 53 (2002), 169–170.

21. I acknowledge Regina Ganter and Shawkat Hossain for the corrections and thank my former student M. Al-Mamun for providing useful reading materials for future research. I am grateful to Sumanta Banerjee, Partha Chatterjee, Ian Hunter, Jawhar Sircar, Debjani Mazumder, Kirsty Gunn, Biswajit Chatterjee, and Meher Ali for their gracious comments.

3 Between Remembering and Forgetting

1971 and an Inheritance of Loss*

MEHER ALI

My grandfather, Colonel Nadir Ali, in the autumn of his life often spoke about 1971. Deployed to Dhaka on 10th April, he served as the second, and then first, in command of the 3rd Commando Battalion until October 1971, when he was sent back to West Pakistan for a promotion. On the morning of his departure from Dhaka, he eschewed his uniform for a traditional *dhoti* and wandered over to the Rangamati lake. He got onto a small *nauka* and shared *dal-bhat* with the surprised boatman. As he would describe it, he imagined himself—in that moment—not as an occupying officer but a resident local. 'I completely lost my mind,' *Dada* would say with a shrug, the bizarre episode marking the beginning of a mental breakdown that would eventually see him hospitalised for six months, temporarily losing his memory, and prematurely retired from the army. 'Were you scared?' I asked him once, understanding his saga—of both war and madness—as one of violence, trauma, and fear. 'Oh no!' he said. 'Once you cross the border as a madman, you go into a fool's paradise.' In his voice was neither pain nor shame but a kind of gentle remorse. It betrayed an attachment, even a fondness, for his old delusions—the impossible imaginings they engendered, the alternative belongings they enabled.

What did Pakistan lose in 1971? A war, certainly, but also a part of itself—akin, as others have put it, to the loss of a limb. As Yasmin Saikia has argued in her work with both victims and perpetrators,

*This essay has been written for this volume, and relates to the author's ongoing research work on memory and archive.

what was also destroyed was *insaniyat* or shared humanity: a loss of the fundamental ethics of tolerance.[1] Pakistan's continued refusal to acknowledge, let alone apologise for, the evidence of rampant army atrocities, rapes, and selective genocide certainly testifies to this immeasurable moral abscess. It also calls attention to the striking absence of public memory around the conflict—summarised in school textbooks only as an Indian conspiracy, virtually ignored in cultural and public life. Many have labeled this silence an effect of 'collective amnesia,'[2] a process of selective erasure in the service of national selfhood and myth-making. When compared to the highly contested and politicised nature of memorialisation in Bangladesh, where the war remains, in many ways, an active battleground (upon which national identity, politics and values are forged and fought)—this silence can sometimes seem deafening.

Against such nationalist agendas of remembering and forgetting, some historians have turned to the realm of individual memory and oral recollection; harnessing the power of the unfiltered voice to reclaim a more human history of the war.[3] Brandishing the authenticity of the personal against the violence of state discourse, the recuperative urge underlying these efforts aims to disrupt and expand the boundaries of the official archive, while nevertheless remaining true to its organising principles of discovery and presence. Confronting silence with the multiplicity of narrative(s), distortions with their corrections, and gaps as an absence to be filled, the logic of recovery aspires, ultimately, to construct a more complete and inclusive truth: as an avenue for resolution, understanding, and even healing.

The indisputable importance of such projects—and the promise of ethical reconstruction and historiographical challenge they hold—is what first drew me to my grandfather's story. His anecdotes were replete with examples of the callousness and violence he encountered at the hands of his peers, beginning with his first action in Faridpur. 'I was given orders to kill as many bastards as you can,' he recounted, 'and to pick out the Hindus.' When *Dada* refused, saying he would neither discriminate between Muslims and Hindus nor would he fire on unarmed civilians, he was told:

'You have just come from West Pakistan, teaching your Bengali students and drinking with your Bengali friends. You don't know what has been happening here.'

Aside from departing from the official army line, *Dada* also expressed a rare readiness to share his account publicly.[4] In 2011, he travelled back to Dhaka to speak about his war experience. 'I, unfortunately, was a witness and participant in those events, though I never killed anyone or ordered anyone to be killed,' he said in his address. 'In the army, you wear no separate uniform. We all share the guilt.' In closing, he offered a personal apology. 'Now, as a Punjabi poet and writer I offer apologies and ask forgiveness from those who suffered so terribly in 1971.'

Dada's apology followed in the footsteps of a small minority of Pakistanis—writers, intellectuals, activists—who have condemned the army action over the years. Progressive poets such as Habib Jalib and Ahmad Salim, activists such as Tahira Mazhar Ali and I. A. Rehman, and journalists like Waris Mir braved state repression to raise their voices against the war as early as March 1971 (and were punished for their efforts). Their acts of resistance—centred around the ethical imperatives of witnessing—form a limited counter-archive to that of silence, by refusing to be mute spectators to atrocity and violence. In an 'Open Letter to President General A. M. Yahya Khan,' written on 7 April 1971, Malik Ghulam Jilani condemned the regime's actions, asking: 'I am not being brave. Who can be brave in fratricide? The days of bravery are over.'[5] Habib Jalib, upon hearing reports of civilian massacres, penned these lines:

Mohabbat golion se bo rahe ho
Watan ka chehra khoon se dho rahe ho
Guman tumko ke rasta kat rahe ho
Yaqeen mujhko ke manzil kho rahe ho

You sow love with bullets
You wash the face of our land with blood
You believe you are forging a path
I believe you are losing the way

The character of this dissent—of truth against silence, of witnessing against erasure, of individual morality against the barbarity of the regime—orients itself, first and foremost, against the Pakistani state. But it also creates the space for a certain critique of the very basis of Pakistani nationalism, throwing bare the violent exclusions at the heart of the nation-project. As Naveeda Khan has powerfully argued, the attempt to reckon with the foundations of Pakistani nationhood can be found, more broadly, in the 'intellectual soul-searching' of the post-71 period: in the growing preoccupation with origins and narratives of failure.[6] The foundational crisis of 1971 reverberates both into the future—in the ethnic tensions and violence which continue to plague Pakistan[7]—and the past, all the way to the tenuous birth of the Pakistan idea itself. The contested relationship between 1947 and 1971 presents dual narrative possibilities: while 'official' historiography reads independence as a triumph and 1971 as a betrayal, an alternative narrative sees problematic origin and inevitable failure. While the first serves the project of nationalism, the other labels nationalism as the cause—with war, violence, and separatism as its effects. Either way, the lens of the nation is ultimately evaluative; the success of Bengali nationalism indicating the intrinsic deficiency of Pakistan's. The question then becomes: was Bengali independence inherent to the Pakistan idea itself? Was the break-up of Pakistan inevitable?

Despite its explanatory allure, the notion of inevitability—establishing a teleological link between 1947 and 1971—has proven overdetermining. The shared history of the interceding years, in particular, has become bifurcated into one of competing nationalisms—limiting the conceptual frameworks available for understanding not only deeper causes, but the role and nature of the postcolonial state, the place of local or transnational contexts, and the existence of alternative ideological commitments and modes of belonging. Fifty years on—as the generations who lived through it are gradually leaving us—our historical insights remain disappointingly limited, constrained by the politics of memory and denial, justice and blame. The finality and violent 'rupture' of the conflict itself—and Pakistan's refusal to acknowledge or apologise for its role—becomes not only a moral and ethical loss, but also a loss of historical understanding. It transforms the war into a festering wound, or rather, a blockage: preventing not only reconciliation and healing but also the possibility of deeper self-knowledge.

Before the war, my *Dada* was posted in Dhaka for four years (from 1962–66), a time he often referred to as the happiest of his life. He joked with his Bengali friends, who would call each other 'general'—the joke being, if East Pakistan went its own way, they would rise in rank. He remembered the real bonds of friendship, but also the feeling of distance between the West Pakistani officers who dominated all the senior posts, and the Bengali officers who made up the majority of his cadre at the Ordinance Depot. 'They spoke in Bangla to each other and in English to us.' *Dada* attended a Bangla language class, which was offered to the officers on a voluntary basis. He remembered seeing the list of verbs and discovering that they were all common with Punjabi. 'Name any and I'll tell you,' he said to me, '*Kore? Kare. Khaoya? Khana*. I even knew some of the words which were not known to most Punjabis in Punjabi—which came from that very rural kind of Punjabi. Like *doka* (to enter). I thought, then, that it won't be very difficult to learn.'

But *Dada* never did learn the language; although he grew to love Bengali culture. Once as a young major, he was made administrative-in-charge of his service—where during lunch-break, music would be played on the loudspeaker. He put on Rabindra Sangeet, although Tagore songs were banned by the government at the time. 'I, in the heart of my hearts, was a very pro-Bengali person, pro-East Pakistan,' he once told me. 'But I suppose it could only go that far—music, conversation, Bengali friends.' Despite his fondness for the people and the culture, *Dada* volunteered for deployment when the war broke out. 'On 25th March, when we heard the news, sitting at the bar—everybody cheered,' he recounted. No one except his brother-in-law, Justice Sajjad Sipra, decried his choice of posting. 'This is a civil war, a people's war,' *Dada* recalled him saying, 'And you volunteered to go?'

When I first sought out *Dada*'s story, I was searching for the potential of memory against loss. But his account, like any other, is replete with contradictions and gaps, ambivalence and uncertainty. His memories of violence sit uneasily with memories of camaraderie and friendship, and the memories of friendship are unsettled by those of distance and indifference. Is it enough, then, to posit witnessing against silence, dissent against repression, remembering against forgetting? What I thought could only be a painful remembering—the flashbacks to a traumatic and bloody conflict—sometimes seemed more like a wistful forgetting. For alongside the guilt and regret in *Dada*'s story, there was also the undeniable presence of nostalgia and loss.

When *Dada* entered, as he put it himself, 'the fool's paradise,' he lost his memory. He told me, often, of the alternate reality he was living in then—before his treatment and recovery. 'I thought Pakistan and India were going to become one,' he remembered, 'I was creating a People's Republic of India; that was the plan.'

What does forgetting enable; what does it allow us to recover? Fantasies, idealisms and utopias are not the stuff of historical event, but they are the traces of the roads not taken, of choices and dreams once imagined and then abandoned. They are reminders of the complexities of possibility and chance, of war and rupture not as inevitable but contingent, of history as always unsettled. I cannot truly know what drove *Dada* back, again and again, to his memories of 1971—but it wasn't simply the pull of a past trauma, an inescapable haunting. Returning to the war was for him entangled, I think, with returning to the pasts it encircled and foreclosed—his happy memories of East Pakistan, but also the possibilities of kinship, the promises of a young nation, of a more inclusive collective imagining. It was the consolation of an old madness—a surrender to contradiction and incommensurability, a place of forgotten dreams and past promise.

When Faiz Ahmad Faiz visited Bangladesh in 1974 and received, as the story goes, the cold shoulder from his old literary friends—he felt this pain of possibilities lost. He returned to write this famous verse:

Hum keh thehre ajnabi itni mudaraton ke baad
Phir banenge aashna kitni mulaqaton ke baad
Kab nazar mein aayegi bedaag sabze ki bahar
Khoon ke dhabbe dhulenge kitni barsaaton ke baad

> We are now strangers again who have known each other as friends
> How many meetings will it take for us to know each other again?
> When will our gaze behold the bloom of green fields
> How many rains will it take to wash away the blood stains?

For Pakistan, at least, a true reckoning with the tragedy of 1971 would mean reckoning not only with the violence and brutality, but with all the things that were lost. It would mean approaching the war not only as an event, but as a doorway: into all of the contradictions, ambiguities, and alternative imaginings of the past. And it would entail, perhaps, an embrace of madness—of history in all of its instability and incongruity, marked by the traces of irresolvable loss.

Notes and References

1. Yasmin Saikia, *Women, War and the Making of Bangladesh: Remembering 1971* (Duke University Press: 2011); 'Perpetrators' Humanity: War, Violence, and Memory After 1971', *ReOrient* 2:1 (Autumn 2016), 73–90.
2. Others have designated this 'apparent amnesia' as more of a willful non-narration, see: Nayanika Mookherjee, '1971: Pakistan's Past and Knowing What Not to Narrate,' *Comparative Studies of South Asia, Africa and the Middle East* 39 (2019), 212–222.
3. Anam Zakaria, *1971: A People's History from Bangladesh, Pakistan and India* (Penguin Books, 2019); Saikia, op. cit.; *Narir Ekattor O Juddhoporoborti Koththo Kahini*, eds. S. Akhtar et al. (Oral History Accounts of Women's Experiences During 1971 and After the War) (Dhaka: Ain O Salish Kendra [ASK], 2001).
4. Colonel Nadir Ali, 'A Khaki Dissident on 1971', *Viewpoint*; 'Liberation War—Historicising a Personal Narrative', talk given at BRAC University, Dhaka, March 2011; 'Aik Fauji Ki Yadasht', interview with BBC Urdu, 2007.
5. Malik Ghulam Jilani's letter of 7 April 1971 to Yahya Khan was reprinted in *We Owe an Apology to Bangladesh*, ed. Ahmad Salim (Shahitya Prakash, 2012), 114.

6. Naveeda Khan, *Beyond Crisis: Re-evaluating Pakistan* (New Delhi: Routledge, 2010).

7. Parallels have been drawn, in particular, with the repression of uprisings in Balochistan. See, Jafar Ghani, 'Of Bangladesh and Balochistan', *Pakistan Today*, 2013, https://www.pakistantoday.com.pk/2013/10/15/of-bangladesh-and-balochistan/ (accessed 12 June 2020; link discontinued).

FICTION

Akhtaruzzaman Elias
Intizar Husain
Selina Hossain
Rasheed Amjad
Papree Rahman
Masood Ashar
Shaheen Akhtar
Agha Sohail
Wasi Ahmed
Sameena Nazeer
Trishna Basak
Tariq Rahman
Jhumur Panday
Raihana Hasan
Razia Fasih Ahmad
Sorayya Khan

Overleaf photograph: Moyna Mazumdar

4 The Raincoat*

AKHTARUZZAMAN ELIAS

The rain started at dawn. Oh the sound of falling drops! According to Allah, this rain would continue for three days; it said so in the proverb: if the rains started on Saturday it lasted seven days, if on a Tuesday, then for three. That was a general statement. Of course, there were general classifications too like if it rained on a Wednesday then it would stop by the evening. He couldn't remember if there were exhortations about the other days of the week. What he remembered was enough to send him back to sleep, bunched into a ball under the thick bedspread. There would be no shooting for three days: in the rain, all ammunitions would want to rest, *na*? So one could relax for the next few days. But that was not to be. On such a lovely rainy morning, the loud knocking on the door managed to rip the blanket of cool air of a late autumn. Military! The military had arrived at his door...Oh Allah! *Allah humma inna anta subanka inni*...he prayed and went to open the door. In the last few months he had memorised a number of *sura*. When he went out of the house, he had at least five prayers ready on his lips: one never knew where the military might catch him. Yet he made a few mistakes: he remembered the prayers but forgot to wear the cap.

After unlocking two locks, one wooden bar and another small bolt, he opened the door an inch and along with the wind and rain, the man who entered was the Principal's peon. Praise be to Allah that it was not the military! He felt like giving the man a kiss but Ishaq Mian's thin voice had taken on a sombre tone, 'Sir

---

*Originally published in Bangla as 'Raincoat', in *Muktijuddher Golpo*, edited by Abul Hasnat (Dhaka: Abasar Prakashana Sanstha, 1997), 230–241.

has sent you his greetings.' Then sucking out the softness of that sentence through his cheeks that were covered with a fuzzy beard, he ordered, 'You have been summoned. *Abbi jana hoga*...You have to go now.'

'What is the matter?'

'There's no time to talk. Last night, someone threw a bomb along the college wall.'

'What!'

'*Miscrian log electiri transformer tor diya*. Some miscreants have destroyed the electrical transformer and while going back they threw a grenade at the Principal's bungalow and broke the gate.'

What a terrible thing to happen! The electrical transformer was next to the college wall; then came a garden and a tennis lawn. The college verandah began after that and beyond was the football and cricket ground. The Principal's quarter was left of the ground, next to a military camp that had been set up in the college gym. If a bomb had exploded in front of the gate of the Principal's bungalow, the motive was to attack the military camp. How did they cross all that distance unnoticed? He asked the peon, 'How did they come in?'

'You would know that.'

What did that mean? How would he know? Did the peon think he belonged to the group of miscreants? His head bowed on its own and like flowing water, the words came out: 'Ishaq Mian, sit down. Have some tea. I will take a few minutes.'

'*Nahin*,' Ishaq Mian turned down the invitation. 'I have to go to the house of Abdous Sattar Mirdha. You come soon. A colonel has reached the college. All the professors have been ordered to come.'

Ishaq left, leaving the college and him in charge of the commanding colonel and the military! The baby taxi that had been waiting noisily on the road picked up speed and rushed towards the geography professor's house. Ishaq now behaved like a military colonel: maybe the appearance of the colonel at dawn at the college might have resulted in his demotion to a lieutenant colonel; maybe he would be pushed lower still, but certainly not lower than a captain. It was not possible to nudge him beyond the rank of a captain. After the military took over, everyone in the college held him in fear. From the beginning of April, Ishaq Mian had stopped speaking in Bangla; he spoke only Urdu, dragging out his family history of a great grandfather or uncle who had served a *saheb* in Delhi. The Principal was a short rotund man; he too spoke to his peon in the new tongue with a certain difficulty: 'Ishaq Mian, there is a lot of trouble in the country. Tell the professors to be on guard and not to spread rumours. *Abhi military sahib ko madat korna ekhon foroj kaam hay*. It is our utmost duty now to help the military!'

'*Zorur, zorur*.' Ishaq, with his thin matchstick-like body and a smallish head like a wet bullet, had agreed with that statement. 'Certainly.'

That '*zorur*' now came to his memory drenched in rain, fresh; it seemed to enter his ears and then burst with a loud bang. Did it start raining again? No, it was the thunder. The rain was probably getting heavier. He had to go out. Allah would protect him.

'Why do you have to go out? If you get drenched in this unseasonal rain, your asthma would again...'

What good would his wife's coy words do? Would she take a bit of the Principal's berating? On top of that, the colonel had landed up in college. God only knew what was in store for him. If he had to face the firing squad would it be possible to entreat the colonel to shoot him right in the centre of his forehead? Wouldn't the Principal also put in a word for him? That man prayed for Pakistan day and night. He sent up entreaties to Allah at odd hours and took some care to keep his colleagues together by shouting at them. In the middle of April, the Principal had respectfully urged all higher ups in the military that if they had to save Pakistan, then all the martyr memorials had to be removed from the premises of schools and colleges. Those unauthorised constructions were akin to the *shivalinga* of the Hindus; they were like thorns in Pakistan's side. To preserve the pure wholesomeness of Pakistan, all these thorns had to be removed. So the military had heard the plea of Dr Afaz Ahmed, the Principal: wherever they had gone, their cannons had pointed at the martyr memorials. Not a single one had survived in the country. If the Principal had given them such meaningful advice, why wouldn't they heed his request to shoot a lowly lecturer not anywhere in his body but only on the forehead? And he had given the Principal such loyal service. Then wouldn't he in turn do his colleague, oh no, his subordinate, a small favour?

As he pulled up his trousers, he heard his wife's voice from the kitchen: 'Come home soon. Before the rain started, I heard sounds of firing from the Mirpur Bridge. Who knows what will happen!'

What was the use of saying all that? Over the radio and the TV, the news continually stated that the situation was normal—the enemy had been completely vanquished. All miscreants were dead. The President was determined to bring back democracy to the country; every other day his speeches resonated over the air: 'Our ultimate aim remains the same, that is, to hand over power to the elected representatives of the people.' Everything was becoming normal. The Bengali, oh no, the East Pakistani Governor and all the ministers who were East Pakistani, they all said the same thing: Everything was normal. Why was his wife talking rubbish? Asma was impossible! Two days ago, in bed, she had complained of not being able to sleep without hearing a few rounds of gunfire: God alone knew what would happen to his family because of her!

'An umbrella would be useless, dear, in this rain,' Asma's soft endearing sentence came wafting to him. 'You can take Mintu's raincoat.'

Oh Mintu again! He had been on tenterhooks because of this brother-in-law of his. Ah yes, on 23rd June to be precise, Mintu went away from his two-bedroomed flat in Moghbazar and as soon as he had disappeared, he shifted house too, in case anyone suspected something amiss. After Mintu left, exactly three days later, the round-faced woman who was their neighbour asked his wife: '*Bhabhi*, I don't see your brother anymore.' It was just an ordinary question but he became desperate in his search for a new flat. He had now changed houses four times after the military arrived. When they shifted to their new flat, the man downstairs had told him, 'I cannot keep my brother in Dhaka anymore. I have sent him back to our village!' His heart had thumped rapidly at that. Suppose the man asked about Mintu? He had come to the new flat because of security—far away from the college, far from relatives, even far from the city. He had thought it was a new area; if he stood at the eastern window, he could see small ponds and rice fields. But oh the danger! It was no secret that boats filled with young men carrying sten-guns were a common sight—people saw boats laden with weapons too! And if his wife began talking about Mintu, then the weapons would come to occupy his home. He knew where Mintu had gone and so did his wife. Oh to see Asma talking proudly of her brother to the children who often declared: 'Uncle has gone to kill the Khan soldiers!' Who knew the danger of such words? If Asma was so brave, why didn't she join her brother too? He didn't utter the words but they hovered on his lips: Asma forget about Mintu, no one was with us, no one. Kissinger saheb said that these were the internal affairs of Pakistan—they killed people, burnt down homes, villages and markets—no one was bothered about that. All that was an internal affair! Oh no, better not to think along those lines. His downstairs neighbour was the owner of a welding workshop whose father-in-law must be a biggish *razakar*. Every other day the old man sent things for his daughter: expensive sofa sets, refrigerators, tape recorders, beds and other furniture. Once he had even sent along a Hindu idol: was it made of gold? Truckloads of things came and went away too. If the man got to know that the brother-in-law of his upstairs neighbour was a miscreant who had gone away to fight against the military, then bullets would fly within the confines of his home. There was no doubt about that. Asma should be careful of her words!

'Let's see if it fits you,' Asma said as she put the raincoat around his shoulders. 'Mintu is quite tall. Will it do?' Look how she compared his height to her brother's! Was it any good to be so overtly proud of her sibling?

'Good, it goes down to your ankles. Your feet won't get wet.' Asma now got the cap attached with the raincoat. 'It is Mintu's doing.' What great work had her brother done now? Oh no, his achievement was different this time.

'The raincoat was hanging in the clothes horse and the cap was on top of the wardrobe. I saw it yesterday when I was taking down the Koran.' Had he kept other things too? He threw a quick look over the wardrobe to make sure. In Moghbazar, the military had found three Chinese rifles under the bed of some houseowner. The man, a simpleton of a doctor, knew nothing of how they had come to be there. It was far better to keep an eye on things inside one's home.

'*Abbu* is now like *Chhotomama*,' the broken baby words from his just awakened daughter made him start: had Mintu entered the house carrying weapons? That meant the military would follow soon: it meant...no, all the bolts and locks on the door were in place. His two and a half year old was sitting up in bed and laughing at his raincoat-clad figure: '*Abbu* is *Chhotomama*.' He had an anxious moment. When he saw himself in the dressing table mirror, he felt a moment of trepidation. The colour of the raincoat was not khaki, neither was it fig-green; its earth colour was faded a bit, but the raincoat looked good. He looked a bit like a military personnel. It was not safe to look like that. If the military thought that wearing a raincoat was the disguise of a military man, they would send him straight to the Cantonment. Nah! He was getting scared without reason. Why should it be a crime to wear a raincoat on a rainy day? The military was not unreasonable. The Principal was right when he said, 'Look, when the military arrest someone they have a reason. That person is, somehow or the other, involved in subversive activities.' He was a thousand miles away from such pursuits. His brother-in-law had crossed the border and was now back in the country, engaged in killing the military. What was his involvement? Why should he feel guilty? Everyday the military burnt down markets, set fire to slums to kill people, abducted women: had he uttered a word in protest? Along the college walls, next to the Principal's quarter, the military had set up camp: no classes took place; there were no students. The teachers had often come to mark their presence but a good number had also absconded. In the staffroom, his colleagues whispered about a bridge being blown off and the bodies of seven Khan soldiers who had been ambushed; they spoke about how many students had joined the Mukti Bahini. He never partook in any such discussions. Whenever he heard such things, he quietly got up and went to sit in the Principal's room. There he sat listening to Dr Afaz Ahmed's hoarse voice predicting the near and inevitable downfall of India and the miscreants. Few people came to that room now. The Principal tried his best to be in the good books of Akbar Sajjid, the Urdu professor, but the man avoided him. Sajjid often made fun of the Principal's broken Urdu. But Dr Ahmed never had the chance to answer back, either because his mind was preoccupied with the preservation of Pakistan's integrity or because it took him time to formulate a correct Urdu sentence. The Principal was in some dilemma because he was never sure when Sajjid was mocking him. One day, after listening to the Principal's overwhelmed response to the latest military skirmish and his analysis of the military's amazing powers, Sajjid had told him, 'You should do a doctorate on Military Science, sir. I know a doctor in Mohammedpur who practises both allopathy and homeopathy. Everyone calls him Double Doctor. You should become a double doctor too.' When Sajjid had laughed at his own joke, the Principal had to keep a false smile plastered on his face. The other teachers, unable to decide whether to laugh or not, had felt caught up in some unknown danger.

After he had worn Mintu's abandoned or perhaps deliberately left behind raincoat, his legs were trembling, he could not stand straight. The Principal had called him a while ago!

There was not a single rickshaw on the road. He had no time to wait for one. He would have no trouble walking to the bus stand wearing the raincoat: the rain splashed on it, not a drop came in. What fun! A few drops came flowing down the visor of the cap. He struck out his tongue to catch them. It wasn't salty at all. Did the water taste different under the power of the raincoat's cap? Was he looking like a soldier? Punjab Artillery or Baluch Regiment or Commando Force or Para Military or Military Police: they had so many divisions, so many guises! Did his raincoat make him look like a member of a new regiment? He began to walk quickly. The autumn rain had brought the temperature down but inside the raincoat he was snug. Mintu was good to leave it behind—when would he come back for it? Where was he right now? Probably hiding behind a river bank, waiting to carry out an ambush. Maybe the Pakistani army platoon had burnt down a village, killed hundreds of men and left their bodies rotting behind as they hurried away in jeeps packed with live women: would Mintu be able to kill all the soldiers and save the girls? Would he succeed? When he saw a military lorry on the main road, he came back to his senses. To hide his betraying thoughts, he looked at the lorry with a layer of devotion in his eyes. Better not to look at them straight in the eye. The vehicle went off northwards and his eyes looked south. But was it easy to obliterate the rain-soaked sounds of the wheels? Asma had heard sounds of firing the night before from the Mirpur Bridge—did the lorry go that way? Nobody knew what happened anywhere and his wife heard the sound of guns everyday. All those were just rumours. His Principal often said that to listen to rumours was as bad as spreading them. The Principal often continued his axioms in Urdu: 'Sajjid, *gujob shob gazab hota*.' And Sajjid had promptly versified:

'*Guzab jo tha wohi sab gazab ho chuka hai*.'

The Principal in his hoarse voice had then said hopefully, 'Is that by Iqbal? Wait, let me write it down.' And Sajjid had said, 'Why Iqbal? *Gujob* is rumour in Bangla and in Urdu it is…'

The Principal had reiterated, 'Let me write it down.' Sajjid had started reciting a self-composed poem: '*Army ke arman purey ho chukey hain…*' and went on to add lines to it.

'What is that?'

'The Army has fulfilled its wishes…' Sajjid had answered. When Sajjid returned to the staffroom, he had said: 'If the Principal recited any of my poems to any army colonel, he would be punished for making fun of the military.' All others present in the room had remained silent: nobody wanted to say anything to Sajjid. Even his friend Ali Kabir from the History department avoided him a little. Meanwhile, the Principal was trying to recite Sajjid's verses to his peon Ishaq. In a few days, he would begin to think the lines were self-composed and as he recited the Urdu words, his eyes would close in reverence and happiness.

The rain fell in a melodious patter on his coat and he thought maybe the Principal was reciting those lines to the colonel at that very moment. Suppose the colonel got angry if the Principal was unable to supply an Urdu synomym for *gujob*? Akbar Sajjid often made fun of the army and its ferocious alacrity. Geography professor Abdus Sattar Mirdha had once murmured, 'This guy uses his mother tongue like a shield to work for the miscreants' and English professor Khondakam had warned everybody, 'Don't listen to Sajjid. He speaks like this to gauge your reactions…the fellow is an army spy.' He kept his distance from Sajjid but standing dry under the raincoat, he felt a sudden urge to talk to Sajjid at that very moment. What did it mean?

These kind of impulses bode no good. It was better to be free of thoughts of satire about the army, either in Urdu or in Bangla. When he reached the bus stop, he had to glance northward to see if the bus was approaching. He couldn't see the military lorry anymore. But neither was the bus there. He was alone at the stop. The small tobacco shop by the roadside was half shut and the shopkeeper was also gazing northwards. Had something happened in that direction? The boy who ran the shop was a talkative fellow. Whenever the boy saw him he would murmur the news, 'Didn't you hear? Two boats full of *muktijoddha* are coming down the Mirpur lake. They have blown off a jeep; at least five Khan soldiers dead. BBC said half of Rangpur and Dinajpur was now free. Did you hear about the Declaration?' He never stood listening to the boy for too long. Suppose someone caught him listening to such rumours? The Principal always maintained that Bengalis were a rumour-mongering lot: to them rumours were sweet, their attraction strong. Like now, when he was sheltered from the rain because of his protective raincoat, he felt a great sense of relief as he walked towards the shop, hoping to hear some titbit of gossip. 'How long has the bus not come?'

'*Arre* bus, where will it come from?' The boy quickly brought the shutter down and withdrew into the shop. Maybe there was some trouble at the bus depot. The sound of firing that Asma had heard, was that it? Did the military lorry go that way? There was a slum just behind the depot; did they set fire to it? The place was not too far away; should he go there to have a look? The rain had stopped. Could he take a walk in that direction? But no, he could not, because just then, in the thinly falling rain, the reddish-coloured state bus came to a halt at the bus-stop. There were a few passengers inside; not like when the conductors yell 'Empty… Empty!' but few of the seats were full. When he boarded, his wet raincoat dripped water over the damp floor of the bus. People could have ragged him a bit for that but no one said a word.

So many empty seats! His lips sported a faint smile: was it because no one berated him for making the floor wet or was it because his raincoat made him an ominous figure and no one had the guts to say anything?

The road was empty and the bus picked up speed. He could choose a seat for himself; he walked up to one and then decided to go for another, unsteady on his feet inside the speeding bus. Just then two passengers stood up from the back, shouted 'Stop' and hurriedly got off the moving bus. He looked at them and realised that they had deboarded to escape him. The pair of them must be criminals: one a thief and the other a pickpocket. Or maybe both thieves or both pickpockets. As they got off, one had looked back at him. His eyes had been filled with fear, only fear. When he found a suitable seat, he sat down heavily and the padding on the seat squeaked loudly. The three men sitting ahead looked back at him. Yes, he could see they were criminals too. Maybe robbers who went to loot slums after the military had set fire to them or who scavenged in places where the military was looting people. The three of them got up in a hurry much before the next stop and got off the bus too. None of the three criminals looked back at him. It was clear they were scared to look him in the eye. Mintu's raincoat was doing a great job! All thieves and pickpockets were fleeing; let other good people remain in the bus. He would travel up to the college in the company of honest men. In the rain, a few people were waiting at the Asad Gate bus stop. Some people held umbrellas while others who did not were trying to save at least their heads by sticking them under the others' umbrellas, and contorting their bodies in order to achieve that. When the bus halted, he saw nine people board. He looked them up and down and when the men felt his scrutiny, four shouted 'Stop' and got off the bus. The last fellow was probably a petty thief; the others were clearly military informers. They kept a lookout for beautiful women and dumped them at the camps and received guns from the military and shouted 'Pakistan *zindabad*' in every neighbourhood. These were the *razakars*, flies that buzzed around the military. Again he felt good to travel in a criminal-free bus. He felt an extra pleasure to see the transparent covering that the raindrops had created in the cold air over the trees, the people, the shops and the buildings. His sense of wellbeing nosedived when the bus stopped suddenly with a screeching of brakes. He had to turn his eyes to notice the half-built mosque. A blast of cold wind entered from the door and went in through his mouth and nostrils to enter his lungs; it jarred him.

When the night had ended on the crackdown, the military had shot down the muezzin *saheb* from the terrace of that mosque. The cold wind suddenly turned warm inside his raincoat; his body felt on fire. He and his family used to live just opposite the mosque in a third-floor flat. That night they hadn't slept a wink amidst the roar of the tanks, the barking of the machine guns and the groans of the wounded. He had lain under the bed with the children and their mother. Around dawn, when the killings had stopped, the children had fallen asleep and he had taken a peep through the crack in the curtain. The muezzin was standing on the mosque's terrace, ready to give the call for prayers. Ordinarily, he would read the Jumma prayers but that morning he had a great desire to listen to the *azan*. He had stood by the window waiting for the call to prayer. There was no electricity in the neighbourhood, the mosque's sound system was not working. In his deep resonant voice the muezzin had called with all his might, *Allah Hu Akbar*. He did not get the chance to utter the greatness of Allah—the man had toppled off the mosque's roof with another kind of sound. It was not raining that day. Was the military trying to reenact that same picture? It was not a time for prayers, who would call the *azan*? Maybe they had passed an official order that anytime was prayer time.

The military was stopping all cars. The passengers were made to stand on the road. Another group of military were pointing their sten-guns at them. Yet another was searching the clothes and the private parts of people. Those that they liked, one or two, they pushed towards the lorry standing at the back. A tall and fair military man got into the bus. It was quiet inside. The heartbeats of all the passengers sounded loud in that silence and resonated inside his head like blows. The sound beats set fire to something under the visor of his cap and the glow of that fire lit his eyes. When he moved a bit, the sound waves in his head and heart came under control and without taking any notice of it all, he raised his eyes to look at the man's face. The military's eyes sharpened like a thorn and came to pierce his entire face. He too made his blunt hot glance travel lightly over the military's sharp nose, piercing eyes, the moustache and the slightly reddish skin beneath and around the eyes. It worked somehow. The searching glances of the military shifted from his face and came to rest on his raincoat. It seemed he was trying to count the raindrops clinging on it. Were the water drops looking a little red, heated by the fire raging inside him? Wasn't it absurd that the military was stupified by water vapours in a riverine country where he had come to kill? Did the man notice flecks of blood in the raindrops? Suddenly the man barked out, 'Go on, go on.' The bus driver had stopped, not knowing what to do. The man shouted again, 'Move!' The bus started with a jerk and the collective sigh of relief from all the passengers gave it added life so that his college gate soon whizzed past. When the bus slowed a bit, he got off the criminal-less transport wearing his drenched raincoat. As he looked at the other passengers with a twist of his lips that showed a glimpse of his front teeth, he had an idea that all of them had no difficulty in recognising that grimace as a smile.

In the Principal's room in his throne-like chair, there sat a fierce-looking military honcho. His lugubrious face proclaimed he was either a colonel or a major general or a major or at least a brigadier. Seeing him, the Principal's dark face turned a shade of violet and Dr Afaz Ahmed, MSc, PhD, tried to summon all of that authority in his statement: 'Sir, here is Professor Nurul Huda.'

The stern-looking military barked out, 'Who has asked you to identify people?' But Dr Afaz Ahmed, MSc, PhD, was unable to stop himself from correcting his mistake. 'Sorry, he is not a professor but a lecturer in Chemistry.'

'Shut up!'

The Principal shut up then.

Before taking him and Abdul Sattar Mirdha to the military jeep the stern colonel or brigadier told the Principal harshly that making fun of the army through *shayari* was an offence. This time he was pardoned but he would be under watch. The Principal's excuse of Urdu professor Sajjid's influence did not cut much ice. Nurul Huda grew anxious. If Sajjid had not escaped, then Allah alone knew what was in store for him! Actually, Allah and the military both knew.

They had been blindfolded. The jeep ran in a zigzag fashion. They were brought to a large room. When he opened his eyes, he could not see Mirdha and the place seemed unfamiliar. He sat there for a long time on a deck chair. Then a military came to sit on another chair in front. He was asked a number of questions in English, which he answered. When the man departed he was taken to another room where another man began his interrogation. The questions were more or less the same and his answers too never varied. Like, a few days ago the college had bought a few iron shelves. Who had carried them in? He answered, 'Yes, three for the office, two each for the Botany, History and Geography departments and one for English, total ten shelves were bought.'

'There is no need to divulge all that information. The shelves had been brought in push carts, and you knew the men who drove them.'

Nurul Huda had asked how he could know them. They were coolies, and he was a lecturer after all.

'Then why were you talking to those men for so long?'

The Principal had ordered him to check the quality, the size, the locks and colour, so it was his responsibility to do just that.

The military said in a quiet matter-of-fact voice, 'The miscreants had entered the college disguised as coolies. Who knew that better than him? They had been arrested, and they had admitted the name of Nurul Huda who was in regular touch with them and who was an active gang member.'

'My name? They have told you *my* name?' the sudden outburst from Nurul Huda did not annoy the military, who forcefully repeated, 'The coolies were disguised miscreants. They have taken the name of Nurul Huda amongst all the college teachers.' Nurul Huda was bewildered. Did they really know him? When one of the shelves was being placed in the Chemistry department, one coolie had stood near him. It was monsoon and Dhaka had been flooded that month. He had commented on the incessant rain, and the man had whispered, 'Monsoon is ideal.' He had repeated that line. What did it mean? In the staff room someone or the other had murmured, 'The bastards don't know Bengal's monsoon. In Russia it was General Winter, here it is General Monsoon.' Had the boy disguised as a coolie also talked about that? Had they so much faith in him? In his excitement Nurul Huda could not sit still; his silence assured the military to some extent.

After some time, he did not know how long, the military asked him the same question again. When there was no reply, he was boxed soundly on his face, twice; the first one destabilised him, the second threw him on the floor. The military hauled him up and asked if he knew the secret hideout. He said, 'Yes.' After an assurance that if he divulged the address he would be respectfully set free, he was fed some milk and bread. The military left him alone to give him time to think. After a while, he did not know how long, the military came back to ask if he knew the address of the miscreants. He again answered 'Yes' but when no answer was forthcoming to the second question, he was taken to another room. His short body was hung from the ceiling. The whip cut through the air and lashed his ass relentlessly. But in that relentless whipping, Nurul Huda began to think them a nuisance. He thought the blows were raindrops that fell on Mintu's raincoat. They had taken away the raincoat; where had they kept it? But the raincoat's warmth still clung to his body. Like the rain, the blows landed on his raincoat-like skin, and he kept repeating that he knew the address of the miscreants. Not only the whereabouts of his brother-in-law, and there was no credit in that, but he also knew the addresses of each of the disguised coolies. They too knew him well and depended on him. Charged of being a miscreant himself and in the excitement of being in conspiracy with them, his dangling body shivered to such an extent that Nurul Huda couldn't pay any attention to the whiplashes at all.

Translated from the Bangla by **Debjani Sengupta**

5 Sleep*

INTIZAR HUSAIN

Zafar was amazed at the sight of him. '*Arre*, Salman! You? You have come back? But how?'

'Don't ask how. I have come back. That is all.'

Zafar didn't know what to say next. 'To come back alive, from *there*—it's a miracle!'

'Yes, consider it a miracle. I was meant to live some more, so I have returned.'

It wasn't just Zafar who was amazed at his return; Salman himself could barely believe it. 'I can't believe I have come away from that place.'

Zafar couldn't take his eyes off Salman. Salman was the only person he knew who had come back alive from there. He looked at Salman from head to toe and asked incredulously, 'But tell me, Salman, how *did* you escape?'

'How did I escape,' he mumbled. For a moment he felt like spewing out his entire tale in one breath. He looked around, then said, 'I can't tell you in a few words; it requires a marathon storytelling session. You will lose your senses if you hear all the details.'

'You are right, my friend. The little that we have heard is horrifying, whereas you—you have seen it all with your own eyes.'

He drew a long breath and sighed, 'Yes. Yes, I have seen it all with my own eyes.'

---

*Originally published in Urdu as 'Neend' in *Kachhuwe* (Tortoises) (Lahore: Sang-e-Meel Publications, 1995). The English translation, published as 'Sleep' in *The Death of Sheherzad*, Intizar Husain, introduced and translated by Rakhshanda Jalil (Harper Perennial, 2014), is reproduced here with minor edits by kind permission of Rakhshanda Jalil, HarperCollins Publishers India Private Limited, and Seagull Books.

Countless macabre scenes danced before his eyes. 'I have seen so much that...Let's just say that I have seen it all.'

'Tell me.'

Once again, Salman wanted to spit it all out, but he looked around and checked himself, 'I have a lot to tell you, but how can I...standing here like this?'

Zafar paused to think, then asked, 'What are you doing in the evening?'

'Morning or evening, nothing matters to me...they are the same.'

'Then come home this evening.'

'All right, I'll be there.'

'I'll phone Aslam. He'll come too.'

'Aslam, the Argumentative. Is he still around?'

'Nothing ever happens to people like him; they are spared both living and dying. Where will he go?'

'What about Zaidi?'

'I'll call that big talker too. So, is it fixed for this evening then?'

'Yes, it is.'

Zafar reached home, and quickly dialled a number. 'Hello? Aslam? *Yaar*, it's me...Zafar. Salman is here.'

'*Salman*? What are you saying!'

'Yes. He has come back.'

'You mean he actually escaped from there? Alive? But how?'

'Come home this evening and ask him yourself.'

'I'll be there.'

Then he called Zaidi at his office. 'Hello, Zaidi?...Please call Zaidi...Hello, Zaidi? It's me, Zafar. Do you know something?'

'Tell me.'

'Salman has come back.'

'Salman! No way, man!'

'Yes, *yaar*. He managed to get away.'

'What a thick-skinned bloke! Where is he now?'

'Come home this evening. He'll be there.'

'I'll come.'

The four friends met in the evening. The three looked at Salman with acute amazement, and Salman looked at them, equally bemused. Aslam expressed their collective astonishment at his escape, then spoke of his sorrow at the state of affairs there. As he spoke, his anger grew. 'How they have tortured people over there... They have killed and maimed the old...children...women...The barbarians! Animals! If I had my way, I would...' He gritted his teeth.

'This is precisely what they should have done,' Zaidi calmly announced.

'This...? Done *this*?' Aslam spluttered in angry disbelief.

'After what we have been doing to them for twenty-five years, yes, this is precisely what they should have done,' Zaidi asserted.

'And *what* have we been doing? What have *we* done to them?' Aslam shouted back.

Then he launched into a long tirade on all the atrocities committed by them on the basis of several sensational newspaper reports. Zaidi countered each one of the allegations and, in turn, listed all the cruelties that we had been perpetrating against them. Salman yawned. Zafar looked at him and asked, 'What do you think, Salman?'

Aslam eagerly pounced, 'Yes, let's ask Salman. He has lived there for so many years. He has seen everything with his own eyes. Tell us, what do you think, Salman?'

'I think that...' said Salman, and fell into a contemplative silence.

Seeing him fall silent, Zafar grew impatient. He prodded, 'Yes, come on, tell us. Say something.'

'What should I say?'

Zaidi sneered, 'Scared of commitment?'

'Commitment?' Salman gaped uncomprehendingly.

Aslam spoke forcefully, 'Let's hear what you have to say about the situation there.'

Somewhat uncertainly, Salman said, '*Yaar*, I don't really know what to make of it.'

Zafar looked daggers at him. 'The last time you were here, you had picked my brains clean by going on and on about that place.'

Salman simply gazed at Zafar, then said in a muffled voice, 'At that time, I had the mistaken belief that I understood the situation.'

'Forget all that. Tell us what happened there.'

'Yes, that I certainly can tell you,' Salman said with conviction. 'I have seen a great deal there. If I begin to describe the things I have seen, you will break out in goose bumps,' he said and then grew silent as though he were preparing to launch into a long, long epic. The three friends sat up in rapt attention and waited for him to continue. But Salman just sat there without uttering a word. Zafar again prompted, '*Yaar,* say something...you haven't told us anything yet.'

'Yes...' Salman again fumbled, 'But *yaar,* I don't know what to say. I...can't remember anything.'

Both Aslam and Zaidi glared at him incredulously, then turned away and started talking among themselves as if they didn't know him.

They talked and argued and squabbled among themselves. Things began to warm up. Tempers rose. Volleys of sarcasm jetted back and forth. Resounding abuse burst from Zafar, sometimes about people on that side, sometimes about those on this side. Salman looked at one friend, then the other. He listened without saying a word. His eyelids began to droop. Once or twice he nearly dozed off. Then he pulled himself up and tried to listen attentively to every contentious word that was being spoken. Again, his eyelids grew heavy and his eyes began to close.

'Bastards! Democratic dogs!' Zaidi banged the table with his fist.

'Bunch of bloody traitors! They are all Indian agents!' Aslam hissed.

Salman looked up at them once with drowsy eyes, and drifted silently into sleep.

He woke up with a start when tea was placed before them and Zafar nudged him saying, 'Salman, here's your tea.' He opened his eyes, looked apologetically at his friends, and sat up straight, rubbing his eyes. He took a sip of tea. As he drank the tea, he could feel the sleep leaving his eyes. He felt refreshed now, as if the doors and windows of his mind were finally opening. He said, 'The way I dozed off just now reminds me of an incident from those days.

That night I hadn't slept a wink.' As he spoke, terrifying visions began to dance before his eyes and a subhuman scream ricocheted through his brain.

'Which night are you talking about? Was it before the Fall?'[1] Aslam asked at once.

Salman thought for a moment, then said, 'I can't remember, but those nights were all the same, except that...' and he fell silent. Aslam, Zaidi and Zafar were listening attentively. Disconcerted by their rapt attention, Salman skittered, 'I forget what I was going to say. Anyhow, after that I couldn't sleep all night.' He paused again and said, 'And after that, sleep became a rarity. I think perhaps I haven't slept at all ever since. Or maybe I have...on one or two occasions.' Aslam, Zaidi and Zafar listened listlessly. Then they got engrossed in their own conversation. Back and forth the arguments raged—did people from the other side exploit them or did our own people betray us? And Salman just sat there and tried to recollect whether or not he had slept at all on any of these past many endless nights. He couldn't remember. And what about after coming here? He couldn't remember that either.

Tired of his futile calculations, he tried to concentrate on the argument raging between Zafar, Zaidi and Aslam. He listened to them, until a yawn caught him unawares and he looked at Zafar with sleep-drowned eyes and said, '*Yaar*, I am feeling sleepy.'

Zafar gave him an insipid look and said, 'So why don't you sleep?'

'Yes, I am going to sleep,' he said in a muffled somnolent voice as his eyes began to close. He slipped down the sofa and rested his head on the headrest and put his feet up on the table. With one worn-off slipper resting near Aslam and the toe of the other foot nudging Zaidi, Salman began to snore.

Translated from the Urdu by **Rakhshanda Jalil**

Note

1. The Fall of Dhaka.

6 The Story of Amina and Madina*

SELINA HOSSAIN

It was time for the *zohr* prayers. Amina and Madina, the two daughters of Muezzin Al-Amin, were standing with spouted pitchers in their hands to pour water for their father's ritual ablutions. It was the month of Baishakh. The scorching heat of the sun had made everything wear a desolate look. Twice the dry wind had churned the dust in the courtyard. The girls had covered their faces with the ends of their saris. Dried leaves from the old jackfruit tree at the corner of the courtyard sailed down onto their feet. But they didn't notice. In fact, they had learnt not to be moved by anything until their father's ablution was over. After a short while, the Muezzin came walking in his wooden sandals, making a continual rapping sound, and took his seat on the low wooden stool for ablutions. He took off his cap and handed it over to Madina. She said, 'Papa, the cap looks dirty. Shall I wash it clean?' The Muezzin replied with a tender smile, 'Okay, my mother. I might as well go to the mosque today with another cap on.'

'Papa I'm crocheting a cap for you. It would be finished by this afternoon. I hope you would be able to say your *magrib* prayers with that on.'

The Muezzin nodded his head in happiness and looked at his daughters. They had covered their heads with the ends of their saris, worn blouses with sleeves going down to their wrists, and their eyes were looking downward. Both the daughters were very gentle. They regularly said their prayers and observed the ritual fast. They read the Holy Quran from beginning to end. They were

*Originally published in Bangla as 'Amina O Madinar Golpo', in *Muktijuddher Golpo*, edited by Abul Hasnat (Dhaka: Abasar Prakashana Sanstha, 1997), 251–260.

polite and sober, did not make much of a sound and did not lift their eyes while speaking to someone. Al-Amin inwardly thanked Allah and sat down for his ablutions. The villagers also knew that no one else in the village was comparable to Amina or Madina in beauty. The girls were so self-restrained that the Muezzin was yet to hear of an occasion when either of his daughters had lifted up their eyes to look at any man. Their mother kept a strict watch over them. The Muezzin was now waiting for two good grooms to marry them off.

After the war had begun, a turmoil arose in the Muezzin's wife, Johra Bibi, about marrying off the daughters. She importuned her husband to make an arrangement soon. 'Please, don't waste time,' she said again and again. Young girls should not be kept unmarried in the house at a time like this.

The Muezzin too trembled at his wife's apprehension, but nevertheless replied with a deep sigh, 'I'm not finding anyone worthy. All the young men are preoccupied with the war. A group of them have joined the freedom fighters and left to work as Indian agents. And the other group have become *razakar*s and are protecting Pakistan. None of them are thinking of marriage.' Carried away by her husband's deep sigh, Johra Bibi slapped her forehead and cried out, 'Oh Allah, what will become of my two daughters!'

In another room, sixteen-year-old Amina and Madina would overhear their mother's lamentations. Both of them would be startled and would whiff at their chests after reciting from the Holy Quran. The next moment the full-throated voice of their father would waft to their ears, 'Have faith in Allah, my wife. Never in life have I lost my faith, nor did I ever commit any sin. The daughters have also never indulged in any shameful act. Their fate will not be bad, my dear.' Their father's self-assured and steadfast voice would bring back equanimity to the two sisters. They did not want to be unnecessarily disturbed and anxious. They noticed that at such times a dark shadow would envelope the brightness of their countenance. They did not then feel like looking at mirrors.

'*Abba jan*...!' both of them called out to their father in unison, realising that he had momentarily got distracted. Why should a pure-hearted Muslim become unmindful at the time of performing his ritual ablutions? The Muezzin started hurrying to complete his ablutions at the soft, sympathetic voices of his daughters. First he washed his right hand upto the wrist, then the left one in the same manner. After gurgling thrice, while he was ritually cleaning his nostrils, three military men entered his courtyard. They entered almost silently, their boots hardly making a sound, nor did they proceed by firing at random from their guns. Muezzin Al-Amin forgot what he was doing and looked at them open-mouthed, and the flow of water from the spout of the pitcher in Amina's hands stopped. Without finishing his ablutions, the Muezzin stood up on the wooden stool and said in Urdu, in a voice thick with emotion, 'Come in, Sir, please do come in.'

The three Pakistani soldiers didn't cast so much as a glance at the Muezzin. Amina and Madina cowered and stood with their eyes lowered to the ground. They might have even forgotten to flee from the place. Of the three Pakistani soldiers, one walked up and, placing his fingers under Madina's chin, lifted her face and said, 'Very beautiful girl, indeed.'

The bright noontide blurred before the very eyes of Al-Amin the Muezzin, and was replaced by a moonlit night. A cyclone kept swirling in his head amidst a supernatural scene like the one playing out even as a piercing cry from Johra Bibi reached his ears. When this cry kept pulsating in full force, the moonlit night was torn to shreds as if the loud lamentations of Karbala were rising and falling all around him. Al-Amin the Muezzin hurriedly got down from the wooden stool and fell on the feet of one of the soldiers, and said in Urdu, 'Sir, as you are a Muslim, so am I. I am the muezzin of the mosque. I call the people to prayers.'

'Very good, we're convinced that you are a true Muslim. Very well, then, very well.'

'Yes, Sir, we are true Muslims. Both of my daughters say their prayers, observe fast and know how to recite the Holy Quran.'

'We're convinced that both your daughters are very fresh things, not stale.'

The swirling inside the Muezzin's head intensified. The loud raucous laughter of the three Pakistani soldiers flew about like a cyclone in the month of Baishakh.

The Muezzin sprang to his feet at the sound of that laughter. But before he could reach the two sisters, one of the soldiers dashed him to the ground. His forehead hit the corner of the wooden stool and blood spurted out of the corner of one eye. Undeterred, Al-Amin the Muezzin again sprang to his feet. By then the three Pakistani soldiers had surrounded Amina and Madina. The two sisters had not looked at anybody at all, had kept their eyes firmly rooted to the ground, and had only once made a slight movement to pull their father up. The sisters had no experience of men at all, but now they felt the presence of the three very close to them. There was a peculiar odour emanating from the hairy hands that touched them, an odour and touch that numbed the sisters. Their trembling hands dropped the cap and the spouting pitcher. When her father's cap dropped at Madina's feet, guilt blurred her vision but she was unable to retrieve it. One of the soldiers grabbed her hand, and the cap got trampled under her feet as she was pulled close to his chest. Another kicked the pitcher, which rolled away on the ground, and he put a hand on Amina's shoulders. 'Beautiful, very beautiful!' their thick tongues kept emitting along with spittle and saliva.

Johra Bibi rushed out wailing, 'Sir, you are our guardians, sir, sir…!'

'Get lost.'

A kick from a boot cut open a wound in Johra Bibi's forehead that started bleeding. When Al-Amin the Muezzin attempted to intervene, he was sent sprawling onto the courtyard, hit by the butt of a rifle.

The men took away Amina and Madina. They couldn't cry because they had not learnt how to. They never cried aloud for fear their voices would be heard by men outside the family. They knew that in times of danger they had to recite verses from the Holy Quran, and one had to whiff at one's chest after chanting praise of the Prophet thrice. But they couldn't do that now because they were frightened into silence, their tongues numb. It was noon, with open fields and undulating green sheaves of paddy all around, as they unwillingly trudged along muddy tracks. They wondered how long they had to walk and if there would be an end to these roads. The girls held each other's hands tight, walking side by side, and their thoughts rose and fell in tandem. Their heads were no longer covered with the ends of their saris. The soldiers of the Pakistani Army liked to see their faces, so they had to drop their veils. Their hair blew in the wind. They could not recall if they had ever seen their village as they saw it now, with fear-widened eyes. To the two sisters the whole village looked flat and naked. The three soldiers would look at the girls from time to time and say, 'Thanks be to Allah, such pretty girls!'—words accompanied by spittle from their mouths. The girls' eyes grew wider, their eyelids refusing to shut as, numb with fright, they thought that they were going to see not just the whole naked village, but Hell itself. Never again would their eyelids close. The muddy tracks of the open fields in the burning noontide were desolate. The sun vanished before their eyes, to be replaced by a strange kind of moonlight. In that eerie glow the faces of the three soldiers appeared to them like those of Satan himself, as they had heard him described by their father. They saw those Satans transforming into different shapes and sizes. They watched as the soldiers suddenly came to a halt to discuss something among themselves in an unintelligible language. They realised that the language did not matter; what the soldiers were going to do was evident.

The sisters cried out pitifully when they were stripped naked on the sands of the desolate village in that strange moonlight. They sobbed uncontrollably. The three soldiers were startled by the sudden sounds in the otherwise silent universe around them. One of them asked hoarsely in Urdu, 'Why do you cry?'

The sisters lay there supine, unfeeling, numb. They did not look at each other. Amina and Madina, the beautiful and cherished daughters of the devout Muezzin—with such care the parents had nurtured them. How zealously they had guarded them! How gently their womanhood had bloomed in the sanctum of their house, safe from all strange prying eyes—was it only for a beginning like this?

Al-Amin the Muezzin could not remember how long he lay in his courtyard. He tried twice to lift his head, but couldn't. He groped and touched the unconscious Johra Bibi. When he opened his eyes again, a moonlit night had taken the place of the noontide sun, and he could remember the birth of his beautiful daughters. He had carefully written down the time, the day, the date and the year of their birth on a piece of paper and got them framed under a sheet glass. Johra Bibi hadn't particularly liked it, because their age had to be continually scaled down as they grew older. What was the use of pointing it out in a glass frame? The Muezzin had replied in a voice choked with emotion, 'You won't understand. An ethereal light had played on the roof of my house when the twins were born. How beautiful that light was!'

The Muezzin had closed his eyes, the timbre of his voice altered as he spoke aloud. Johra Bibi was alarmed: had the man gone mad? No, that was impossible. Al-Amin was a devout Muslim. He never delayed in saying his prayers, nor ever forgot to observe his fast. He always offered his early morning prayers. After suffering such a grave loss, a man could not be mad. But Johra Bibi had to hear this story from her husband: the story of the birth of Amina and Madina. How the man had behaved at that time! Johra Bibi's heart started to palpitate. It was as though the voice speaking to her was not that of her devout husband. And yet, she had to listen to his story.

'You had been moaning with labour pains that day, and listening to you groan as I waited outside in the courtyard I felt as if the very earth was splitting into pieces. The old midwife was guarding your door, with her back to it and her limbs spread out in front. For her the universe may well have been silent, and even if there were terrible sounds it did not matter to her in the least—she waited only to hear the cries of the baby.

'My mother sitting behind in the verandah asked, "Has the moon risen to your rooftop, Al-Amin?" I went running to my mother. She could not see, but a light seemed to have filled her eyes. Seeing that light I felt like playing the flute, but I could not bring myself to do so. Because of shame. Being a muezzin, if I were to play the flute, then people would…' The Muezzin stopped here and his face brightened with a sheepish smile as the light played on his fair-complexioned features.

At that moment Johra Bibi had said to herself, Oh, what a beautiful sight! But what she said to her husband was, 'You didn't do the proper thing; you might have played the flute.'

'I was afraid to. I sacrificed my wish for fear that the villagers might not let me continue my job as a muezzin in the mosque if I played the flute.'

'But you so wanted to play the flute in your boyhood.'

'Hush! Don't say this to anybody! Seeing the moonlight shining on the roof, I ran hither and thither in the courtyard and kept praying for divine blessings. In the early hours of the morning you stopped moaning, and I could hear the cries of infants. My mother said, smiling, "It seems your wife has given birth to two children, Al-Almin."

'I was thunderstruck. Expressing my gratitude to Allah, I wondered what my mother was saying. "Ma, have you gone mad?" She said, "No, son, I haven't gone mad. The midwife is going to come out with the news herself."

'I couldn't hold myself back any longer. I rushed to your door and called out to the old midwife. The old woman shouted back, "*Chander moton duida maiya oichey tumar*…You have got two moon-like girls…"

'I touched my mother's feet and told her she was right. I announced the names of my two daughters: Amina and Madina. My mother replied, smiling, "Very blessed names." The next day, after touching her two grand-daughters, my mother died in robust health.'

The Muezzin's voice at this point became a little choked. Throughout the rest of his life he could not forget that ethereal light. Still, Johra Bibi was happy with him. After giving birth to two beautiful daughters, Johra Bibi did not conceive again. The

Muezzin had nurtured the desire for a son, but he did not regret not having any. He was happy with whatever Allah had bestowed on him.

From his very boyhood, the Muezzin had acquired the art of attaining happiness within himself. In his adolescence, he had learnt to render songs full-throated just by listening to the rural folk singers sing. His father, who happened to hear him one day, had rebuked him harshly and said, 'Scoundrel! A Muslim's son does not sing! I do not want to hear any songs from you again.' Without ado, Al-Amin had promptly obeyed his father's command. The father enrolled his son in a religious school for fear that he might go astray otherwise. Whenever the school remained closed, the boy would stealthily go to Ashish Mondal in the neighbouring village to learn how to play the flute. Ashish used to say, 'Your melody is very sweet. Al-Amin, you'll be a renowned artist.' The father came to know, and gave the boy such a severe beating that it left him unconscious for two days. The mother's wails brought home a doctor, and when he was better, Al-Amin went back to the madrasa. The father said, 'Sir, the boy is prone to go astray; please make him into a good man.' But the teacher did not have to undertake any trouble on that count, because Al-Amin possessed the art of being happy. He devoted himself to his studies so attentively that he never thought of the flute, even by mistake. When he recited from the Holy Quran, the teacher and students alike of the madrasa listened engrossed. Everyone admitted in one voice that none of the students who came to the school in the last twenty-five years could equal Al-Amin. He was happy, and believed that the melody of the flute lay in the tune of the last chapter of the Quran. If the mind was attuned to happiness, a tune could spring out of anything. He had no regret and no sorrow. Whatever the religious teacher asked him to learn, he did so with perfect devotion. The teacher said, 'We will make you a muezzin. People will come rushing to the mosque at the sound of your call to prayers.' Al-Amin had nodded in agreement.

He could not remember how many years had passed since then. The eyes of the supine Muezzin had been fixed on the moonlit night sky all this while. He was searching for that supernatural light he had seen at the time of his daughters' birth. The Muezzin's eyelids drooped after a time.

But the eyelids of Amina and Madina did not droop. They gazed unblinkingly at the trickle of blood running down their knees. Their bodies were convulsed with agony. They could also see zigzag lines on their bodies furrowed by human nails. Drops of blood spurted on them. In places they could see that dust and dried grass had created patches, somewhat resembling the patterns of embroidered quilts. How strange their bodies had become! The three soldiers pulled them up by their arms and made them stand. They gave them their clothes to wear. One of them pointed a finger at the girls and barked out, 'Do you know the *Kalima*?'

The two sisters nodded their heads.

'Recite.'

The two sisters recited effortlessly, 'There is no God but Allah, and Mohammad is his Prophet.'

'Well done!' The soldiers raised their guns skywards and opened fire in delight.

Amina and Madina read the pleasure of rape which was evident on the faces of the three soldiers. They forgot about their bloodied bodies and the lack of ablutions before prayers and they kept on reciting the *Kalima*. Their devout father had taught them many things with care. They tenaciously held on to all that he had taught them; they did not want to forget anything at this moment. They discovered that their bodies were on the verge of collapse and that they could walk no further. The three soldiers lifted them on their backs and carried them to their camp. 'Very pretty girls,' the soldiers repeated, bursting into cheers as they did.

Al-Amin the Muezzin cannot recall how he went rushing to the Imam and fell at his feet. Between heart-rending sobs he could utter only two words: 'Sir, my...'

'*Khamosh!* Silence! Don't be impatient. I have heard everything. These are all tests of your faith.'

'Sir...!'

'Don't offer religion as an excuse. Islam is in danger in this country. It is the responsibility of each one of us to save it. You have only sacrificed your daughters. Life has to be sacrificed after this. Go back home.'

The Muezzin could not return home. The Imam had threatened him. An old man with a flowing white beard and hair, one whom he had for so long regarded as a heavenly being, had turned into a polecat. The Muezzin wept helplessly, realising for the first time the perverted use of religion in politics.

Some ordinary people, watching him walk along the road weeping, came up to him and held his hands. '*Kainden na huzoor*. Don't weep, sir, please, don't weep. You will see that God's curse will befall the enemies. Allah will do justice against this wrong.' Another one proposed to go to the chairman of the local peace committee. 'The chairman is on friendly terms with the commander of the camp. The commander may send your daughters back if he so wishes.'

They all went to see the chairman of the peace committee. He spoke with a smile in a calm voice, 'I have been serving this union for the last thirty-five years and have never seen such a calamity. We all should jump up to face this calamity. Go back home, my dear fellow. Express your gratitude to Allah. Your daughters are saving Pakistan.'

The Muezzin could barely whisper and weeping, murmured, 'Sir, the honour of my daughters…'

'What does honour matter, my dear fellow? First come religion and the country.'

'What kind of religion is this?'

The chairman stopped the discussion. He scolded the Muezzin into silence and said in a harsh voice, 'Why do you worry? If these daughters die, you will get daughters again.'

'Sir, after my twin daughters were born, my wife didn't give birth to any others.'

The chairman's voice softened. He replied, smiling, 'You can marry again. You may take a second wife. She may give birth to a pretty girl.'

The Muezzin hurriedly went away from the presence of another polecat. He realised that he had nowhere to go. The sky and the netherworld had merged to become one before his very eyes. He realised that an ethereal light was swirling inside his head. Like a demented soul, the Muezzin kept going round and round in the field and suddenly, with both hands raised over his head, he started to dance. His companions, the common village folk, burst into tears at this sight. They took the Muezzin back home with much effort. The next morning it appeared that Al-Amin the Muezzin couldn't recognise anyone. Johra Bibi threw herself down on the verandah with heart-rending moans.

Amina and Madina were carried away in a military jeep to some army bunker. The two sisters watched the countryside wide-eyed. Never before had they undertaken a journey along such a wide road to any place in a jeep, where the scenery on both sides kept up with the moving vehicle. The wind rushed along from the opposite direction as if competing with the jeep—what a wonderful touch, their lungs were left gasping—it made one feel heavy, empty and silent. They pressed each other's hands. They didn't speak, as if a rare thought flowed in each of their blood-streams. Was it a lament for the lost innocence of adolescence? For whom did they sacrifice everything? After a while the scenery changed and they roused themselves. The trees looked different. The large trees stood in a strange manner; the bamboo groves seemed to be posturing; at places human bodies walking along the ridges of earth demarcating fields kept metamorphosing into scorpions; elsewhere the necks of humans squatting in potato fields got shortened, giving them the roundish look of domes on the roof of a mosque—it was as if the whole sky had somehow come down; it was not deep blue any more but greyish black, and the pervading colours, like the melodious voice of their father, kept rushing along with the jeep, only to dwindle into nothingness. How charming! In their minds the two sisters began a silent lament. Their father had said that Sheikh Mujib wanted to sell this country to India. That the Pakistani Army was fighting, betting their lives to avert such an eventuality. But their father had also told them that the Pakistanis were true Muslims, and that so were we. They would not commit any sin. But now? The two sisters covered their eyes with the ends of their saris. What kind of a Muslim asked them to recite the *Kalima* after raping them? Their tears did not cease to flow. Their eyelids grew swollen with weeping. One of the soldiers lightly boxed Amina on the chin and said in Urdu, 'Why do you weep? Don't weep anymore.'

The two sisters remained silent. They thought that they should understand the language of Muslims. But they understood nothing. They racked their brains about it. They thought that perhaps the soldiers were speaking the language that the girls had memorised without understanding in their childhood from the last chapter of the Holy Quran. If only their father had taught them the meanings instead of making them commit it to memory! They would have then engaged in loud-throated quarrels with the soldiers. They could in no way reconcile the description of Muslims that they had heard from their father with these soldiers. That melodious voice came floating back to them: 'Remember, you are Muslims. I have chosen sacred names for you. I want you to be like the devout Rabeya.' The hearts of the two sisters cried out in lament, 'Our father had asked us to be like Rabeya, but how could we possibly be like her? We'll never get back our old lives.' They couldn't recite praises to the Prophet to their heart's content with their ritually unprepared bodies. If the two sisters wanted to remember something to give them strength in the darkness of the bunkers, the exquisitely beautiful landscape came floating before their eyes. Madina burst into sobs in her sleep. 'We didn't want to be girls like these! We wanted to recite verses of the Holy Quran from memory to our heart's content.'

Amina wrapped both her arms round Madina's neck and said, 'No, we cannot. Our bodies are not ritually prepared. We don't have any cloths. They have kept us naked.'

The two sisters woke up in the darkness. In that darkness, their bodies shook violently with nausea. Then they felt hairy hands were pulling them along, beastly men were riding their bodies, taking in the scent of them, and then it was all darkness again. Evenings began that way inside the bunker, and mornings ended there that way. There were ten soldiers. And there were only two girls for them. If they saw the girls weeping, they would bark out in

Urdu, 'Why do you cry? You are Muslims, so are we. You know the *Kalima,* so do we. Recite, recite the *Kalima.*'

Everyday the sisters recited the *Kalima* fluently and without interruption.

Once Amina had kept silent, thinking of something else. The ferocious giant had caught her by the braids of her hair, lifted her up in the air and hurled her to the ground. As a result Amina could not leave her bed for the next two days. Scolding her, Madina asked, 'Why did you have to do that?' Amina replied tersely, 'Can *Kalima* and rape go together?' Madina looked at her strangely and said, 'Hush! Don't talk like that. Our father will hear.'

When they felt each other's backs with the palms of their hands, they knew that the soft smoothness had been replaced by roughness. There were many wounds, big and small. In the same soft voice Amina said, 'Our bodies are no longer ours.' Madina laughed a strange laugh and said, 'After all, we are defending Pakistan.'

Amina could not say, 'Hush! Don't laugh. Our father will hear.'

The two sisters in the army bunker thus tried to keep their father away from their agony. They didn't know how many days or months rolled by. Or was it a year? They very clearly remembered the month of April; it could now be October. The faint stirrings of winter were already discernible in the air. For the last two days the soldiers had been looking worried. They kept talking among themselves. Guard duty at the bunker had been beefed up. The two sisters whispered between themselves, 'Has the war begun?'

Madina cried out, terrified, 'Shall we die in this hole? Won't we ever meet our parents again?'

'We may even survive. All these devils will be finished off in the war.'

'You are right. The freedom fighters will come and rescue us. They are our own people.'

'But how can we possibly face them? They have kept us naked.' The two sisters covered their faces with their hands at the thought.

Two days after this, the sisters were awakened from sleep by the loud sounds of shooting. There was uproar in the Pakistani camp, 'The war has begun! The Mukti Bahini soldiers have attacked us!'

The sisters looked on stony-eyed. They had heard talk of independence from other village girls. They did not know what independence was; their father had not explained it to them. But looking at their own selves, they wanted to find the meaning of independence. One soldier, holding Madina by her braids and shaking her, cried, 'You Bengali traitors! You pigs!' Madina gritted her teeth in anger.

Deep into the night, the two sisters realised that the sounds of gunfire had now become deafening. Were the *muktijoddha* advancing heroically? Their eyes sparkled with anticipation. They expressed their heartfelt gratitude to the freedom fighters. The two were huddled in a corner of the bunker, their backs against the wall. Despite the constant sounds of gunfire, sleep kept overtaking them. They had not had one full night of sleep in so many days. When their eyelids began to close again, they had a vision of the long-lost path through an open field at noontide. They had heard their father recount many times the glow of supernatural light on their rooftop at the time of their birth and the light that had rested in the eyes of their sightless grandmother. That same incandescent light now illumined their dreams. There was no one around. Just a lone figure draped in a golden cloak coming up along the path they had traversed. The two sisters craned their necks to see who he was. They saw that the man was holding a rifle in his hands, which at times disappeared under his cloak and at times the tip of its barrel pointed towards the sky and the bullet burst forth. The two sisters peeped out of the bunker. He came forward and said, 'Come out.' They felt ashamed and covered their bodies with their arms. The fighter took off his golden cloak and offered it to them. 'Please wrap it around yourselves. You have nothing to be ashamed of. It is we who must be ashamed. Please do come out. See how an unseen light is spreading all around.'

Both sisters awoke at the same time.

They looked at each other.

Amina spoke up, excited, 'I dreamt such a strange dream, Madina!'

'So did I!' said Madina, her voice ringing with joy.

The sisters plunged back into their dream despite being awake. A handsome fighter was approaching through the dense fog inside their skulls to cover up all their shame, rage, hurt, humiliation. A strange shiver ran down their bodies—a pleasure they felt for the first time in the sixteen years of their lives.

Clasping Amina's hands, Madina said, 'I want to love a man like that.'

Amina said, 'So do I.'

The deafening sounds of the firearms made them ecstatic.

Translated from the Bangla by **Ali Ahmad**

7 A Long Conversation between Cain and Abel*

RASHEED AMJAD

Putting the luggage in the car, Cain asked Abel, 'So, you are really going?'

Abel looked for the sadness in his eyes, 'You still do not believe it?'

Cain shook his head. Abel said, 'The bond of our siblinghood has grown feeble. The old land has distanced itself from me. The new land now beckons.'

Cain looked incredulously and said, 'Your own roots have become hollow. When the roots become hollow, the earth spits them out.'

Abel escaped the clutches of silence for a few moments and replied, 'Perhaps you are right. But if a wall cracks, destruction is its fate. I cannot wait for that to happen. And so I want to escape to avoid it…far, very far away, where I have no name, no face, no identity. Name and face are our sibling identity, and if you break free of them, there is no name and no face.' Abel then gazed at Cain's face, taking in each of his features, but he encountered only drops of strangeness.

'Still. Going away doesn't make any sense.'

Abel shrugged. 'Nothing makes sense. We are born here. Does that make sense? Sense…sense…sense.'

'Who is this man?' Cain asked himself. Surely, he is not the man I have known for years. 'Then who *is* he?' He reached out and touched Abel's body with his hand, but Abel remained unmoved. Cain tried to catch the light that emanated from Abel's eyes.

---

*Originally published in Urdu as 'Habeel aur Qabeel ke Darmiyan Ek Taweel Makaalma', in *Zameen Zalim Hai* (The Earth is Cruel) edited by Bashir Mansoor, 2015.

In these desolate and gloomy ruins, where was this light coming from? Cain tried to capture the light, but it eluded him.

Cain asked, 'Where did you get this light from?'

Abel laughed and moved away. Then the laughter turned into sadness. 'The winds have lost their name. Now instead of rainfall, hunger falls from the sky. And all old relationships have been broken. Do you know why the lamp always flickers before it dies out?' Abel asked.

'Yes. And I also know that those who have sold their voices live in closed rooms,' Cain answered.

Abel looked stricken, like a horse that had been whipped. 'Whatever happens, I have always valued my voice. Do you know that when all voices were being hushed, it was I who stoked the dying embers?'

'Yes. I know,' Cain conceded. All the pages of Abel's life fluttered in Cain's eyes. Cain touched Abel's face, but he could not find in it that sweet familiarity. 'Whose vacant face is this?' he wondered. Both were silent. The shroud of fear enveloped them both and the pebbles of parting were thrown at them. One thing kept rising to his lips; he finally blurted it out: 'Are you going away to earn money?'

Abel hesitated for a few moments then said, 'Do you think I am a vulture to leave a stale corpse for a fresh one?'

'Then why are you going?'

'Now the clouds do not bring forth greenery but only barrenness. I do not want to see hunger and starvation. I want to escape all that. The bosom of the earth is drying up. I was chasing after butterflies. Her lap always welcomed me. It was I who did not go. I was not allowed to do so. Believe me, I wanted to but they released colourful butterflies around me. And now that bosom has dried up, I cannot face her with my embittered self.'

Cain grasped his hand. 'There are others.'

Abel freed his hand. 'But my curse is that I know.'

Silence descended upon them, drop by drop. As the veil of stillness lifted, the noise of the platform danced around them. *Hai Jamalo...Hai Jamalo...Hai Jamalo.* Jamalo also proved disloyal.

Cain's voice began to dry up. 'We forgot that Jamalo also drank the milk of those disloyal winds. We are, in fact, blind. Blindness, haziness and silence melt within each other.'

The guard blew the first whistle. Cain was reminded yet again that Abel was indeed leaving.

'So you are really going away?'

'Yes,' he said, placing his hand on Cain's shoulder. 'And before I go, I will leave my name and identity behind.'

The guard blew another whistle.

Cain shouted, 'When will you be back?' But the vastness of distance engulfed both his voice and the gesture of his waving hand. Slowly, as if in a dream, he walked homewards. Sadness and numbness dragged alongside him. He thought that if people keep leaving, he would be the only one left in the city.

Absolutely alone!

Just himself!

God above, the earth beneath.

And just him in the middle.

He looked up at the sky. 'Come, my friend…come down. You are alone and sad. Let's stay together.'

A speeding car went past him. The driver leaned out of the window and yelled, 'Are you blind?'

He snapped back to reality. He remembered Abel had gone. The distance between them had grown, spreading its arms outwards. He ran back but the platform was bare and desolate. The shining railway tracks had taken the train far, far away. He ran along the tracks, shouting, 'Abel, kill me before you go, just kill me!' But his pleas went unheard. He asked a passerby, 'Do you know why, many years ago, Abel killed Cain?'

The stranger looked taken aback and proceeded to walk away.

'Don't you know?' The words fell from his mouth like drops from a cup of tea. 'The city is emptying out, and someone has come between us. One day, Abel took on Cain's identity and killed him. But where is he now—the nameless one? He searches his own self. He was not inside either him or Cain. He looks, smells, touches, laughs and tastes like him but now he is not within anybody. He casts a web of lines on faces and destroys like termites. Abel's face also had that same web of lines, and now it will be on my face too. So the earth closes its eyes for me, and I too will go away. He wants everyone to leave one by one so that he can possess everything, but I will not go.' He looked at the receding plumes of smoke and shouted, 'Abel, I will not run away like you! I will go and face him. I will hug him and his shriveled chest. I will say to him, "Open your eyes".'

But who was this who weaved webs of lines on faces? What was his name?

Translated from the Urdu by
Tabinda J. Burney *and* **Alvira Burney**

8 Durba Grass, Tin Roof and Alakananda*

PAPREE RAHMAN

Although we couldn't tell the difference between autumn and late autumn then, we could clearly tell the difference among the many kinds of grass. We could easily identify which was *durba* and which *mutha*, which was *chapra* or *fulka* and which one *shama*. *Durba* was very fine, just like the vermicelli cooked on festivals. *Chapra* was flat and wide. *Durba* was thin as a blade, so dewdrops always hung on it, glittering. On the way to school our feet would get soggy with dew, and we felt strange whenever the dead yellowish grass got mixed with the morning dew. The light was still dim and the morning hadn't yet revealed itself fully. Even at that hour, we dragged our mushy sponge sandals flecked with bits of yellowish grass clinging to them like a dead photograph. We had to walk to school on wet soggy feet. School had not yet begun; our school office-keeper Sanaullah's wooden hammer had not yet struck the brass gong. But by then we had already crossed the *durba*-filled meadow and started walking on the plump tarmacked road. As we walked, the dew-drenched grass on our feet lost its moisture, and the itching began. We would then take off our sandals and start walking barefoot. We would fiercely shake and rub our legs and feet to get rid of that persistent itchy dampness. But it was no use—that wet grass still stuck to our skin like a photograph. And like a photograph it stared at us.

---

*Originally published in Bangla as 'Durba Ghash, Tiner Gher, O Alakananda' in www.banglanews24.com in 2010. The English translation, first published in *Lilies, Lanterns and Lullabies*, edited by Niaz Zaman (Dhaka: Writers.ink, 2014), is reproduced here with edits by kind permission of the translator Shehreen Ataur Khan.

Before crossing the *durba*-filled meadow, we had to pass through the zamindar's house. It was a house covered with trees and creepers, bushes and shrubs, and it also had a flock of swans. We used to stop and gawk at the large birds in wonder. To us it appeared as if a fleet of milk-white ships had emerged from the ground and glided towards us. But our stunned immobility was only momentary because that white fleet would promptly come charging at us, and half dead with fright we would run for our lives! The aggressive behaviour of the swans bewildered us. Why did the creatures come to peck us and why did they honk so hoarsely on seeing us? When the birds chased us, we would often fall with a crash straight into the lantana bushes.

Lantana bushes—an intense wild fragrance and hundreds of bright multicoloured flowers. Small shy flowers with prickly stems. We didn't pay much heed though to the scratches we got from the lantana's thorns. By that age we had learnt the colours of a rainbow, and happily chanted V-I-B-G-Y-O-R as we sat spread-eagled on that prickly bush. The flowers were stripped off their stems as we crash-landed on them. But we never could pluck these flowers; they had probably already uttered tiny screams before their fall. As we hid from the aggressive cackling swans in the lantana bush, our wet feet would invariably slip out of the sandals because of the dew-drenched grass.

Every morning we headed to the Abeda Khatun Girls' School. No one lived in the zamindar's house anymore. It looked dead, as if everyone there had turned to stone; the trees, flowers and fruits were the only living beings, and there was no shortage of these at that place. There were plenty of flowers and creepers on both sides of the spacious lawn that was surrounded by gigantic trees. In the midst of all these there used to be a tree with clusters of red flowers that we adored the most—they were full of honey. We sucked the butts of these flowers and could instantly taste their sweetness on our tongues. We would crave for them. But as soon as our hands reached for these flowers, three or four dogs used to run out after us, and we forgot all about the honey and ran for our lives. What a mean zamindar! They were all long dead and gone but they never forgot to guard their garden! There was one more flower other than the honey-filled *rangan* that used to hold us in its thrall, just like our school bell. It was the dazzling yellow of bright sunlight. Seeing its radiance we forgot about the school bell. Blinded by its beauty we would circle the flower-laden bush in a daze. And sometimes during those very moments we would hear the vendor calling: *Ice-cream! One paisa, two paisa, one aana, four aana…Ice-cream!* Ice-creams wrapped in plastic, carried inside a wooden box on wheels. The colours: red, green, white. Those bright yellow flowers and colourful ice-creams made us forget all about school. By then, Sanaullah *Bhai* had already rung his bell for the first class. We saw the ice-creams right in front of our eyes and school was still far away, but we could not buy them for we never had any money. If I were lucky, *Dadajan* would sometimes open his cloth wallet and give me two paisa. His *botua* was khaki in colour.

When we learnt the colour of *Dadajan*'s purse, we also recognised the khaki of the military. Did the military also put their money in a *botua* like *Dadajan*? He used to tie the long strips of his purse around his waist. Whenever we needed any money, he would untie them in a leisurely manner and give us one paisa or two *aana*.

Ice-cream…Kulfi ice-cream: that cry would reverberate in our minds. One could buy an ice-cream for two paisa, but it was pointless for I could never have it all by myself. I had to give Kakon, Juthi and Kona at least a lick. Often they would also have a bite. Though I didn't know the answer, I sometimes wondered which one of these had entered our country first: *Dadajan*'s *botua* or the military? I often heard that the military would kill us all and take control of our country. But the *durba* grass and the bright bunches of *rangan*: how could *they* belong to the military? And if they did not, then why would the military kill us? The elders whispered that they were already very near, killing people on their way to our village. Schools and colleges were about to shut down. I felt a chill run down my spine. If the school was closed, we could never get our feet wet in those dew-drenched meadows again. Never fall with a crash into the lantana bushes again. We heard that they were killing people—are children people too? If so, then the military would kill us too! And that yellow flowering shrub bright as the sun whose name we only learnt later—*alakananda!*—what would happen to our *alakananda?*

The cobbled road began right at the end of the zamindar's house. We didn't walk along that road but on the narrow path that led through the field. The roof of the school could be seen the moment we stepped into the field. The tin roof shone bright in the morning sun; under it was our school: one white verandah and one yellow. The yellow verandah looked like the *alakananda*; Sanaullah's brass bell was kept here. All our teachers sat in the white verandah while our headmistress and the school office room were in the yellow one. We had our classes in that tin-roofed building. When it rained heavily, it made such a racket on the roof we could barely hear our teacher's voice. Among them, two were my aunts. Whenever one of them entered the class, I would say: *Salaam alaikum Apa,* in my mind still thinking of ice-cream. Aunty would glare at me; then she would open the register and start the roll call.

Roll 1: Fatema Ferdousi

Roll 2: Jinnat Ferdousi

In between the roll call, she would look up and again frown at me. *If you call me 'Apa' again, I will punish you!* Class would end with glares and frowns.

We remained homebound. But we couldn't forget those *alakananda* flowers. The flower looked just like the bell in Sanaullah's hand, as if it would ring whenever the wooden hammer struck it and I would run for school. But I didn't run for school. Instead I learnt to run for the trenches. There was a large area at the back of our house, swampy and overgrown with bushes. There, *Dadajan* had dug trenches deeper than graves and covered them with tin sheets. Whenever the gunfight started, we were thrust into those trenches. Once, right in the middle of that frenzy and chaos the straps of my sponge sandals got ripped. Such rotten luck! In that overgrown swamp there were pieces of broken glass and sharp dry brushwood...how on earth was I to run barefoot? So I quickly seared the plastic straps of my sandals together using a burning kerosene lamp, and then ran for the trenches again!

Meanwhile *Dadajan* started running out of money. And the Pakistani military entered the zamindar's house with loaded guns. *Dadajan* did not look for money in his *botua* anymore. We also stopped attending school. We didn't get any news about our ice-cream vendor, our school office-keeper Sanaullah *Bhai* or even our peanut vendor, Jabbar. From the low voices of our guardians we got to know that the situation was worsening day by day. We couldn't go to school, couldn't even step out of the house. Our mothers, aunts, elder sisters, everyone started hiding themselves under burkhas.

What exactly had happened? Why on earth were all these things happening to us?

Dadajan anxiously caressed his beard, his eyes grave. When *Dadijan* asked him for money for the household, he kept rummaging through his purse. I noticed that its colour was fading—it had become paler—and wondered where its khaki colour had gone. Did the military take away the colour of my *Dadajan*'s purse? Otherwise why would it look so pale?

My dear, school is not going to open again.

What was the old man saying? I was feeling sick with giddiness like a spinning top. What would happen if school really did not open? There were so many things under that tin roof…slates-pencils-books, white and yellow verandahs, Sanaullah's bell. Its ringing sound meant that school was over for the day. And we would start flying homewards, carefree as dragonflies, rushing towards the *alakananda* bush, running to see the honking swans. And if we crashed into the lantana bushes all the little lantana flowers would again fall.

They said the military had raped Sanaullah's wife and had left her in front of the school.

What was rape?

We could not understand but whatever it meant, why did it happen in front of our school?

Didn't they have anywhere else to go?

A military camp was set up at the zamindar's house. And another one at Basaile.

We heard that they had blown up our school with bombs.

What was a bomb? And what was the fault of our school?

The elders wanted to shelter us and hide us. We started fleeing the place with our families when we saw that our school was on fire.

We cried as we ran.

We heard that Sanaullah's wife could no longer feel her legs.

We heard that they had killed Sanaullah.

One bullet went whizzing over my head.

They urged us: *Walk faster, my dears, walk faster!*

How could we walk fast? Our school was on fire. Our houses were on fire. Bazaars were on fire. Fire. Fire. Fire. Oh the terrible heat of that fire. But as we ran, in our mind's eyes we could clearly see our school, the dew-drenched grass, the lantana shrubs, the *alakananda* blossoms.

Then a sudden thought struck us—the Pakistani military could burn down every single thing…let them! Let them destroy the trees, shrubs and all. But they could never destroy our soil. This soil was incomparable, this soil rich with the warmth of love. Even if they burnt down everything, life would always spring back here again. How many would they kill? Let them kill. There would always be someone alive. There had to be. The trees and creepers and flowers would all grow again. Sanaullah's bell would never ring again, but we would be able to tell the time.

And when the *alakananda* bloomed again, we would walk to our school once more through the grass-filled meadow. After all these days we knew that the *alakananda* also had another name: bell flower.

Translated from the Bangla by **Shehreen Ataur Khan**

9 Versions of Truth*

MASOOD ASHAR

'Baby, there is blood on your finger. Did you hurt yourself?'

'No. It is nothing. I did not hurt myself,' the little girl says.

'Okay, but let me wash it away.'

'No, I won't let you wash it. It is my mother's blood.'

I look around. I am unable to decide how to react. Everyone looks occupied. Their faces show no emotion. Perhaps, even their hearts are empty. They are trying to scrub the walls clean. I tell myself I should control my anger; I should pull myself together. Anger is the abandonment of reason, the end of all argument. I have so much to say. I should not get angry.

This time, I try to talk to them with new arguments based on reason and logic. I want to capture their eyes as well as their ears. I want them not only to listen but to see, to open their eyes to all those things which my sinful eyes have witnessed. I want them to listen to everything which has been poured into my ears over the years.

I am happy that they are listening to me intently. Words flow from me unceasingly, spilling across the room as it were. Words and images of people, places, incidents—an unending stream. Suddenly I gaze into the eyes of my listeners, eyes I had thought I had put under a spell. My monologue comes to an abrupt end. Their eyes are desolate like my heart—and dead. Why are their eyes so desolate and empty? Why do I feel such elemental sadness while they are busy scrubbing the walls clean of blood and new residents are being put into old houses?

---

*Originally published in Urdu as 'Apni Apni Sachaiyan' in Masood Ashar, *Saare Fasane* (All Stories), 1987. English translation by Khalid Hasan previously published in *Versions of Truth: Urdu Short Stories from Pakistan*, edited by Khalid Hasan and Faruq Hassan, 1983; reproduced here by permission of Jeffrey Hasan/Estate of Khalid Hasan.

I say a prayer: 'May God give me the courage to accept what I cannot change; and the courage to change what I can; and the wisdom to tell good from evil.'

Everyone bursts out into laughter.

'It is a political prayer.'

'A compromise formula, pure and simple.'

'Playing politics with God.'

Why has this prayer come to my lips? It is a strange prayer. Who has taught it to me? Time itself? Has time robbed our eyes of light and our minds of reason?

On the night of March 24 and 25, I was in Hotel Miskha. It was an absurd name. It had a lift which never worked. The lift boy who, in fact, was an old man, always carried a tool kit with him. Whenever we went to that hotel, the children would make fun of the old man. He would try to scare them with his tools. He would tell them, 'This lift can take us to the moon. All of us will one day go to the moon and all you naughty children will be nailed to the wall.' The children would laugh and I would wonder why this hotel had the absurd name of Miskha.

In front of the hotel was the railway colony. It was surrounded by green, fertile hills. We used to live in the colony in a small bungalow on a little hill. On the night of March 24 and 25 the guns began to roar and reverberate in the hills. We did not know what was happening. In panic, we ran towards Hotel Miskha. Why we ran in that direction nobody really knows, but at the time it seemed as if the only thing that made any sense was the absurdly named Hotel Miskha. Nothing else mattered any longer and everything for which we had struggled and undergone such pain had suddenly been rendered meaningless.

They came in the night while the guns roared in the hills and told us to hand over our men to them.

I said to them, 'This is my son, who is not yet a man. He is just a boy.' They looked at me as if they did not understand me, as if my voice had not reached their ears.

'You will not leave this place,' they said to me.

'Where can I go?' I said, 'But don't you see...?'

'We'll see everything,' they laughed. 'You get out of the way.'

I did not understand what they meant by that, but when they moved towards my daughter I knew. 'She is my daughter,' I said to them. 'She is like your daughter. She is not a man.'

'Daughter! Whose daughter?' Their eyes were like a blank sheet of paper.

And then the womb of the earth burst open. They tugged at her sari and the sari wasn't interminable. It came into their hands. My daughter wasn't Draupadi. My daughter lay naked in front of her father and her brothers.

But why is my daughter not Draupadi? I have no answer. I look at their faces for some sign, for some meaning, but they laugh at me. My eyes go dark because I am gazing at the nakedness of my daughter.

'Who suffers when wild elephants fight? The grass.'

I hear their guffaws.

'And when wild elephants fight playfully, who gets trampled? The grass. Always the grass.'

I am walking down Jinnah Avenue. I stop and look around. We construct new buildings with great speed here and just as rapidly as we build them, they grow old. Rain and salinity age them in one season. And every time the season changes, they have to be given a facelift. But the great rivers flow and their waters never age. They renew themselves endlessly. And the buildings of the new capital have been designed with wide arches and semi-circles. Through them the water can flow without hindrance.

'I feel as if a dry rot has set in my body. I need to be freed,' someone whispers in my ear. I turn around and the whisper becomes a scream.

'All meaningful things have an absurd dimension,' I say to myself. Then tears roll down my cheeks.

When they refused to unload the ships in the harbour and locked up the crew in their cabins, I took a vow of silence. When they came to take away our men, I shut my eyes. It seemed supremely irrelevant in what particular school the walls and floors were splattered with the fresh blood of little flower-like children. Nor did it seem to matter any longer in what rest-house the bed-sheets were covered with the blood of young virgins or how many women were abducted and raped in what quarter of town.

I only know that when they came to the hotel room, I hid my children under the mosquito net overhanging the bed. It was almost comic.

I distinctly remember the puppet show given by a group of visiting Germans in the club on the hilltop. One of the puppets, which was supposed to be a professor, was talking high-sounding gibberish in an exaggeratedly grave manner. He was trying to explain some theory and sounded so funny that the audience burst out laughing. The puppeteer fell silent but as soon as he resumed his talk, pandemonium broke loose. People were hysterical with laughter. The puppeteer would thump the table every now and then and start again but the audience was beyond control. My own children were delirious with laughter. Somehow, I was feeling sorry for both the puppet and the puppeteer.

I asked some people sitting next to me, 'Who are you laughing at? The puppet or the puppeteer?' They replied with more laughter. I am being ridiculous, I thought.

'Long live the first Khan!'

'Long live the second Khan!'

'Long live the third Khan!'

'Long live all Khans!'

I turned my face in the direction of the posts and pickets which marked our territory. These slogans were obviously being raised for the benefit of the people on the other side. No longer could gunfire be heard from the hills. It now came from the direction of the harbour. The ships were being unloaded of their cargo, which was being transported to the city.

In the dining hall of Hotel Miskha, the faces were different. However, the mosquito nets were still as unsafe as before.

'Hello! Where is number one?'

'Booked.'

'Where is number two?'

'Booked as well.'

'Who are you?'

'I am number three but I do not like civilians.'

They came again under cover of automatic fire and said, 'Hand over your men to us.'

'There are no men here,' I say. 'Like grains of rice they lie scattered in the fields and have taken root.'

They look at me suspiciously and tear down the mosquito nets over the beds, nets they had made themselves. I close my eyes.

Who shall defend whom?

The lift boy has already reached the room. The wooden staircase is old and moth-eaten.

I try to pray but somehow nothing comes to my lips. What is there to pray for and whom can I pray for anyway? I have a powerful urge suddenly. I want to disintegrate completely and let the wind blow away my remains. I do not want to open my eyes ever again. I do not want to see anything. There is a limit to how much and how long your eyes will see.

Then suddenly, involuntarily, my eyes open. I see that I have turned into stone. There are strangers tugging at my daughter's sari and she, who is not Draupadi, is stark naked. I want to close my eyes but they will not close because no longer will any daughter be born as Draupadi.

I try to remember the times when it was not like this and we did not have to shout slogans and fresh air belonged to everyone under the sky. But I am no longer sure it wasn't always like it is now. In my heart, doubt like a serpent raises its head. Was there ever a time unlike the present? I can no longer trust my memory.

I try to talk to them. Old stories come to my mind.

'Oh, son of man, I was hungry for food and you let me starve.'

'Oh God of all creation who feeds all of mankind, how could I have given you food?'

'Do you not know that one of my sons begged you for food and you refused it to him? Do you not know that if you had fed him, you would have found me closer to you?'

A shiver runs down my spine. My body is stiff. All questions have become futile. I am tired of asking questions of myself repeatedly. I do not know the answers any longer, not even one.

I feel very sorry for myself. At my helplessness. I do not know what there is to do or what anyone wants.

No one listens to me. How hard I have tried. 'Listen,' I said, 'One can only talk in parables. These are the signs of the times, the writing on the wall.'

'Oh son of man, I was thirsty.'

'Oh son of man, I was without raiment.'

The body becomes numb after injury. Pain comes later.

'No, it is nothing. I did not hurt myself.'

'Okay, but let me wash it away.'

'No, I won't let you wash it. It is my mother's blood.'

Does it matter if this happened before or after March 25? In a dark and narrow grave, I try with my fingers to feel my wounds, now caked with blood, but there are dead bodies piled all around me and I cannot move without suffering excruciating pain. I try to raise my face and breathe but the chill breath of death rushes through my nostrils. I am struggling to stay alive.

And then all the women sheared off their long black hair and gave it to their men so that they could use it to string their bows and keep their arrows on the ready. The women threw out their men from the houses so that the men may die fighting. And I found that I was among those women who had sheared off their hair. My own hair, shorn by my own hands, was strung across a bow. I was not sorry why it had happened; the great tragedy was that no longer was there a dividing line between sorrow and happiness. I was not even sure if this was a moment to mourn or rejoice.

Over my head is the sky black with clouds, and I am standing knee-deep in mud mixed with gunpowder and blood. The air is heavy with the lamentations of women and children. It is difficult to breathe. As the night deepens, the screams of the children in the distance intensify. Is it not strange that despite the thud of heavy boots and screeching jeeps and trucks, the screams of children can still travel through the air and reach us? Then there is silence but it is suddenly pierced by the children's screams—but only for a moment. Heavy hands are slapped across their mouths. I cannot see how many they are or even who they are. I say to them, 'Get out of this darkness or you will suffocate to death.' I try to see the hands that are slapped across the screaming children's faces. I suddenly feel that it is darker outside than where I was. I huddle back into the grave.

Mothers are strange creatures. Every mother thinks she is different from the others; that her children are unlike other children; that they can never do wrong or suffer pain.

How wrong they are!

Who had said that the past is like the dark side of the moon? All tomorrows are strapped in mystery but when the mystery is unravelled, then...

Ten years were spent in loving, another ten in recapturing the magic of that first love. But what about the rest of the years? Is there any point in thinking about them? Is it not enough to accept that the past and all the memories connected with it have been swallowed up by Mother Earth? Do we not know that even the Earth's tolerance of the extremities of nature has a limit? I look up at the walls which are now being raised to construct new edifices and see the doors open and close. And I say, 'You must now listen to me. You never listened to me before.'

'Truth has so many faces. One man's truth can negate another man's truth. And when so many versions of truth clash, everything becomes an absurdity; all meaning, all sense is lost.

'Let us scrub the walls clean because if life is to begin anew, the spots of blood must come off. The realities of the past and the future must remain in our consciousness.'

But then I wonder if reality means anything any longer. The serpent of doubt raises its head again and I cannot take my eyes away from its hypnotic gaze.

I laugh at my helplessness. What strange creatures we mothers are.

Translated from the Urdu by **Khalid Hasan**

10 She Knew the Use of Powdered Red Chillies*

SHAHEEN AKHTAR

On the Silver Jubilee of the Liberation, a stone was flicked into a calm pond. A group of researchers spread out in all directions, like water-hyacinths, in search of female freedom fighters. They traced one woman-warrior who knew the multiple uses of powdered pepper. In 1971, she vanquished a number of Pakistani soldiers by flinging powdered red chilli on their eyes and noses. The problem was that her name was not on the list of freedom fighters. Her identity was also an awkward issue. In the birth-hour of Freedom, the Mukti Bahini Commander of the Mohakhali area had included her name in the list of collaborators. On the other hand, the interviewer at the Women's Rehabilitation Centre had filled in the identity box of the form by writing 'Birangana' because the medical examination had revealed damage to her reproductive organs that could only occur with a rape victim. In addition, an Irish doctor identified her varied versions of what had happened and time-confusion as post-rape mental disorder. Despite having these significant details close at hand, the interviewer at the centre was completely confused about the woman's identity. Hence, at the top of the report, the sentence 'She knew the use of red chilli powder' was written in thick block letters. Because of this, she even managed to get a job in the spice-grinding section of the centre at the time. A few days after that, in the deep of night, she threw powdered pepper into the eyes of the uniformed guard of the Women's Rehabilitation Centre and ran away. The team of researchers learnt from the former director of the centre that her aim

---

*Originally published in Bangla as 'Gura Morich' in the *Daily Sangbad* on 16 December 1997, Dhaka. The English translation, first published in *Fault Lines: Stories of 1971*, edited by Niaz Zaman and Asif Farrukhi (Dhaka: The University Press Limited [UPL], 2008), is reproduced here with minor edits by permission of the author, translator and publishers.

was as deadly as a skilled archer—as a result of which, although the guard survived, he lost his eyesight forever. Hence, the authorities did not attempt to again locate and rehabilitate such a dangerous woman. When the centre was closed down and the thousands of filled-in forms were poured into a dry tub, doused with kerosene and set on fire, her 'Birangana' identity was also reduced to ashes. The collaborator file had disappeared before that. Twenty-five years after Liberation, the team of researchers interviewed her again. Their report was titled in accordance with the title of the Women's Rehabilitation Centre report. Despite the fact that the story of the powdered pepper had not seemed credible to them from the very beginning, they thought about it deeply and realised that if one left out the tale of the powdered red chilli, one could not even label her a collaborator, let alone a freedom fighter. And if they called her a Birangana, then that was an insult to the whole group of Biranganas, wasn't it? Then who was she? Attempting to explore all this objectively a quarter century after the Liberation War further muddied the issue of her identity. In this situation, the researchers felt that publishing the interview would be risky and meaningless. This story has been based upon that discarded interview. The interview has been presented exactly the way it was, including the titles. The author did not feel any desire or responsibility to invest her with any specific identity. All that the author has attempted to do in this narrative is to break the boundaries of human credulity, maybe just a little.

This could even be a dream

Two months after March 25th, my husband decided to go off to the Liberation War. I was such a fool! I grabbed his hand, fell at his feet, wept, 'Take me with you, make the arrangements to take me along.' He said, 'All right, I will.' And then he left. He just disappeared. There was this abandoned house owned by someone, where I had been living for two days. Since my husband left this place, they haven't called me for meals. They're whispering among themselves. They're thinking I'm a woman of the streets. Does anyone's husband just leave his wife in an unknown house! Even if it is wartime? The man of the house woke me up in the morning to ask me, 'Where did your husband go?' I replied, 'Who knows where he went.'

'Do you have anywhere to go to?' He holds the door to the street wide open.

I come out on the streets. I have no sandals. I have lost everything as I've been on the run for two months. I roam the streets without rhyme or reason. Where shall I go? Where can I stay? I've had nothing to eat at night. I feel pins and needles of hunger in my stomach. Suddenly, a Bihari boy called Chullu shows up. Chullu comes up to me and said, '*Apa*, you here! Do you want a job?' I don't know if people have jobs during wartime. For the past two months I have been fleeing with my husband from one place to another. Now he has gone and left me on my own. I said, 'I do want a job Chullu *Bhai*. Or else what shall I eat, where shall I live? But how can I get a job? I can't go that way. They'll kill me.' *That* way meant Mohakhali, the part of the city that we have left behind. I had worked at a private company there before March 25. The boy gestured towards the sun-grilled, almost empty city and said, 'Come with me. No one will say anything to you.'

I'm going to Mohakhali by rickshaw with Chullu. I don't have a single penny in my pocket. I can't open my mouth and tell him, 'Chullu *Bhai*, buy me something to eat before I start at my new job.' Except when I kept on looking at my bare feet and made sounds of pain, Chullu said, 'Nothing to worry about, you'll get everything.'

Chullu sat me down in an abandoned house and went out looking for a job. There were several guards at the front and back of the house. I sniffed around the kitchen. Empty bottles of marmalade, jelly and pickles; the remnants at the bottom of coffee and Horlicks containers had congealed into hard rocks. There was nothing in the fridge except a few bottles of whisky. Beside it a huge piano, with a family group photo atop. Their faces and clothes made me think that they were non-Bengalis. I felt spooked. I opened a bottle and poured half of the whisky down my throat, absolutely raw. Then suddenly I noticed the house-guards. Although they were scattered here and there, they were guarding me in a circle. It was late afternoon. What should I do? I had to escape from there and that too before evening.

When I found a guard by himself, I asked him, 'Who lives in this house?' He turned his face away pretending he couldn't hear me. I had come out of the house and was walking on the lawn. My throat stung, my innards were burning, and amidst all this I was making plans to escape. There were a few rickshaws on the other side of the open iron gate; they even had some passengers. But it would be no use shouting. No one would have the courage to stand face to face with armed guards.

They had surrounded me now and were circling me. Gradually the circle was closing in. 'Look, I'm very hungry. I haven't eaten all day.' They pursed their lips in laughter, as if what I had said was very funny. I was stubborn, 'Can you tell me where I can get some food?' I looked at all of them when I asked the question this time. Chatting and jabbering, I actually wanted to break out of their circular formation. One guard said, 'Yes, yes, you'll have everything in the evening,' and asked another to bring some tea. As soon as he moved away, I raced towards the street. With a tremendous roar, the five thugs ran after me.

I am running. I hold my life in my hands and run.

It was like it happens in dreams: I was running but could not move forward. At one point they surrounded me in a ring again. I stood with my face lifted up towards the sky. Oh, I'd forgotten to mention, I had packets of powdered red pepper with me. Not one but many. I flipped open the packets and tossed them. Once, twice, thrice…The skies of Mohakhali turned as red as Karbala that day, as if a blood-rain was pouring from the sky. The booming cannons of the *ferishtas* in the sky sounded at the same time. I would throw a packet and run. Where to? I didn't know. When I think of it now, all of this seems a dream.

Then I wanted to live or die

My husband was taking the dog Pinky instead of me. Not a sound emerged from my lips either in sorrow or humiliation. I stared and stared as he put the chain around the dog's neck, and began to pace from this end of the room to the other. After a long time Pinky had been bathed in hot water mixed with a little Dettol. He was looking at the clock repeatedly; Pinky stood wagging her tail. When the horn blows from downstairs, they will leave the room and go off to the Liberation War. I couldn't stand it anymore and grabbed hold of my husband's collar and tie and shook him with all my might, grinding my teeth. 'If you're not going to take me with you, why did you marry me? Is Pinky your girlfriend or your wife? Come on, tell me, girlfriend or wife?' He loosened the grip of my fingers from his collar and tie and said, 'Oh brother! You are all worried about yourself, and here I am...' He began pacing again. I ran towards him to shake him again. He shoved me onto the floor with a single push and walked out with Pinky. With all the commotion, I hadn't heard the horn sounding from downstairs. It was when the green jeep gunned its engine and sprayed dust as it climbed onto the main road that I saw they were leaving. So if you are leaving, go on, leave. Guerrilla wars, liberation wars aren't fought with dogs. Were they actually going to the Liberation War at all? As if I didn't know. It was all a ploy.

That man had tricked me into marriage in the very month of March 1971. Believe me, I hadn't wanted to marry. The people in my house said, 'So how long are you going to live by yourself? The way things are, who knows what will happen when!' Tell me, can you trust a man that quickly? And that too someone who owns a bitch named Pinky! So it was because of their words that I got married to this brute.

My husband left me and went off to the Liberation War, or to hell, with Pinky. I spent the night at that abandoned house and came out on the streets while it was still dark. Back then I wanted to live or die. So I appeared at the office at ten in the morning. The non-Bengali boss jumped up from his chair when he saw me, '*Arre larki, tum kahan se aayi?*' The others were in an uproar. Which is what happens when a prey walks into a trap. 'Sir, I need some money. If you could give me my salary for March.' The big boss called a peon in and immediately wrote me a cheque. I snatched it from the peon's hand and I ran. All the Bengali and non-Bengali employees of the office ran after me. I zigzagged down the staircase, only a step ahead! Just as I was tearing open a packet of pepper, Chullu appeared from somewhere and blocked my path. That Bihari boy I had tricked yesterday and escaped from that abandoned house.

My trance was broken when the peon entered the room. I stood up and accepted the money from his hands. It's because he was a non-Bengali that I showed him this respect. Then the big boss said, 'Start at your job here today. You're not going anywhere now. Have lunch with me in the afternoon. You can't stay anywhere else at night; you have to stay at my quarters.' I staggered and collapsed onto the chair with the cheque in my hand. My head was reeling; I hadn't had anything to eat in two days. The boss brought his lips near my ears and whispered, 'You know I'm alone now. I'm living a bachelor's life. I need you...'

A thousand and one Arabian nights

There's no work at the office. All day I just stare at the air without comprehension. And I think, what would I be thinking or doing if the war had not happened. All the people of my household, they all went every which way! Who knows where home is? Now I am part of the big boss' household. At times I am even called into the air-conditioned office of the big boss to feed paper into the typewriter. I stuff carbon paper into the machine. The boss unbuttons my blouse and plunges his face into my breasts, whining like a puppy, as if he has a tummy ache. Then he stuffs money into my cleavage—whatever he feels like that day: five takas or ten. He deducts all of it to account for my keep—food and boarding. When I return to my desk, I see not a mountain of money but red powdered chillies.

One day after the office hours were over, the big boss said, 'Commander Selim is waiting for you in a car downstairs. The Naval Commander.' Naval Commander Selim from whose clutches no woman ever returned, no matter how pretty or ugly. When the night was through, he killed the girl and dumped her into the Rupsha. I was being sent to this Sultan of the Arabian Nights! I pleaded, 'Sir, I won't go. I'll stay with you. I won't ever be disobedient again, Sir. Save me!' The big boss didn't agree. His family was arriving from Pakistan. He was kicking me out to purify his household. I was being sacrificed for this purity. The middle-aged killer Commander stood holding the car door open, saying, 'Come Memsahib, come.'

The car sped towards the naval jetty. This was my last day surely. Life or death would be decided today. When we arrived in front of the level crossing, the signal barrier descended. Commander Selim stopped the car but left the motor running. The signal light turned on and off, on and off. A train had been passing for an eternity, crawling on its chest. Finally the light turned off altogether. The crossing barricade was rising upward. I opened the car door and jumped. The naval commander's car disappeared under the powdered red chilli pepper. As I escaped, I turned back and threw packets and packets of it. Once the sachets were gone, I was weightless. I left as a plane leaves the runway and flies into the sky—fearless, free.

That night there was no pause in the chop-chop sounds of the slaughterhouse by the port jetty. My eyes had closed as dawn neared. Countless army vehicles surrounded my quarters. They had encircled the house in a honeyed-ring. It was still dark outside. There was no light in the stairwell. What if the freedom fighters lay in wait there? So no one had the courage to climb upstairs. I stood at the top of the third floor stairs and threw them a challenge. I was well turned-out, my ammunition pouch filled with red chilli powder. That was my weapon. I would throw it on whoever climbed up those stairs. A call came from downstairs, 'Come down, you bitch. You've murdered Commander Selim. You have to go down to the cantonment.' I responded from the top of the stairs, 'Why don't you come up?' A brave *jawan* raised his arms above his head and climbed up the stairs. When he reached the second-floor landing, he raised his face, puffed through his nostrils and sniffed the air. I lobbed a packet of powdered chilli at him, the same way that dynamites or grenades are thrown. He collapsed and rolled down the stairs into the garage downstairs. Then another one climbed up.

I flung my packets. They couldn't stand the burning of the powder and jumped into the river one by one, where the corpses from the slaughterhouse were dumped in the night.

No one in the world will believe it

The country was liberated. The first few days, interrogation followed interrogation. One group left, then another arrived. Each time the same words: 'You were Commander Selim's mistress. You are a collaborator.' Each time I gave the same answer: 'It takes money to buy packets of powdered chillies. If I hadn't stayed with him, where would I have gotten the money? Who would have given me the money during wartime?'

'Why, your husband would have. He could have given you money.'

'He was in the Mukti Bahini.'

'No, he wasn't. We have made enquiries.'

'Perhaps he couldn't make it. Every time he tried to cross the border, Pinky started barking so loudly—she's a Pakistani supporter, see—that he couldn't make it across.'

'Pinky? Her name isn't in the list of collaborators.'

'It isn't. Because Pinky is a bitch.'

They exchanged looks. They thought I was crazy. But I wasn't crazy. I started telling them how I had flung powdered chilli like dynamite and felled the Pakistanis. They were bewildered. They couldn't figure out whether to believe me or not, whether they should continue with the interrogation.

In these twenty-five years I have answered whatever questions anyone has asked me. But I have never been able to open my heart. Now I am fifty years old. I've heard that at sixty, even whores become innocent in the eyes of God. They can enter the community if they want. If I live for another ten years, if I did not die in 1971, I will open my heart and speak then.

Anyway, I was set free. They let me go. Besides, why shouldn't they? The Indian Army had rescued me from the cantonment. They were witnesses, those men of our allied forces.

They had abducted and taken me to the cantonment. That day, when several carloads of Pakistani Army men had surrounded my quarters in a honeyed-ring. Their accusation was that I had murdered their commander. The man was about my father's age. One day while playing cards, I had implored him: 'Teach me how to shoot a gun. I want to see whether I can.' His hands had grown still in the midst of riffling through the cards. His eyelids were motionless. I was scared. 'Oh no. I was just kidding. Please don't be angry. It's your turn now.' I shook and shook him awake. That day we didn't play cards anymore. He took me to the shooting range and all afternoon he taught me how to shoot a gun. In point of fact, he had wanted to die. He had aged, and he had committed so many murders and atrocities in the past few months that he couldn't sleep, day or night.

We were returning from the range to the naval camp amidst the light and shadows of the evening. Commander Selim was driving; I was sitting in the seat next to him. I was playing around with the pistol in my hand; it looked rather like a toy. When we reached the level crossing the commander stopped the car but kept the engine running. The night train was entering the city just then. That was my chance. I opened the car door and jumped out. I still remember, just before I jumped, Commander Selim had extended one hand in front of him like a blind man to block the bullet.

Translated from the Bangla by **Shabnam Nadiya**

11 The Dagger's Tongue*

AGHA SOHAIL

If it is easy to introduce a tree, a pole or a lamp-post then I can certainly try and introduce 'him' to you. 'His,' 'he' and 'him' are all pronouns but I am not using them instead of his name; rather I am using them as his name because I don't know his name. All I know about him is that I had always seen him standing still exactly at this spot on this road in Dhaka, like a tree or a pole or a lamp-post. On the footpath beneath the lamp-post stood this thin, scrawny man—so thin that he seemed merely a string of skin and bones—and black as coal, too! So much filth and grime had collected in his matted white hair that they looked like the hanging roots of an ancient banyan tree. Peering from beneath those filthy locks of hair, two grime-encrusted eyes looked like the flickering flames of a dwindling lamp. He was always seen standing in exactly the same pose with his hand outstretched, a lock on his tongue, a silence, an immense silence encircling him like a halo. Seeing him, it seemed as though he had been standing there, still and silent, since the beginning of Time and would continue to stand exactly like this till the end of Time. And if he were to speak, Calamity would surely befall! Therefore, it was best if he were to stay silent.

I am not the only one; in fact, the entire population of the city had got used to seeing him standing there like this. I had been seeing him, with his hand outstretched, peering into some vast abyss of unknowingness, for a quarter of a century. All manner of passers-by—young and old, men and women, children, everyone—had got accustomed to seeing him like this, as though he was an inseparable, intrinsic part of that footpath and that road. Standing beneath that

*Originally published in Urdu as 'Zabaan-e Khanjar' in *Zameen Zalim Hai* (The Earth is Cruel), edited by Bashir Mansoor, 2015.

lamp-post since an eternity he had become an indivisible part of the road. Those who travelled in rickshaws or moved about in cars and buses as well as those who went about on foot had become habituated to seeing him like this. No one knew who he was, where he lived, where he came from, or where he went.

For one thing, there was no shop or bazaar anywhere close. If, perchance, a passerby or a hawker stopped to talk to him he was met with such a silence that he would give up and go away, or at most mutter to himself and carry on. Some people thought he was mute. Others said he was deaf. Some believed that, at midnight, the earth split open and swallowed him up and spat him out again in the morning. Others maintained that he did not move in the slightest and it was entirely possible that he was a lifeless statue, made of stone. Some jesters were known to swear that he was actually a jinn or ghost or evil spirit who would appear with the day and remain standing there till late in the night, and then suddenly disappear.

But the truth is he was neither an evil spirit nor an apparition, nor a ghost or spectre but merely a human being. He was just a man who had been standing continuously on this footpath, under this lamp-post beside this road for the past twenty-five years, with his hand stretched out. Though it must be said that his impressive silence had a great role to play in the speculation and gossip that swirled about him.

The one thing that troubled me the most about him was not his silence but the manner and condition in which he stood still—never would his outstretched hand move in the slightest nor would he scratch himself or move the flies that buzzed around. He seemed as though he was an ascetic from the early period of Islam. Ascetics are known to stay immobile for long periods of time as part of their meditation; the only difference between him and those ascetics was that he would move from his place when the night deepened and walk down the footpath like a robot or someone walking under the influence of a hypnotic spell, or someone walking in his sleep.

The stream of people moving up and down this road in Dhaka were not all of the same type; there were the truly rustic folk, foreign visitors, those who looked and sounded like foreigners, students, teachers, labourers, doctors, engineers, pedestrians, those riding cycles, scooters or rickshaws and everyone had got used to seeing him like this here. So much so, that even the seasons came this way and went away on tiptoe lest any difference was noticed in the routine.

Dhaka would bathe itself in the river of happiness during a national festival but he would be planted in that very spot, still and solitary. Or else there would be strikes in the city, parades and processions, cries of 'Long Live!' or 'Down With!' would rent the skies, stones would be pelted on crowds or by crowds, sometimes bullets too would be fired but he would remain completely unaffected by all these events. He seemed to be lost in his own being so much so that those who went past him or those who were trapped in the crowds felt sorry for him lest some stone or a stray bullet might put an end to his life.

Perhaps no such stone or bullet had yet been discovered that would put him to the eternal sleep of Death because, time and again, there would be stone-pelting and firing on that very stretch of road but not one of them would touch so much as a hair on his head. Nor would he move or shift or budge the slightest from his place as though he was carved from stone.

I personally thought that he indeed used his eyes—that were directly beneath his forehead—to see but he put to greater use the eyes that he had opened inside his heart. And that was why he seemed so unaffected by what was happening in his immediate vicinity. First and foremost, I addressed the curiosity as to whether he stood there all day and night or did he, in fact, go away somewhere at night. One day, I saw the last show of a film and came and stood across the road. I saw him move from his spot and start moving down the footpath like a wound-up toy or someone under a hypnotic spell. I watched him till as far as the eye could see as he turned into a black shadow and finally disappeared from my sight.

On another occasion, a friend trailed him on a cycle only to discover that he went far beyond the city outskirts and disappeared in some graveyard. I have always found him here in the morning on this very footpath. In fact, I have even placed some coins by way of alms on his palm and never found the slightest quiver in his still form.

At first, there was much slaughter and carnage in Dhaka. Then suddenly, war was announced. But there wasn't the slightest change in his routine. There were airstrikes and bombings on this very road and a large part of the road disappeared in the shelling. I had to go from one place to another in search of shelter. After all, life is the dearest thing; people have been known to sacrifice their mothers to save their life. I, too, sensed danger and left my home and hearth and found it expedient to run away. I searched high and low but could not find a safe place. On this very road, where a bomb had fallen and a large crater had formed, there was a trench where an underground pipeline was running and a pipe had been placed. I found this to be the safest place of all. I entered this pipe and lay hidden. But as I hid there I thought what if he were to tell someone that I was hiding here?

From my hiding place beneath the ground, I could hear the barbaric clamour above me. I could hear the loud slogans and the sound of bullets being fired. Every moment, danger seemed to be closer and closer to me. I lay there holding my breath, barely breathing till finally it seemed as though the danger had passed. And when I stuck my neck out of the hole in the ground, like a turtle peering out from its shell, I saw him standing beneath the lamp-post as always.

I spent thirty-six hours in my hiding place. Having starved for all these hours, I didn't have the strength to move. Perhaps I fell unconscious as I lay hidden in the underground pipeline. At some point, I became conscious of someone bending over me and sprinkling water on my face. When I stirred a little, someone helped me get up, gave me a sip of water and handing me a small packet wrapped in paper, began to move away. That was when I realised: Dear God, it was him! He who stood immobile under the lamp-post! So, he knew everything. He could see everything and understand what was happening. He was not unaware and insensate to the world around him.

The next day there was even greater commotion on the road. The crowds were hoping to catch me and tear me apart limb from limb and chop me up into tiny pieces. They had searched everywhere for me, from my home till every nook and cranny of the city. Now they were creating a ruckus on this road. Several hours passed in this manner till finally, they grew weary and went away. Someone tapped my shoulder. This time it was a friend of mine who had come looking for me. He had hidden a jeep among some bushes in the distance. When I emerged from my hiding place, the very first sight I saw was his corpse lying beneath the lamp-post. A dagger was stuck between his mouth and neck.

Translated from the Urdu by **Rakhshanda Jalil**

12 The Odd Bird of the Cage*

WASI AHMED

Suleman was being dressed in fresh clothes after a long time. The heady smell of naphthalene coming out of the newly laid out dress tickled his nostrils, eyes and maybe the ears too. It's been a long time since he'd last smelt that scent. The layers of his brain were elated by it and his head danced a bit as one or two slow dizzy bubbles rose causing the mud-soft indent of the brain lobes to tremble, just as someone grimaced—*Nice, nice!* Suleman closed his eyes as the bubbles of the scent rose one by one. How nice! Good!

The jangling inside the head increased. Suleman opened his eyes. There was nobody around.

Last night Habildar Jamal came to him in his disturbed sleep. He was short and stocky with a lively deep laugh in his betel juice-reddened mouth, his teeth blackened by *khayer-jarda*. These days, his appearance disturbed Suleman. Jamal probably knew this, and that was precisely why he came, laughed with his blackened teeth and grimaced—*Nice, nice!* Suleman could find no reason for such behaviour. What had made Jamal so mad that he wouldn't leave him alone? Was it envy or a joke?

In earlier times, Habildar Jamal would stand still, dark-faced, without making a sound, without uttering a word. His head would sway like a raft over the waves. He would arrive so many times in Suleman's slumber and half-sleep during the day and at night. Recently, his manner of presenting himself had changed. He had become keen about playing with Suleman. He would smile, exposing rusty teeth while repeatedly playing his games. Sometimes

*Originally published in Bangla as 'Khancha O Acheen Pakhi' in the literary magazine *Nirontor* edited by Naim Hasan in February 2000, Bangladesh.

he would confine himself in the softest layer of Suleman's brain and sometimes emerge just to grimace at him. But amidst all these, like the sound of clouds roaring from a distance, Suleman also heard an utterly different sound—a single shot of rapid-fire.

Suleman noticed that his tiny room had undergone a quick makeover. Dust had been cleaned, garbage removed, pillow covers and bed sheets replaced and the soot on the wall swept away before giving it a fresh coat of paint, although in a hurry. Outside the room, amidst the swishing leaves of the coconut tree peeping from across the balcony, the hot March morning had swollen up like a balloon. Suleman looked around to find the morning full of light and air. No one seemed to be about. A crow's silent flying shadow caused a ripple in the coconut fronds.

Some people were coming to visit today after a long time. Suleman tried to regain his mental composure!

There was a time when Suleman was enthusiastic about the visitors. Besides the usual natives, there were the white-skinned British, American, French and Scandinavians who came frequently, sometimes the soybean oil-complexioned Japanese too. Different faces, body odours, voices, heights and shoes: the diversities were enjoyable. But for Suleman, it was a different kind of fun.

The visitors got stumped at their very first meeting when they tried to exchange greetings with Suleman. Seated on his wheelchair, with only his left leg on the footrest, he would extend his handless right stump and ask with an amused expression, 'How do you do?' Seeing the tiny skin-wrapped shard of bone sticking out of the emptiness of his right shoulder, they would be shocked. To reassure them, Suleman would dance the 'hand' fiercely in front of them pointing it heavenwards like a spear.

He always enjoyed their first reaction. Day by day, the limb was getting thinner like the pointed edge of a weapon.

The visitors would want to know about him but their questions always had the same pattern. Their stereotypical and monotonous conversations bored him. Suleman would change the monotony by taking control of the conversation and steering it as he willed. If the visitors were foreigners, local officials would escort them. They would be enraged by his behaviour, but Suleman did not bother. He enjoyed that too. Here's how it went:

'Do you live here?'

'Sure,' Suleman responds with a silly pointless smile.

'How many of you are here?'

Suleman tells a number.

'What about this place? Is it a comfortable place to stay?'

'Good.'

'Food?'

'Good.'

'Medical facilities? Recreation?'

'Good, good.' (So many 'goods' for the sake of the escorting officials.)

'How long have you been here?'

'Haven't counted, eight or nine...'

'Months?'

'Years...years.'

'Oh! Don't you get bored?'

'Ha ha...Yes! Can I have a cigarette?' (Suleman breaks the conversation pattern).

'Of course. Your brand? I have Camel, will that do?'

'Oh, Camel! Roasted tobacco. Of course, it will do. Don't see it these days. Triple Five and Benson are everywhere. The taste of Camel is different; the others are nothing compared to it. See the picture of the camel on the packet here: it's not an ordinary picture, it is highly imaginative. Do you remember that advertisement—the famous one—can you remember what it said?'

'Take the whole packet if you wish.'

'Thank you, thank you! You are so nice! What's in your bag?'

'A camera.'

'Just a camera?'

'A few books and a laptop. Why do you ask?'

'I thought you might have a small one, a really cute small one, ha ha…a bottle of champagne. Take a look inside, you might find one there. Aren't you French?'

'How do you know that? I haven't told you yet. Oh, I understand, it's my accent. Otherwise you would think me a Scandinavian, as many people do. Anyway, your observation is very good. But I don't have any champagne in my bag. If you like I can send you some from my hotel.'

'I don't think you will.' (Suleman looks away, gritting his teeth.)

'Pardon?'

'Nothing. I'll sleep now.'

'I haven't asked your name yet.'

'Napoleon.'

'Pardon?'

'Napoleon Bonaparte…living here since the Waterloo.'

But the same thing cannot be repeated for years, the same old play of games with names. The elements of amusement were always the same and had become clichéd. And now Suleman understood that monkey-play is interesting but monkeys do not prosper.

Over time Suleman lost his interest in visitors. Visitors hardly came anyway. He too didn't feel any eagerness to know if anyone came. In the past, visitors used to come frequently. The Rehabilitation Centre was kept neat and clean. Kamrul, the caretaker-cum-cook, walked about busily from room to room, singing filmy tunes every now and then.

The visitors brought rustling cereals, apple juice, chocolate drink, instant soup and other expensive gifts for the inmates of the Centre. They would hand them over to Kamrul with a strange sense of guilt before they departed. Kamrul generously consigned the gifts to the shop next door without much bargaining. The visitors also left cash for the residents, and Kamrul would receive the cash too. At that time, his income from the cash and the goodies was much more than his salary.

With the decline of visitors, the goodies and the cash flow also stopped. Almost no one came anymore. And if at all someone did, the officials would remain glued to the visitor so that nothing could escape them.

The officials would tell the visitors in advance not to leave any gifts for the inmates. The government was taking care of the Centre and every need of its residents, they would claim, adding that it was a priority sector and well-looked after. They would brief the visitors that there were more then five hundred such centres all over the country, of which three hundred and thirty four were in Dhaka itself. If the government didn't look after the inmates, who would? They were our most immaculate national pride, the officials would further add. And that is why no one should meddle with matters concerning their welfare. Only the government had that right.

But the present times were lean. Kamrul had to rely only on government rations—rice, lentils, flour, salt, cooking oil. From the allotted fish, meat and vegetables, he couldn't save anything as nothing remained after meeting the hunger of the inmates. One litre of Australian apple juice could easily be sold at two hundred takas without bargaining. Cereals also had a great demand.

The situation had not changed abruptly or without reason. One-legged, one-handed Suleman knew the reason well enough.

It was a convention at the Centre that if the visitors were foreigners, the residents must be presented as properly as possible. They had to bathe properly and comb their hair. All of them would be given freshly laundered clothes that were kept for such occasions. They must wear those; no objections would be entertained. They would then be put into wheelchairs, beds, on crutches, or wherever else they could be fitted in.

If the visitors were very important, an advance team of officials would come. They would brief the inmates and threaten them elaborately that if anything untoward took place or something disconcerting was said, the culprit would be thrown into the streets to live on begging or rag-picking.

The briefing would be directed mainly at Suleman. Only Suleman annoyed them by his impudence. He was dangerous—the most educated and obstinate of the lot in the Centre.

One day, a distinguished team of foreign visitors was expected. The advance team of officials came to examine the Centre. They inspected the rooms, clothes, crutches and wheelchairs and briefed the inmates, and as usual, warned them with prospects of begging or rag-picking.

They admonished Suleman sternly, 'Don't you say a thing, not a word, be careful.' Suleman moved his head with a smile to indicate assent. His head was still swinging a little from the scent of the naphthalene wafting from the freshly laid out clothes.

The noted foreign team appeared on time. It was made up of a couple of British MPs, British journalists, and accompanying them were local TV crew and government officials. In the two-storied building of the Centre, ten people lived in six rooms. They were waiting for the visitors. As they entered, everyone scampered around, agitated, making a lot of noise with their crutches, and wheelchairs banged the floor in saluting the visitors. 'How do you do? Nice to meet you!'

Suleman's room was at the far end of the first floor. It was smaller than the other rooms and he was the sole occupant of that room. The entire armada of visitors entered his room after finishing with all others, though for so many visitors the room was rather small. When the lights of the TV cameras were turned on, Suleman felt dizzy amid all the glowing bulbs and curious faces.

There were rapid-fire questions for him from all sides. There was too much light and noise and he suddenly felt sleepy. He kept silent. The scent of naphthalene prowling about his brain cells seemed to cause a strange numbness, but he was jolted into wakefulness when he was asked his name repeatedly.

'Your name, please?'

He heard the question again and again as he drifted between sleep and sense. What is your name? Your name, please?

The team was eager to know his name, Suleman was certain. But in his half-awake state, he could not understand why he was repeatedly being asked his name.

Someone inside him whispered: what's in a name? There were so many names spread all over! Does the world need more names? Abraham Lincoln, Pablo Neruda, Adolf Hitler, Charles Chaplin, Karl Marx, Ishwar Chandra Vidyasagar, Kamrul: different names, different smells. He was so overwhelmed by so many diverse names that he became exhausted remembering them. Surya Sen, Maulana Bhashani, William Shakespeare, Mir Jafar Ali Khan, Rabindranath Tagore, Habildar Mohammad Jamal. He was shivering and trembling because of the names.

In this state of excitement, Suleman opened the shutters of his eyes. All around him were other eyes eager to know his name. Surely they must already know his name. One couldn't imagine how stubborn they were to insist on hearing it from his lips! Even the officials who had earlier warned him not to open his mouth tried to cajole him to say his name. 'Why don't you tell them your name? We have given them all the necessary information about you. We have shown them all the records; they have even taken a handful of them. But they cannot take all the records; it will be a burden for them. They already know your name; they just want to hear you say it. Do please pronounce your name.'

For the first time in his life, he was not interested in making games out of names. But where had his name gone? Why couldn't he remember it? He shook his head as if a raging animal was shaking its head in desperation.

Suleman hunted for his tiny name in the forests of forgetfulness. Where had his name gone? And then, as if in some strange joke or in rage, he felt two burning teardrops roll down his cheeks and he was instantly stung to his senses. When a mortar shell had furrowed his body years ago, his eyes had remained dry. But after all these years, they had betrayed him in such a meaningless effort of stating his name.

His handless right limb was itching to act. He glanced at the gushing faces, and as if to avenge the betrayal of his eyes, he did something he had not thought of before. He stretched out his still-able left hand from the arm of his wheelchair, the five fingers and his palm, full of intricately crisscrossing lines, in a gesture of supplication.

The lights of the local TV camera shut down, while the foreign cameras flashed and sparkled intermittently. Suleman's agitated left hand lengthened. He was possessed with a strange feeling about his hand; he kept his hand stretched out. He could feel his twisted body trembling in excitement. He was stunned and could not remember how many times he had felt this way in his life before. He only gazed at his hand stretched out in front of him—it was silently was growing larger and larger.

The incident provoked a great reaction in the media. The 'mad, deviant, crippled freedom fighter' the newspapers screamed the next morning. It was a national scandal, the media said, adding that every palm shared the same desire, openly or in secret: to stretch out for alms; but does that mean it had to be done so shamelessly?

Suleman had thought that the foul left hand would be cut off and hung around his neck. If needed, it could be shaped out as an exact match of the other hand. He became somewhat curious as to what would follow. How would they do it? After putting him to sleep in an operation theatre or just by slashing it off with the stroke of a dagger?

There was always the possibility of something happening and what ultimately did happen was quite extraordinary. A two-member enquiry committee was set up. Suleman was totally confused when he faced the committee members, the barrage of questions they put to him. Apparently, their purpose was to bemuse Suleman. When one asked him a question, the other immediately followed by asking another. If one asked how many hands a man had, the other at once wanted to know how many legs? If the purpose of one hand was to eat rice, what was the other one for? Everyone had legs and hands in pairs, but why was it that Suleman had less—just one each?

Suleman could not decide whether or not to answer their questions. He also couldn't make out if the purpose of the cross-examination was simply to make fun of him. If it was so, then he could also make appropriate jokes. But the attitude of his interrogators confused him. One looked almost like Habildar Jamal with his salt and pepper moustache, while the other one's bearded face was contorted with what looked like self-inflicted dignity and righteousness. He looked at them with blank eyes, in a daze. And then he realised that the two had not come to crack jokes; they had specific tasks in hand.

The man with the moustache suddenly grabbed his left thigh and dug his nails into his flesh, saying, 'Having just one hand and one leg is a lot of fun, isn't it? Where is your other arm and your other leg? Where have you hidden them? Come on now, show me. You know magic? I see you are enjoying hiding your entire thigh inside your belly. You have stuck your thigh inside your belly? Tell me how did you push it in? Which one entered first—the leg or the hand? For how many years have you been going on this way? Hasn't the hand or the leg been digested inside by now? Are you sure they are still intact? You have only one hand, and with that hand you eat, you clean your ass and you beg! A multipurpose hand…marvelous! Now tell me why did you stretch out your hand that day? What do you want? Money, cigarette, wine, women? Done. You will have them all. But first tell me why did you stretch out your hand? Or do you need that arm to fight again?'

Suleman felt the man's nails clawing deep into his thigh. Simultaneously the man took his handless right limb—the skin-wrapped bone—and began to twist it. As he wrenched the stump, the man asked him in a soothing voice, 'Does that hurt? Does it pain too much? It will hurt my dear. How famous is this hand and this leg! Do you remember how they once looked like? Or have you forgotten them entirely? Because of these two, the nation is now free. Is there a nation on earth freer than ours?'

The man kept on talking and twisting the bone from right to left and left to right, as if pulling out a stake dug into the earth. Suleman kept on looking with steady eyes and pricked his ears to listen to any sound the pulling and twisting would make. The man kept on saying, 'Oh, your sweet leg! Your delicate hand! Where have they all gone? Where are they now? Where?' The man kept lamenting and, with great regret it seemed, kept on twisting his stump.

But for how long could one enjoy twisting a thin insipid piece of bone? The monotony of the action bored the man. Giving one last parting twist, he muttered, 'Bastard!' and let go. Suleman was surprised that the matter had ended without any further ado.

After the incident visitors stopped coming to the Centre. It began to look more and more rundown everyday as sweeping and dusting lessened and the rubbish was strewn all around. Visitors were not going to come, so who would take the trouble to keep it clean? Kamrul continued to be there although he rued it all the time. No local or foreign visitors came and the only people who did were the itinerant hawkers who took shelter on the verandah from the rain or the sun. They would sometimes venture in and peep into the rooms and if anyone stretched out his palm, they would generously throw a half-rotten cucumber, a fistful of puffed rice, perhaps a few groundnuts too. At night, some decrepit prostitutes would take over the room in the attic and light a few flickering lamps, courtesy of Kamrul.

Suleman was relieved as the Centre lost attention. No visitors about, no anxiety, no excitement made the place look good. There was no undue haste to know a name, no extra effort to make up one. Just have two meals a day and somehow pass the time sleeping or waking or doing both at a time!

As he passed his days idly, Suleman often became intrigued by the questions of his interrogators who wanted to know about his missing leg and arm. It was true that he hadn't paid any attention to his unseen limbs in years. He hadn't yearned to remember how they had been or how they would look had they lived. He hadn't washed them for a long time or cut his nails. They were no ordinary nails; they were sharp and strong like talons. Who could tell how long the nails had grown after all these years!

He could, however, remember that his leg was tough and stubborn. When it kicked a ball, it didn't care about its life or death. When it ran, it pounded the ground like a hammer. And once when it suffered a split on the knee in a soccer game, it was laid down for long but when it recovered, it returned to ferocity and strength.

Compared to the leg, his hand was soft, his fingers delicate. Night after night, it wrote poems holding the tip of the pen tight. But when it took up grenades, it was as if they were better pens.

He wondered why he hadn't looked them up for so long. They were not with him, but they must be somewhere. Could they be lying together, the hand and the leg, or moving about as an odd pair through hills and forests and deserts? Wouldn't he be able to catch up with them, see them for once, caress them, wash them or scratch them if bitten by mosquitoes?

Memories of the lost limbs haunted him. Sometimes an unbelievably fleshy part of the missing arm seemed to appear on his right hand's dry bone and then disappear like magic. Sometimes a soft skin would cover the tender fingers and immediately vanish. But despite all his efforts, the miserable thigh, knee and ankle would not wake up to answer the call of the vast emptiness of the lower part of his body.

As he thought and tried to remember them, his missing limbs played hide and seek with him in his moments of wakefulness and slumber. In such a state, Habildar Jamal would appear, whether to save him or sink him he couldn't tell. Jamal's short robust body had remained the same as it was long ago, as had his betel-chewed red lips and his teeth like melon seeds!

Suleman would sometimes wonder, was it the man he knew long ago? His style of standing had not changed—hands at his waist, the legs unwavering and still. But why was the face so grave? Where had the liveliness of his eyes gone? In those days when the man led them to parade on soft wet earth at dawn, taught them how to pull the lever and shoot with a three-naught-three rifle, his mouth would spew words like a torrent of fireworks.

Abuses would rapidly flow from his tongue and he would twist his face and shout in accompaniment. 'You sons of *nawabs*… have you come to fight a war? Can't you move your asses? You have come to fight? Do you know what fighting is? Fighting and fucking aren't the same. Use your hands; God hasn't given them to you for nothing. Pull the lever with your left hand and cock the trigger with your right. How many times do I have to show you! Your heads are full of words and junk when it comes to work…can't do a single thing! Fuck you, you useless eggheads! Take a single shot at a time, a *single* shot I said, not rapid-fire!…Who will give you bullets if you spend them all in one go! Bullets won't come from heaven. Not rapid-fire, single…'

In his trance-like state, Suleman saw a shadow. The shadow quivered and Habildar Jamal's face also quivered in waves. Why was he so silent? Why didn't he have any words? Rapid-fire or single, couldn't he decide what to say? Or had he forgotten all those scoldings? Should Suleman remind him? The still dark face did not seem like his. Where had he been all this while? How did he find Suleman after all these years? Suleman examined the face closely and waited for the stream of words. Or was it that after all these years Habildar Jamal had also forgotten how to abuse?

It was at that time that Suleman began to live a new life. He felt that the difference between day and night was dissolving. A thick, deep, unfathomable hypnosis behind the light and darkness was pulling him down. Habildar Jamal appeared to be behind it. The discontented soul had returned from his grave, lured by the attractions of war. He wanted to entice Suleman to join him. He would take him to the battlefield, pushing his wheelchair. There was no definite time for his arrival. He appeared whenever he wanted to before Suleman's dimly lit eyes and he vanished gradually, dissolving as it were, in a shroud of mist. There was no screaming or shouting, just a stunned look on his calm face.

Suleman would closely examine Jamal's face as it drifted between his slumber and waking. Sometimes he seemed to be grieved by Suleman's handicapped body, and sometimes in his eyes burned sparks of envy. Suleman looked at the face, and in his discomfort and helplessness, shriveled. How strong and powerful the man was! His harsh and deafening voice was an extra weapon. During the training periods, he would compensate his miserly shortage of bullets by the fireworks from his throat. But when it came to real fighting, he was not a miser at all. In fact, he was quite extravagant while laying an ambush. Then, it was just rapid-fire and rapid-fire and rapid-fire…

That restless fiery mouth was suddenly frozen shut by a single shot that went through the middle of his forehead. Suleman could find no trace of the shot as he closely examined the forehead. There was no sign of the tunnel that had burrowed through the middle of his brows. The tidy forehead confused him. Had he gone into hiding all these years just to seal the tunnel, fill it up so that Suleman never found any trace that it had ever existed? And now that it was gone, sealed impeccably, he had come to steal Suleman back!

Slowly, day by day, Habildar Jamal's face changed. There would be the small expressions visible on his face—a crumbling of the stiff shoreline around the edges of his lips. And finally the day that his face trembled, his salt and pepper moustache shook and his mouth fell open, Suleman looked at him in surprise. He was stunned to hear the man demanding an explanation—why did Suleman stretch out his hand in that fashion? As if the action of his hand had reached him deep down in his grave and disturbed his peace!

In a voice at once stiff and controlled Jamal explained how lucky Suleman was! Although Suleman did not have a leg or a hand, his crippled body was a witness to so many things. It was only because people like Habildar Jamal had cleared the path that someone like Suleman had become a sight to be viewed. But what had he done? Suleman could hear the voice swirling around inside his head. There was no arrogance, no hope, no aggression in his voice, but somewhere at the bottom of it all lurked dim flickers of envy.

Suleman thought about what the man was saying. Didn't he know that by dying he had been saved, and that Suleman, who lived with his eyes and ears open, was condemned to be more dead than alive? Let the man judge which one was better and which worse. Or had he lost the brains to judge facts? Was this the reason he had returned from his cold home buried deep beneath the earth to be ravaged by agony and envy? Did he have the right to demand an explanation? Being dead, he was freed of all responsibility. A single shot to his forehead. And Suleman, who should have been blown away by the mortar shell, was left with a single leg and a hand on a wheelchair. Why had he stretched out his hand? Did he really do that? It didn't matter anyhow because if he had the chance, he would do it all over again.

A single shot to the forehead was better than a mortar shell. He would make the man understand this. After such a long stay in his grave, his head was not there anymore. It had become a pile of mud.

After observing Habildar Jamal for a few more days, Suleman realised that the man not only thought him lucky but seriously envied him. When Suleman would see him in his waking hours, the man appeared subdued but in his dreams, he was quite eloquent. In a halting voice he would speak of many things, of the pain and drudgery of his long imprisonment inside his grave. At the same time, he would whine that he had never had the chance to savour the air and light of life outside. Reminding Suleman of his perforated forehead, he would poke at it and remove the earth that had filled up the hole, exposing the tunnel the bullet had bored.

He showed the hole to Suleman with great care. The bullet had gone right through the skull without turning an inch, straight to the back of the head, opening up the lid. He twitched his face in frustration. If only the hole had been somewhere other than his forehead! If only it were in the belly or the chest or the shoulder! Or, if instead of a single shot, had it been a mortar shell crumpling his hand, leg and body! Why only one hand, why not both? Maybe even the face could be charred. But if only the nose was spared for sucking in free air and the eyes...maybe just one eye spared for seeing with! If only one could somehow pull in air and had an eye to see with, one could have spent the rest of one's life in the grave even with a shortage of oxygen.

Listening to all this, Suleman could only think of a trick. Fooling the man into his wheelchair, he would set out looking for the cold grave. Let the idiot sit like a clown and suck in a belly full of free air!

Suleman would drift in and out of the trance of his tangled mind. Shapeless, meaningless images would dance in his head. Some days he would see that the right leg had returned to its original place. It seemed a little unfamiliar after all that time—the taut skin on his thigh and knee, the muscles looked different than before. But what surprised him was that the entire leg seemed to be smeared with tiny drops of blood from mosquito bites. Holding the drops in their mouth, hundreds of small fleshy hives covered his thigh, knee and ankle.

On some days, he would see Habildar Jamal with a pair of rusty old pliers. He would measure the length of Suleman's right leg in the emptiness and then swing one of his hands like a magician as if he was going to conjure up a red rose or a pigeon from thin air. But what Suleman would see in his hands was his missing leg. Snatching the heavy fleshy leg from mid-air, Jamal would start putting it in place, tightening the nuts and screws with his pliers.

Suleman realised that this was a game for Jamal. He also played another trick with his leg. He would bundle Suleman up in his arms and leave him in an empty field. Suleman would find piles of legs strewn everywhere. All of them right legs, severed from the hip. Thin, fat, heavy...all kinds of legs! Some were bent from the knee, some were lying on their sides and others were in prone positions. Jamal would ask Suleman to quickly search for his leg, find it and fit it where it belonged.

Suleman would hop about on his solitary leg desperately looking for the missing leg in the pile. Not finding it, he thought maybe another would fit him. But there was a problem in that as well. He would put them on and pull them out one after another—they wouldn't fit. Some were too tight; some were so loose that if he walked wearing one of them, the leg would fall away. Watching Suleman hard at work, Jamal would smile widely with his blackened teeth to say: *Good, good!*

For Suleman, it was appalling and shocking—the man was making fun of him! But how was he to believe that he had heard or seen right? He could barely see a thing because of the foggy shroud swelling all around. He strained his eyelids and pushed at the fog. Some of it shifted as he kept on pushing. And it was then that he saw he was lying inert in a cage for a long time.

The cage would be wet with rain, dried by the sun, and it trembled gently in the wind. No one was pulling him out of the cage, and couldn't even if someone wanted to. The bars seemed to be made of mercury and they appeared to shiver and tremble. One was afraid even to touch them…afraid.

The Centre was alive after a long time. There was the hustle-bustle of cleaning up. The air was heavy with the scent of incense. People with busy feet were moving from room to room, pushing, shoving and moving things about.

Suleman had been dressed in freshly laid out clothes. The smell of naphthalene wafting from the folds of the clothes tickled the nose, even the eyes and ears. He pulled at the smell after a long time.

Despite the tickling, the freshly liberated and slightly pungent scent reached the layers of his brain. And amidst all this, came the words: *Nice nice, good good!* Sitting in the softest ante-room of his brain, Habildar Jamal was mocking him.

Suddenly, everything seemed different to Suleman's eyes. Outside, the mid-morning sun sparkled with light and the air shimmered restlessly on the drooping coconut fronds. A long hushed buzz blew like silent music, on and on.

Suleman's surprise grew. Was it the moment…was it? He felt an exhilarating shiver in his body and soul. The smell of incense and other herbs was rising above the odour of naphthalene and churning the air in the room. He said to himself, hey, what's up? Then he noticed the dress he was wearing. He was draped from head to toe in a white dress that he had never worn before. Suleman wondered, ah…well, well…

So he was going to be taken out of his cage after all these years? Was the smell too pungent? Someone else would replace him in the cage, someone valuable as an object of curiosity. Suleman felt excited. In the vacant limbless parts of his body, the excitement was the highest.

People were coming in a line, moving around in a circle. So these were the visitors. They had a serious problem. They weren't able ask him his name. In which sector did he lose his arm, in which the leg; which one went first, the hand or the leg; did it hurt, how bad was it…so many questions wriggled inside their heads.

Suleman realised that nobody could touch him now or make him dance at the snap of a finger. He also saw standing in front of him Habildar Mohammad Jamal. But he was not mocking him at all. There was no envy, no jealousy on his face. Then whom did he see all these days? Suleman was startled to see the face. No, there was no mistake. There he was, lips reddened by tobacco juice and betel nuts, bushy moustache and the hole in the forehead from the single shot.

Suddenly, he heard the piercing howl of a voice like a thunderclap: 'Rapid-fire!' Suleman got down from the wheelchair, sprang to his left foot and started running. As he ran behind the man he could not see himself, neither his body nor his shadow. It would have been nice if he could, his lone leg was moving so well… running on and on.

Translated from the Bangla by **Afsan Chowdhury**

13 Betel Leaf*

SAMEENA NAZEER

Standing on the *ghat* of Barishal, waving her handkerchief at the departing launch, Ritu said goodbye to Shakir with tears in her eyes. She did not know that she will never be able to meet Shakir like this again.

Shakir and Ritu studied together at Dhaka University. Shakir studied commerce, and Ritu was a student in the music department. She was Shakir's senior by two years. She wanted to do research on Bhatiali folk music after getting her Master's. They met each other in a political rally, and in the short span of two years, they crossed the long passage of love. Shakir was studying commerce, but he was also an extraordinary artist. Pencil, pen, coal, paint—he used whatever was available to him. Shakir's grandfather had migrated from Patna to Dhaka at the time of Partition. His mother was Bengali, and his father was Bihari. A mixture of both languages was spoken in his home.

Ritu lived in the university hostel. Both her parents were Bengali. When Shakir found out that Ritu was from Barishal, he could barely contain his excitement. One of his aunts was married to a man who lived there. That was all he needed. After that, if he had any break from college, he took a launch with Ritu and left for Barishal and Banaripara. He could always say that he was missing his aunt and wanted to visit her.

The flowing streams of Barishal, the thin boatmen rowing their boats, their rhythmic songs and sweet *ragas*, the betel leaves that were rolled to make paan, the lakes full of fish, the lush paddy fields,

*Titled 'Paan ka Beeda', this story was originally written in Urdu in 2020, especially for this volume.

and the small wooden houses dotting the landscape—for Shakir and Ritu, Barishal was made of love and romance, not timber and cement. They always took the night launch from Dhaka to Barishal so they could better embrace each other in the darkness of night, which was only faintly lit by the tender light of the moon. They were both completely lost in each other's trance.

At the same time, the atmosphere of East Pakistan was being punctuated by chants of 'Bangla is our national language' and 'Stop shooting at your brothers.' Ritu saw many soldiers on her way back to her house from the *ghat*. It was already late at night. She decided to leave the road and take the boat tied behind her friend Rupa's house. She thought she would get home faster this way. She was wearing a red floral sari. She had made sure to leave the house before her father noticed the sari. Behind a tree, after showing her all his love, Shakir had put *sindoor* in her hair to declare that their relationship was now unbreakable. He had placed a marigold flower in her hair with his own hands. Ritu pulled her sari up to her ankles and rowed as fast as she could. 'I will speak to my father about Shakir today. He will not refuse. Shakir's father has many successful businesses; they make glass, they make carpets.'

'Ritu!...Oh Ritu! Come quickly.' Her father was restlessly pacing the *ghat*. He had spotted his only daughter from far away. Pakistani soldiers were marching everywhere. They were supposedly there to protect Bengalis, but their expressions told another story. It looked like they were waiting for their orders—but what would the orders be? The elections were over. Only the Prime Minister's name needed to be announced.

Both father and daughter ate their dinner silently. Her aunt, Anisa, was used to sleeping early; her snores were ringing loudly through the whole house. Ritu's lips were red with the colour of paan. Her father, Howlader Fazlur Rehman, noticed the *sindoor* in her hair, but he swallowed his anger along with his dinner. He was waiting for a better opportunity to bring it up with her. Ritu ate the lentils, boiled rice, dried fish paste, and the curry made from the head of the rohu fish as she thought about her aunt's incredible cooking skills. I will learn it all too, she decided. Shakir loves Bengali food.

The next day, when twenty-year old Shakir reached his home in Narinda after taking a cycle rickshaw from Sadarghat, the main port of Dhaka, he quickly realised that something was wrong. His younger siblings were weeping. His sister and brother-in-law had arrived at the house from Narayanganj that morning. His newly-wed aunt, who looked deeply aggrieved, was sitting next to his mother. His mother was wailing loudly and lamenting in Bangla. She only spoke Bangla when she was angry or sad. Everyone was in the house except his father. He found out that his father had been arrested because the Mukti Bahini had caught him sitting in the middle of the market and expressing opinions against Bengalis and in favour of West Pakistan. He didn't know he could be considered an enemy of Bengal for expressing his opinions. The police were not willing to release him. Shakir's mother was waiting for him to arrive. As soon as she saw him, she covered her head with her sari and rushed off to Dhaka Jail with him.

On the way there, Shakir tried to think of ways to talk to his mother about Ritu, but he eventually decided against saying anything in the midst of this new crisis. Anyway, his mother, his sister and his aunt had already met Ritu once or twice. It was his father, Alauddin, who had no knowledge of the relationship. He would never accept a Bengali daughter-in-law. They arrived at the jail. They waited for hours before they were allowed to see an officer. When they tried to walk into the office together, the guard told Shakir to stay outside. His mother marched straight into the office. She spoke in pure Bangla, telling the officer that she and her whole family were Bengali, and asked why Alauddin was being kept behind bars. Then there was silence. When she came out of the office, she had lost all her temper to the brute force of the police officer. While waiting for his mother, Shakir had gotten hungry and left to get some *jhalmuri* from the street. He even had some tea. When a long time had passed, he returned to the jail and stood outside the office. The door was locked from inside. The guard was closely watching the door. Then, the door opened and his mother walked out. Shakir looked down at the floor. Soon his father was brought there.

Shakir and his mother climbed into a decrepit cycle rickshaw with Alauddin, who was completely oblivious to the situation and busy insulting Bengalis in Urdu. Shakir's mother sat in the rickshaw with her disheveled hair and her rumpled sari. She was completely silent. Alauddin thought that she looked so overwrought due to his absence. Shakir wanted to go back and murder the police officer. He wanted to cut his hands off. But then his family would need to send his younger sister to get him out of jail. He didn't move. He sat quietly and looked at the army trucks passing by Ramna Park.

There was dread in the air that day. Ritu practised Raag Malkauns on the *tanpura* just like she did every morning—except that today her performance didn't satisfy her. She played Abdul Alim's LP, but it didn't make her feel any better. She took her *ektara* and went to the lake; she played the *ektara* for a long time. She closed her eyes and tried to remember the feeling of Shakir's breath on her skin. She kept singing her favourite song, '*Shadher laau banailo more boiragi.*'

She started preparing for her friend Rupa's *haldi* ceremony early in the day: taking out the yellow sari she wanted to wear, collecting flowers to go with her clothes, putting on silver jewelry. Her humming filled every part of the house with melody. When she put a round red *bindiya* on her forehead, she remembered Shakir's words: 'It looks like a shining red moon on your beautiful face.' It started pouring. It got even colder.

Howlader Fazlur Rehman was a respected teacher of Bangla and History at Banaripara High School. He had lost his wife, Ritu's mother, a few years back after a long, protracted illness. He was holding a newspaper. He read the various news reports about the sensitive conditions in the country for the tenth time. His frown was fixed on his face. He understood what was about to happen in the country. 'Radio Ceylon will give the correct news.' He was tinkering with the radio when Ritu walked past him, dressed and ready to leave for Rupa's ceremony. She smelled like a fresh, blossoming flower. He wanted to erase the glow of Shakir's love from her face.

'That idiot Bihari! Who gave him permission to put *sindoor* in my daughter's hair?' He cursed Shakir in his heart and threw the radio, which wasn't catching the right station, on the ground. He remembered the day when the thin, fair-skinned Shakir had come to visit him in Barishal. He had tried to impress him with his broken Bangla and English. It didn't seem like his family cared much about education. Howlader Fazlur Rehman had decided to reject Shakir even before he met him. His friend's son, Robin, was doing a doctorate in Sweden. He wanted Ritu to marry Robin when she was done with her Master's so she could go to Sweden, or even to Oxford, and continue her studies. 'The idiot didn't even consider that he is younger than my daughter.' He punched the radio, and a voice—'This is Radio Ceylon'—came out of it. He had heard the Bangla and English news already.

'Baba! I'm leaving. I will come back late. Don't worry about me.'

'Cover your head. It is evening. And it is dangerous in the country right now. Should I come with you?' Howlader Fazlur Rehman's otherwise calm voice betrayed a hint of restlessness today. Ritu's boat was already disappearing from view.

Rupa's courtyard was crowded with women: young, married, unmarried, mothers, sisters-in-law, and daughters-in-law. The elder women were grinding rice and preparing *pethas* with brown sugar and coconut. Everyone was wearing yellow saris with red borders. Rupa was rubbed with turmeric. When the girls got done with singing and dancing, they applied henna on each other. Jokes were flying around. Ritu wrote an 'S' on her hand with henna, and then felt embarrassed. Shakir had promised to come the day after tomorrow, the day of Rupa's wedding. 'He will be very happy to see his name.' She smelled her wet palm. Suddenly, the sound of soldiers' boots punctured the joyous air. A surge of panic and fear spread over the courtyard. The thud of boots overtook the beat of the drum. The courtyard turned into a scene of terror, cruelty, harassment, and rape. Innocent laughter turned into agonising screams. Not just saris, but humanity itself was torn to pieces. Ritu witnessed Rupa's rape with her own eyes. Then Nazneen and Mona's bodies jerked in the arms of the soldiers. Ritu's eyes couldn't bear the terror. The men and children were beaten with rifle butts and locked inside a room. Ritu succeeded in jumping over a wall and escaping from the house, but two soldiers were waiting for her outside on the road. She fainted on the spot and didn't remember what happened afterwards. When she woke up, she couldn't recognise herself.

It was Khalil Ahmed's last day as an employee of Karnaphuli Paper Mills. Four years ago, he had left his home in Hyderabad Deccan to try his luck in Dhaka, and then Chittagong. He had a degree in chemistry, but he could never get promoted due to his poor grasp of the Bangla language. He decided to leave his job and move to Karachi in West Pakistan. In any case, he didn't like the romantic atmosphere of East Pakistan. Everywhere you looked, someone was falling in love or talking about love, singing or dancing, or busy wasting their time in some other artistic activity. He believed this plague was a result of eating too much hilsa fish, which warmed the body. He even found reasons to be agitated by the way Bengalis wore their dhotis and saris. 'The whole atmosphere is indecent. The people are unaware of religion. They still seem more Hindu than Muslim. I will leave this place and go to Karachi and get married to a pure woman who wears the veil.'

He had got off at the Barishal bus stand and was now walking towards his uncle's house, lost in his thoughts. He held his bag, stuffed with all his belongings, in one hand, and his leather briefcase in the other. 'I will repay everything.' Khalil Ahmed remembered the day when, after three years of living in his uncle's house, his aunt had tried to send him to Karachi via a ship on an eighty-rupee ticket. Everyone else was travelling by air. 'The air ticket is two hundred and fifty rupees!' His aunt's voice still haunted him. 'Where will we get this money, Hissam's father? Does money grow on trees?' Hissam's father, his uncle, looked down in shame and continued scratching the soil with a stick. My aunt wanted me to vomit and suffer for fifteen days until I died on a ship! Humph!

Khalil Ahmed was a self-made man and a very calculating person. He ate a measured amount and spoke a measured amount. The distance from the bus station to his uncle's house felt much longer to him than usual because of the soldiers patrolling everywhere. He got irritated by the army trucks, checkpoints, the endless interrogations and searches. Why did he come all the way to Barishal? He could have just sent a money order. He started regretting his decision, but then he reminded himself that nothing will give him more pleasure than seeing the embarrassment on his aunt's face when he puts a wad of cash in her palm. How could he miss that opportunity? He patted his briefcase decisively—it held his air ticket to Karachi and the money for his uncle and aunt—and walked into the house.

He settled his accounts with his aunt, but his uncle was nowhere to be seen. Khalil started to get impatient. He needed to catch the evening bus back to Dhaka. Seeing no other option, he left with Hissam to go to Howlader Fazlur Rehman's house, where his uncle had gone to pay a visit. Hissam was rowing the boat. Khalil was irked by the slow pace of the village. 'I will go to Karachi and become the Director of the number one factory in that city. I will have my own car. I will also travel by tram. That will be my Pakistan!' He was jolted out of his thoughts as the boat collided with the *ghat* near Howlader Fazlur Rehman's house. A quick, forceful burst of rain added to Khalil's annoyance. He worried that his new shirt and trousers would be ruined. They both started walking towards the house. Khalil didn't speak much, so Hissam also kept quiet. All around them people were going about their day on cycles. Soon the market ended and they arrived at their destination.

A heart-rending scene awaited them in the red, tiled courtyard of Howlader Fazlur Rehman's house. Ritu's long hair was open, and she was standing by the well, adamant that she needed to jump into it and end her life. Both her father and her aunt were trying to stop her. Khalil's uncle was not there. He must have left after offering his condolences earlier. Both Khalil and Hissam stopped in their tracks. Hissam whispered the details of what had happened two days ago in Khalil's ear. How the soldiers had unleashed hell. How nearly every house was going through the same ordeal.

Khalil heard everything and shrugged his shoulders dismissively. His uncle was not there, and his bus was leaving in an hour. 'Let's go back,' he told Hissam, but right then Ritu's loud, harrowing scream reached his ears and pierced his heart. It was the scream of someone who could not bear life anymore. Even her father gave up any remaining hope. She touched her father's feet and walked towards the well, saying that an honourable death was better than a life full of insults and humiliation. Suddenly, Khalil started running towards her. He was surprised by his own spontaneity. He arrived at the well before Ritu and spread out his arms, as if trying to block her from reaching the well. Everyone's breath, the rain, the time—it all stopped.

Shakir was sitting stiffly in a colourful kurta-pajama on the floor of his small courtyard. There was no other empty space left to sit down. Countless boxes, bags, copper and brass pots, six or seven suitcases with the family's clothes, and all other sorts of luggage were strewn around him. Every suitcase was addressed to Syed Abrar-ul-Haq, Water Pump, Karachi. Abrar was Alauddin's good friend, who had left for West Pakistan many years ago and started a successful business there.

When Shakir woke up in the morning, he was more excited to meet Ritu than to attend Rupa's wedding, but none of it mattered because his father dropped a bomb on him as soon as he stepped out of his room. His father informed him that he was leaving for Karachi that very day. His mother, three younger siblings, two cousins, his married sister, brother-in-law, and two nephews—Alauddin delegated the leadership of this small caravan to twenty-year old Shakir, and abruptly left for the market. Alauddin had already booked everyone's air tickets. He handed his wife some money to open a glass business in Karachi and left before Shakir could say anything. He instructed him to leave for Karachi like he was asking him to go to the zoo or Ramna Park. Alauddin had always been like this. 'Never bothers to speak to his children. Only speaks with my mother, and that only when it is absolutely necessary. Hates Bengalis. How did he even marry my mother?' Shakir wondered.

When his airplane was about to take off from Dhaka airport, Shakir felt like someone had removed the very ground from under his feet. As the plane ascended, it didn't feel like he was going to another country, but like he was leading his own funeral to the heavens. 'How will I ever explain to Ritu that I'm not disloyal?' For a long time, he stared from the tiny window down at his Bengal. How can a language divide the hearts of people? I speak Bangla. I know Nazrul *geeti, polli geeti,* and Bhatiali songs by heart. My sister plays '*O Amar Bangla Ma Tor*' on the harmonium. But we are still Bihari? Non-Bengali? This is not our country? Why should we go to the other Pakistan? Bury our hearts, our souls in this land and leave? Why should we go?

I will come back to Dhaka after helping my family settle in Karachi. I will never leave again. The scene below started to blur. He thought he saw Ritu playing the *ektara*. Somebody on the plane took out a paan and put it in their mouth. The scent tore open Shakir's heart. His eyes overflowed with tears. He remembered that Ritu had picked up the habit of eating paan from him. Every time he fed her a paan with his own hands, she bit his finger and ran away, laughing.

The airplane and time, the sun and moon—they journeyed together. Soon after, an impenetrable wall of language, prejudice, disloyalty, and then hatred was erected between East and West Pakistan. It could never be brought down.

Bilqees tried to light the stove. She was going to cook a curry of meat and potatoes. But she kept going through one match after another without any success. Bilqees checked the packet. The matches were made in Thailand. 'Only my country makes real matches!' She looked displeased. There were many servants in this huge house in Karachi's P.E.C.H.S neighbourhood, but Khalil Ahmed only liked to eat food cooked by his wife. He had got all his mother's recipes from Hyderabad Deccan translated into English, so he could make a recipe book for her. The annual diary from Koh-i-Noor Chemicals was thrown in the waste every year. This way Khalil Ahmed found a use for it. Most of the recipes required tamarind. Since trade relations with Bangladesh were suspended, they used dried mango powder instead. They also used more plastic now; sackcloth was rare. Books and newspaper prices were increasing due to a lack of paper being imported from Bangladesh. But none of it mattered because Pakistan was stubbornly developing towards the future!

It was Sunday. 'Bilqees! It's one already. Please serve some food. Did you finish your prayers?' As soon as he returned from the mosque, Khalil Ahmed called for his wife. 'Yes, the table is set. Come and eat.' She had avoided her prayers again. She had never been able to accept Khalil Ahmed and this country wholeheartedly. Mutton instead of fish, wheat instead of rice, or basmati rice instead of the thick rice grown in her country, beef instead of mustard greens, a Mercedes instead of a boat, devotional hymns instead of music, shalwar kameez instead of sari. Even if you are inside your car, you must wear a veil. And Khalil Ahmed himself—she was finding it impossible to accept him, whether in the privacy of the bedroom or the sprawling lawns outside. When she was a child, she used to play with Rupa around the lake in Barishal. They would try to grab fish with their bare hands, and when they succeeded, they would pull the fish out of the water, put it on dry land, and watch it thrash about for a few seconds before throwing it back in the water. Today, she felt like a fish out of water, thrashing desperately on dry land.

Khalil was employed by Pakistan's biggest chemical company. They lived in a mansion, went around in a chauffeured car, took annual holidays to Singapore, Thailand and London, but her heart was still stuck in Barishal and Dhaka. It rained abundantly for six months there. Karachi, on the other hand, experienced nothing but dust storms. 'Is this a city? This is a desert where people made of iron and stone live!' It wasn't even possible to send or receive letters for four years. But now, there was some possibility of routes opening in the wake of the Islamic Summit Conference. She wanted to take the first flight to Dhaka. She remembered her father, her aunt, Rupa, and then she remembered that evening when her body and soul were torn into a million pieces. How could she go back? How could she face everyone there? She tried to commit suicide many times, even after moving to Pakistan. When she found out she was pregnant, she tried to overdose, cut her wrist, everything she could do to end her own life. Then one day the baby in her body decided to commit suicide before her, and so Bilqees was left with no other option but to continue living. 'Five years have passed. How is Shakir? What does he do? Does he still wait for me? He must've come to see me and met Baba.' What? When? Why? How? Where? All these thoughts assaulted her day and night. She had forgotten her own name, Ritu. Perhaps Ritu really did die in the well that day, and Bilqees survived in her place.

Trrntrrn. The ringing of the telephone jolted her out of her thoughts. It was Khalil Ahmed. He was reminding her that they had to attend a New Year's party tomorrow. The company's highest-ranking officers, even a few Englishmen, will be there. He wanted her to wear a nice sari with a small blouse. She agreed to the request without commenting on her husband's hypocrisy. The sun was setting in Karachi. The sky was full of screaming crows. She couldn't become a mother anymore. This thought strangely comforted her. 'It's good that I have been spared this useless journey in my life.' Sometimes Bilqees felt like she had got on the wrong bus. Even if she reached the last stop, she wouldn't reach her destination. So why not get off the bus at an earlier stop?

She stared at the box of paans in front of her. These paan leaves came from Ceylon, of course, but they always reminded Bilqees of Barishal and Shakir. Baba hated Shakir's habit of eating paan. Khalil loved paan too. This was his box of paans. He ate a paan after every meal and cup of tea. He only used the best ingredients, which were prepared meticulously for him. He spared no expense on this habit. But Bilqees never fed him a paan with her own hands. He thought that she hated paan. She never corrected him. She had written the last letter addressed to her father today. She looked calm. She put the last letter in the same bag as all the other letters she had written to her father and sealed the bag. She wrote the address on the bag:

Howlader Fazul Rehman
Banaripara High School
Barishal District, Bangladesh

She wrote the address first in Bangla and then in English. She never learned to write in Urdu. In the letter, she asked her father for forgiveness and told him that five years later, she was still standing at the edge of the well. There was nothing between her and the well anymore.

'Get lost, you Bengali! You are lying that you are Pakistani! You don't have any old paper, any certificate, any identification...Grab him, Ghuncha Gul...That boy is illegal...Don't let him get away... Oye!'

That is all Shakir heard before he turned around and started running towards the exit. Outside the passport office, he was confronted by Saddar's chaotic traffic and a crowd of hawkers, beggars, passport agents, and swindlers. Thin, lanky Shakir slipped through the crowd, lost Ghuncha Gul, who was trying to follow him, and got a rickshaw to the Water Pump neighbourhood. He kept looking behind him. Were the police following him?

This was his third attempt at getting a passport. He already had a fake identity card, which he had acquired by bribing an agent. Now he needed a passport so he could go back to Dhaka. He remembered how his brother-in-law had torn all their passports upon their arrival, warning that no one will ever try to return to Bengal. His father had gotten stuck there after the war. He was taken into custody along with other relatives. He was still living in Adamjee Camp, still celebrating on the 14th of August with a green and white flag instead of on the 16th of December. His mother repeated the same assurance every time: 'Your father will come soon, and he will bring everyone with him.'

'Get lost, you Bengali!' The sentence kept replaying in his mind at night. He felt like he had murdered someone or committed some unforgivable crime. 'There, the Bengalis told us that we were Biharis…Here, everyone tells me, you are Bengali…Why can't I just be Pakistani?' His two little nephews played on his back, fighting, laughing, screaming, as he hid his tears in his pillow.

The shop Shakir Glass Works was a commercial success. Shakir was an expert. He cut glass cleanly and quickly with his diamond-studded pen. His brother-in-law opened another two shops next to Shakir Glass Works. They bought two apartments in Yusuf Plaza. Karachi's population and construction projects were expanding like the bellies of the bourgeoisie.

Shakir loaded the next delivery—some glass for a dressing table—in the Suzuki pick-up. Munna *Bhai* complained of an upset stomach and ran away, so Shakir had to accompany the driver himself. They took the glass to the P.E.C.H.S neighbourhood. Munna *Bhai* had brought the order for the glass yesterday evening. He had gone to the house to take the measurements of the dressing table. Upon his return, he had whispered in Shakir's ear: 'The begum of the house broke the glass herself. She was wearing a bandage on her wrist. There's some marital problem there, I'm telling you.'

'I don't care about any woman anymore. If I can't have Ritu, they can all go to hell,' Shakir muttered under his breath and got in the front seat of the pick-up.

A servant kept guard while he fitted the new glass on the dressing table. The begum was taking a shower. He could hear the falling water. After he was done, he picked up his tools and turned around to leave. That is when he noticed a copy of a Zainul Abedin painting, which showed a frail farmer working with a pair of famished cows, on the wall. He had gifted this same watercolour to Ritu many years ago. He even recognised his own signature: Shakir '70. His feet turned to stone, but the servant kept pushing him out of the room.

The cook had laid out tea and some snacks in the lawn. Khalil Ahmed was sitting in his gown, reading an English newspaper and sipping tea. Perhaps this was their daily ritual. It was the year's last evening. The begum and her husband were leaving soon for some party. Khalil asked Shakir if he wanted some tea. Shakir needed an excuse to stay, so he quickly agreed and sat down. Blood was flowing inside him like an electric current. His temples were throbbing. His heart was in his throat. Bilqees walked out, wearing a flaming red sari, dark circles under her eyes, wet hair wrapped over her head. She was not wearing a *bindiya* or any *sindoor*.

She didn't look at Shakir. She sat down and pulled the tea cozy off the teapot. Khalil Ahmed addressed Shakir, just to say something: 'So where did you study? What does your father do?' Shakir spoke with great difficulty: 'Dh...Dhaka University. Commerce. My father is still in Dhaka. He was jailed twice.' He tried to get up, but Khalil told him to sit back down: 'Bilqees, he is from Dhaka! My brother, you must eat a paan before you leave. Yes, we should eat some paan to celebrate this meeting.' Bilqees started preparing paans without saying anything. Khalil continued talking: 'It's good that you folks came to Pakistan. Those poor, hungry Bengalis. The place gets flooded every year. Serves them right. That's their punishment. You just watch—Bangladesh will never be able to progress. And they want to separate from us? They want to support India? Treacherous, disloyal people! Humph!'

He stopped talking. Bilqees had finished preparing two paans. He stretched out his hand, but instead of passing one to him, she put it in Shakir's mouth, and then Shakir took the second paan and fed it to her. He couldn't believe his eyes.

Khalil Ahmed knew then that he will never eat a paan from Bilqees's hands again.

Translated from the Urdu by **Haider Shahbaz**

14 The Green Card*

TRISHNA BASAK

Kabita was getting ready to leave for school. Bukun called out 'Ma, come and look.' He didn't wait for her but entered the room on impatient steps, where Kabita was, trying to arrange the pleats of her sari. Just a touch of the comb to her hair, a *bindi* from the rows stuck on the mirror on her forehead and she would be ready. To do even this small task was making her tense today. She was really late. By now Kathakali Kindergarten would be full of twittering children. And here was Bukun troubling her, urging, 'Ma look, look…!' Kabita could tell without turning her head that he was showing her something on his phone. The boy could not rest without showing his mother whatever new things he saw: a video of the Niagara Falls or a picture of the shortest girl on Earth or a cruel scene of a tiger attack while on safari. Moreover, on Facebook under 'People You may Know', everyday he found one or two familiar faces, and excitedly ran up to his mother to share. Kabita expected something similar. In an irritated voice she said, 'I'll take a look when I return. Where is the time now? I am late today.' She picked up the *bindi* from the mirror as she said this and took her shoulder bag from where it hung on the wall. From her house there was a walk down a lane towards a huge pond. Along the pond stood a row of tall palms. Kathakali Kindergarten lay just beyond. It took little more than five minutes to reach it, but when she was late, the walk appeared a thousand miles long. Slipping her feet into a pair of sandals from the shoe rack on the verandah, Kabita said, 'I've kept your *nashta* covered with a lid. Eat it. If you go out, leave the keys with Munira *Apa*.'

---

*Originally published in Bangla as 'Shobuj Card' in the literary magazine *Kathasopan* (October 2020, Kolkata).

Paying no heed to these words, Bukun lifted his phone up to his mother's face and said, 'Look Ma, there's *Mama*.'

Mama! Kabita's heart jolted. As soon as he had opened his Facebook account, Bukun sent Tamal a friend request. Tamal had accepted it. Since then, via Bukun, Kabita was able to see their house, their car and their children in Canada. She had looked, not wanting to hurt Bukun, but she had felt a sharp pain in her heart every time. She hid her hurt and said, 'Okay, show me what you want.'

Smiling, Bukun showed her a photo. 'Look Ma, there's *Mama, Mami*, Esha and Isha. Can you see what they are holding in their hands?'

Without her spectacles Kabita couldn't see clearly. She faintly saw the four of them holding something aloft like victory flags.

'What is it? I can't see properly.'

Bukun answered with a bright face, '*Arre*, it's a Green Card! *Mama* has got his Green Card at last. That is why they have posted a picture on Facebook, holding it in their hands.'

A Green Card!

'Now don't ask what is a Green Card. Okay you leave for work. I keep asking you to buy me a bike. Then I could take you every day.'

Kabita heard none of that. Their home was in Sitakundo, near the entry to Chattogram. From the verandah of the house, one could see the Chandranath hill. It was now covered with vivid green after the fresh rains. The poet Nazrul had once visited the place. He had composed the song:

Akashe helan diye pahad ghumoe oi
The hill slumbers leaning against the sky…

Kabita had been to the place many times. Once she had taken Tamal too. The waterfall was dry, but the slopes were still green. However, at that moment, a different kind of green floated before her eyes, obliterating all other shades of green.

The road ran towards Korutia College, crossing Nalsonda village. On other days, there was much talk, laughter and banter. Today, well not only today, since past several months, all was silent. There were no crowds of college students. Those who stepped out did so for the sake of empty bellies. Jyotsna looked out of the window as she performed her household tasks, and thought it would have been better if she had not come from Mymensingh. Her father was so well known there, he had such influence and prestige as a doctor. All one had to do was to enter the house on Number 6 Natok Ghar Lane, and no one could touch you! But would her mother-in-law understand that? Not being able to see the first grandson of the family made her heart palpitate. Yet it was only in February that Jyotsna went to her father's house after the *annaprashan*. She had hardly rested for a few days before the frequent summons began: 'Come back immediately with the child.' Angurbala, her mother-in-law, couldn't bear the separation from her grandson. Jyotsna's third brother-in-law Subal made frequent trips bearing her missive.

Subal used to work as an usher in Chayabani theatre, and lived in Kadu *Pishima*'s house. Those days, Subal would be regularly invited for dinner to Jyotsna's father's house. Now that he had left Mymensingh, naturally he became the conduit to keep in touch with Jyotsna's paternal home—whether it was to accompany Jyotsna to her father's home or to fetch her back! It was Subal who had brought Jyotsna to her father's home along with Kobu, Sobu and Tomu after the *annaprashan*. Before fifteen days were over, it was he who arrived with Angurbala's urgent summons: the situation everywhere in the country was bad. Who knew what might happen? Angur wanted to see her grandson's face before she died. There was no way of finding out what Parimal thought about all this. He was a busy doctor in the hospital at Mirzapur; it was not easy to get leave. And quite possibly, Angurbala didn't mention all these feminine wiles to him. She didn't think it was necessary to talk to her son. She couldn't have managed to drag *Bouma* and the child home so easily in those dangerous days if Parimal had known about it! Even then Jyotsna had thoughtfully left behind

Kobu and Sobu with her mother. Angurbala had no attachment to her granddaughters. After all they were girl children. She could bear to die without seeing their faces!

Subal did not dare contradict his mother, but he was very fond of his nieces and nephew. Along with passing on his mother's command, he had whispered, 'Whatever Ma says, you must not leave, *Boudi*. This is a town area. Everyone is a patient of Uncle. No one will dare to lay a finger on you here. And if the *razakar*s come to the village, where will you go? The house is close to Korutia College. Half the students are with the *razakar*s and half with the *muktijoddha*. How will I save you then, tell me?'

Subal had kept looking at Jyotsna as he spoke. His *Mejoboudi* looked exactly like Suchandra, the one he saw on the screen when he was ushering at Chayabani. His mother's irrationality was dragging *Mejoboudi* into danger. His heart thumped at not being able to do anything.

Jyotsna had glanced at her father; surely her father would stop her from going. He would say, 'No point in jumping into the fire with a nursing infant. It isn't justified for your mother-in-law to insist.' But to Jyotsna's surprise Nirmal Doctor said, 'Go my dear, since your mother-in-law wants. Let Kobu and Sobu stay.' Hurtful tears had sprung to her eyes, but still she understood why he had said that. He didn't want to take a risk by keeping the male child. If something had to happen, let it be in their place! Kobu and Sobu were girls; what was the value of their lives? It was true that after two daughters the much-desired son had arrived. If anything were to happen to him while staying with Baba, how would he be able to face them? Subal had said nothing to *Tauimoshai*. But he had taken some steps on his own. He bought a burkha for Jyotsna from the market in Mymensingh and as they travelled to Nalsonda, he had taught Jyotsna how to recite the *kalma*.

'*Mejoboudi*, repeat after me: *La ilaha illallahu Mohammadur Rasulullah*...'

Jyotsna had laughed aloud and said, 'What does it mean, *thakurpo*?'

Subal had answered, 'Don't laugh. It is a very holy saying in Arabic. It means, there is no God but Allah and Hazrat Muhammad is his messenger. Learn this by heart. I'll teach you five more.'

The second *kalma* was even longer.

Ash-hadu alla ilaha ill Allahu, wahdahu la sharika lah, wa ash-hadu anna Muhammadan abduhu wa Rasooluhu.

Jyotsna didn't ask for the meaning. Subal interpreted it for her on his own: 'I bear witness that there is no god but Allah, the One alone, without equal and I bear witness that Muhammad is His servant and Messenger.'

With great effort she had memorised the first verse. It was by the power of this *kalma* that Jyotsna was able to save her son's life.

Now, Kabita thought, the owner of that priceless life was holding out a green card in a photograph.

She had heard all about it from Ma. Those days, she and her sister were in Mymensingh in their grandfather's house. Ma had to leave for Nalsonda with their brother. *Thakuma* was calling them over incessantly. Once they reached home, *Thakuma* had hugged their brother to her chest, while Ma silently did all the household work. She didn't allow Ma to do anything for the boy.

Angurbala had kept the child close to her heart. One tumbler of sago was always kept ready for him against the necessity of having to escape if the *razakar*s came. It wouldn't be possible to take anything at such a moment except the infant clutched to her breast and the brass pot of sago. Behind their house in Nalsonda there was a large pond. Baba's younger brother had drowned in it at the age of six. So *Thakuma* never went near that water body. Another small one next to it served for her ablutions. That pond was no better than a pool, but only a few trees surrounded it, plenty of sunlight fell on it and the water was clear. Ma however went to the pond at the back, where many trees provided cover. The jungle began beyond that. People called it the Pakura forest. *Thakuma* had thought that they would hide in the jungle. She had a faint hope that the Louhojong river would act as a magic amulet. Like her, many had thought that the trouble was confined to Dhaka. And that the West Pakistan Army would not be able to cross all these rivers and streams and reach the villages. But soon it was evident that the Khan Army had reached even the remote places. Nor was Nalsonda beyond their reach.

That morning after a breakfast of puffed rice and coconut *laddu*, Jyotsna had settled down to clean some greens. Angur had asked for *saak* with garlic and nigella seeds, *mashkolai dal* and fritters with *gondhopata*. Fish was rarely cooked in the house and that too mostly small ones. Late afternoons, her father-in-law bought small fish from the market; sometimes a few were spoilt. They were washed thoroughly, then rubbed with salt and turmeric. Angur dried them on the dying fire after the meal had been cooked. On special days when visitors arrived or after a long fish-less month, she allowed them to be cooked with vegetables or in a curry. There was no sign of that happening that day. After having ordered the preparation of two vegetables, Angur walked around feeding Tomu some mashed banana. Though Jyotsna's breasts were aching with the weight of milk, there was no way she could feed Tomu. Even breastfeeding her baby had to be done at her mother-in-law's will.

As she cleaned the vegetables, Jyotsna thought that her sisters were lucky not to have such a mother-in-law. Nor did they suffer from such hard living conditions. Her brothers-in-law may not be doctors like Parimal, but they all had adequate jobs or businesses. Their families were not so penurious that they would have to eat dry fish or vegetables growing near the pond. At her father's house in Mymensingh, all three meals included fish, and they were large in size. Small fish were only cooked with mixed vegetables. She felt close to tears as these thoughts passed through her head. She felt even angrier watching her mother-in-law walking around with the baby. On some days Angur went visiting neighbourhood houses with the baby. Contentedly chewing on betel leaf, she would exchange all the news and gossip, and roundly criticise Jyotsna: Jyotsna couldn't do anything well; Subal had to fill water for her bath; a bamboo shelter had to be especially built for her near the pond; Jyotsna looked glum if there was no fish on her plate. According to Angurbala, all these things were to be criticised. Who could Jyotsna blame if not her father? Baba had married her off after being impressed with the groom. In his opinion, Parimal was a determined young man who was destined to go far. Besides, doctors never had to starve!

The day after the wedding, he spoke to Jyotsna in private, 'My dear child, let me say one thing. The in-laws' home is never a happy one for any girl. One has to make it happy. Whenever you feel hurt at someone's words, don't open your mouth to retort. If you feel angry, look down at the ground. Think how much the earth has to bear.'

As it was, Jyotsna always looked at the ground. Her tears soaked the earth. And now there were deep pools of blood there. Her heart jumped. Were Kobu and Sobu safe? Ma, Baba, her brothers, her sisters? Every day bad news flew in from all over.

Suddenly she heard a scream. No, not a scream, a kind of roar, a woman's cry, and earsplitting gunshots. Subal ran in from somewhere, his eyes popping out in terror, and said, '*Boudi* throw away your greens. You have to run! Pick up Tomu and hide in the Pakura jungle.' Angurbala was reluctant to part with Tomu. Subal gave her a push and said, 'You want to kill Tomu? Can you run as fast as *Boudi*?' Chastised, Angur gave Tomu to Jyotsna, and Jyotsna lay her *boti* down and ran towards the Pakura jungle. A heap of greens and *gondhobhadali* leaves lay abandoned. Left behind were the trifling household of the hearth and cooking pots, the bamboo bench in the courtyard, pumpkin vines on the roof. Outside, there wasn't a soul to be seen. Not a cat or a dog on the roads. Emptiness reigned.

As she entered the jungle, Jyotsna's heart thumped. In the middle of the afternoon it seemed as if night had descended. Tall trees surrounded the path from all sides. Only the most daring ever entered the forest. It would be someone having an affair, or someone who wanted good quality grass for their cow; some people would also come to collect wood. But that was not why Jyotsna's heart trembled. She had left behind Tomu's pot of sago. Who knew how long they would be stuck there in the forest? What would she feed her son? Her head swam even to think of it. As she settled against a tree trunk, she saw Angur standing under a *pakur* tree nearby, holding the pot of sago. She calmed down; in relief and gratitude, tears came to her eyes. But what was Angur holding in her left hand? Reading Jyotsna's glance, Angur pointed to her neck, wrists and ears. Jyotsna immediately understood—they were the ornaments Baba had presented to each of his daughters: twenty *bhori* worth of gold jewelry. All that jewelry was in Nalsonda. Angur wanted to keep her hold on Jyotsna's ornaments just as she did over Tomu. So, despite everyone's protests, the jewelry stayed with her in that remote village. That day, even while escaping, Angur had not forgotten the bundle of gold.

Beyond the jungle, the sounds of heavy boots and gunshots came nearer. Angurbala swiftly buried the bundle of jewelry under the *pakur* tree, and signalled to Jyotsna to remember the spot. Much later, even after a hard search, that tree could not be found. And that day, when they had returned home, they heard that the *razakar*s had entered and killed their eldest uncle and his two sons. When they had asked for water, thorns of the date palm had been rubbed inside their throats.

Jyotsna was once again at her chores, chopping spinach on the *boti*. Menu for the day: spinach, dal and fried bitter gourd. Those days it was the same fare every day. There was no chance of fish during the fourteen days of mourning when a close relative died. Food was not the only problem. After the funeral, Angur would drive her mad, almost killing her by forcing her to wash bed sheets, mosquito nets, pillow covers. That would be followed by cleaning the whole house and spreading cow dung all over. It made Jyotsna feverish just to remember all that.

But who knew if they would survive till then? To Jyotsna it appeared that the whole country was in mourning. Every home was destroyed. Who was left behind to follow rituals? She wondered what Kobu and Sobu might be doing right now. She had no news of her man working in a Mirzapur hospital either. She wondered how it would have been if at that moment she had been with Parimal and her three children. Who would dare enter Ronodaprasad Saha's hospital? That hospital was a shelter for so many! Ronodaprasad did not let the doctors suffer any kind of want. There were family quarters for married doctors. Before Tomu was born, Jyotsna had stayed there for some time. That was where she first got a taste of running a household of her own, and there was no Angur to breathe down her neck. Parimal used to buy fish like in Jyotsna's paternal home. Though not in such variety, in Mirzapur Parimal would buy at least one kind of big fish. Then there was a full-time girl to help Jyotsna and another woman to look after the children. Needless to say, they were all hospital staff, so there was no need to give them wages, only meals.

Jyotsna wept thinking of those few brief days of happiness, when her heart was stopped by a familiar earth-shattering cry. She swiftly laid down the vegetable chopper and went into the room to take out the burkha. She wrapped it over her sari, picked up Tomu from Angur's lap and the pot of sago from the fireside, and ran towards the *pakur* forest without waiting for anyone.

That day she didn't feel so scared like last time. Armed with the burkha and the glass of sago she calmly waited for the inevitable. Soon the sounds of heavy boots rang out. The sounds approached nearer. There were others too in the forest who waited with their hearts in their mouths. The shock of finding that the *pakur* forest they had thought a safe haven was no longer so almost overcame their fear. Were the Khan soldiers more in number than all the inhabitants of Nalsonda village? That was not true, but they had fire-spewing guns. They were armed with the conviction of their superiority, and an inbuilt addiction towards crushing all Bangla-speakers under their feet. Jyotsna faintly remembered the two tender faces of Kobu and Sobu; images of her mother, father and Parimal floated before her eyes. She felt neither anxiety nor fear, but under the burkha her body felt paralysed.

A tall, broad Khan soldier stood in front of her. Even in the dark shadows of the *pakur* jungle, the huge shape of the man and his fair skin were clearly visible to her. The man was looking at her very closely. It felt like the end of time. Jyotsna's complexion was a rich cream. Noting her fair colour and the burkha, the soldier asked her in a rough voice, 'Are you a Muslim?' Jyotsna nodded, unable to speak. Another soldier approached from the side and said, 'These Bengalis are bastards. Burkhas are sold in the market. What's so great about buying and wearing one? Remove the burkha and take a look. The bitch looks an excellent piece,' and guffawed.

Jyotsna didn't understand all that Urdu, but she understood the laughter. She felt a tremor of fear run through her. A chill terror that spread from her spine. Instantly she remembered some words whose meaning she didn't know. The fear of death and worse made her repeat those unknown words, clutching Tomu to her chest: *La ilaha illallahu Mohammadur Rasulullah*... The words acted like magic. The two men were startled. A kind of respect and admiration showed on their faces. They spoke amongst themselves, and the first man softly squeezed Tomu's cheeks. His eyes looked sad to Jyotsna. She thought perhaps he had left behind a child like her son back in West Pakistan.

As soon as she finished taking two consecutive classes, the bell for recess rang out. Kabita had had some bread and tea at home but brought no tiffin with her. This was not a government school. It ran on the generosity of a local businessman. Sometimes he sent cakes and biscuits for the children, which included some for the teachers. There were only two of them, Kabita and Salema. Salema's husband lived in Abu Dhabi. They were childless. She came to the school to while away her time. Kabita came in the hope of earning a little extra money to make life easy. Radharaman, Bukun's father, worked in a small factory and his earnings sufficed for bare subsistence. These days, education cost so much. At least *Didi* had taken her daughter to Rajshahi to stay with her. Kabita's brother-in-law was a professor at Rajshahi College. They wanted to encourage Brishti to be a doctor. The girl was intelligent. But Kabita did not dream too much. Just then, before her eyes floated the *pakura* forest, Tomu in her burkha-clad mother's lap. That day her almost uneducated mother had remembered a sentence from an unknown tongue and saved Tomu's life, so he could become a doctor one day.

Tamal had met Runa Choudhury when he was a student. Runa's father Kartik Choudhury was a well-known businessman whose close relationship with the ruling party had concealed the stigma of being a patron of the *razakars*. His experienced eyes recognised Runa's excellent choice. Consequently, it didn't take long for Tamal to reach Dhaka Medical College, plucked adroitly from Pirpur Grameen Hospital.

Tomu had once taken Jyotsna to see her first granddaughter, to his grand flat in Gulshan, given as a gift by Kartik Choudhury. He had brought her back in his car to the house in Kishoregunj after two hours. At home, he had put some coloured strips of paper in Jyotsna's hand.

'What are these?'

'You'll be able to measure your diabetes on your own. Dip it into your urine.'

In front of the huge house in Kishoregunj, in the middle of a desolate field, Jyotsna had stood holding the coloured strips to measure sugar in the blood, watching Tomu's foreign car vanishing in the distance. By then she knew, distance no longer meant just Dhaka, but Canada. Kartik Choudhury had an old establishment there: a son and another daughter already lived in that country. Watching Tomu's vanishing car, Jyotsna had thought, however far Tomu might travel, he would never be able to leave behind the foliage of the *pakura* forest.

Salema offered Kabita some sweets she had made, served on a plate with a floral design. '*Apa*, have some sweet potato *pitha*. You never eat any snacks.' Kabita picked one up. Salema said, 'You know *Apa*, I found my aunt's diary the other day. She used to work in Dhaka University. She used to stitch flags of our soon-to-be independent country in secret. She was killed trying to save her orderly, Gopal.'

At that moment, Mostapha Kamal's car drove up to Kathakali Kindergarten. Mostapha alighted, followed by his driver Rajab Mia holding a big bag of cakes and sweets for the children. This time, an addition was the national flag.

Mostapha was an excitable man. He called out from outside: 'Salema and Kabita *Apa*, listen, this year you must make plans for *Bijay Dibas*, Victory Day. You do know that Nazrul had come to Sitakundo, right? And he wrote that song of his: *Akashe helan diya...* Kabita *Apa*, you must write a musical about our *Muktijuddho*. The children must know what fire storms we had to come through.'

The words flew over Kabita's head. All she could see through the folded flag in Rajab's hand was a red globe and a deep green spread around it, like that green in the *pakura* forest as her mother had once described.

The photo Bukun had showed her that morning, of the green card held by Tomu's family—could that green ever compare with the green of the flag?

Translated from the Bangla by **Kalyani Dutta**

15 Bingo*

TARIQ RAHMAN

It was miserable in the first term at the Pakistan Military Academy (PMA). It was. They made us stand in the snow in our underwear at night and I was given a cold shower and frog-jumps too. The battalion sergeant-major was a sadist. He made me hop around catching my ankles till I fell down and my legs ached like hell. But the cadets of my platoon were idiots. Each one of them broke the orders once, and lo and behold we were all up to our neck in the soup. When I was the senior gentleman cadet—the 'bloody SGC' as I was termed—I made them fall-in ten minutes before time. It's idiotic to be late, so I made them double around as the seniors told me. Why should a chap be lousy when the staffs and the seniors are all around to nab him by the neck and do the dirty on him? So during my days the sergeant was pleased and the CSM[1] ragged us only twice.

'You bloody Jitter,' my cadet corporal said to me, 'you will be a good soldier.'

'Yes, sir,' I shouted as he liked us to do.

The fellow beamed at me and omitted to make me front-roll when he left.

Tajassur, on the contrary, was such a fool that the whole army spat on its hands and got down to the onerous task of making a soldier out of him. He didn't care. He let the cadets get late and stood like a statue who has had its behind kicked. He chatted around from room to room and didn't do his class work. He let us walk if he could help it. Naturally, whenever we were caught, Tajassur was the one who never heard the last of it. He gave away

*Written in English in 1973, and reproduced here with minor edits with the kind permission of the author.

some of the articles of his FSMO[2] and was the first one to be on restrictions. But he always walked around casually and smiled. It was foolish. The funniest thing was that he was my room-mate. It gave me creeps to see him sleeping in the morning when I was almost in my shirt for the PT or the drill. He was a sub-human creature and knew no discipline.

Yet Tajassur had soft baby-looks and large black eyes. If one talked to him he smiled and spoke nicely. The seniors called him a sissy and said he was fit to be a heroine in a Filipino movie. He often had one or two sadistic senior slave-drivers who delighted in punishing him or feeding him on sweets in the canteen. It was awful to be his room-mate. The seniors came into our room just to enjoy themselves by punishing him or talking to him—he was witty. 'Hey you heroine,' one would say, 'have you got girl-friends?'

'No, sir,' Tajassur would reply, standing to attention.

'Why, you bloody goof?'

'I don't know, sir.'

'Get down on your hands, idiot,' and Tajassur would fall to the ground on his hands and feet.

'And you too, you priceless imbecile.'

So I, cursing the bastards, would go into the same position. And the ragging would go on at my expense. Had Tajassur been less popular nobody would have bothered us so much.

I was good at drill and P.T. and Tajassur was lousy at both. Yet he managed to pass. In the map reading the platoon mates often did his work. They enlarged the map for him and even found the grid reference of his own position. In exchange all the fellow did was tell them jokes. And in spite of his innocent looks Tajassur knew jokes which could send the angels running after the chaste houris in paradise. I like jokes but I detest stupidity. Of what use are jokes when the officers are just around the corner. All these immature things did make Tajassur popular but at the expense of his marks and position.

He was a cadet platoon commander once and, at the end of the exercise, he brought us back in a truck. It was a big risk. We were supposed to have walked back 20 miles and there was a competition with the other platoons. And yet this grinning baby brought us back on this truck. Naturally, we reached before midnight. So what does he do? He takes us to a hotel of all things and there he makes us dance all night and eat and drink and have a rollicking good time. Oh boy! It was fun; but he could have been withdrawn if anyone had noticed. Well, we reached the Academy gates and were told that we were third. Tajassur seemed so tired that the cadet sergeant sent us to rest after the rifle cleaning—the fraud!

He passed out twentieth in the course. And, I bet, it was all because of his wonderful oral expression in English and wit. He read his lesson half an hour before the model discussion and gave cogent arguments. Besides, he was liked by our immature platoon-mates and they thought he was a good sort. He had given his water-bottle to thirsty people who had been foolish enough to have wasted their supply in the exercise. He had cheerfully carried the light machine-gun—the most goddamnest pain in the arse—in the 'initiative exercise'. He had a smile for most of us and, in the Academy, chaps are nit-wits enough to get impressed by these kind of trivialities.

But just before our passing out, things were against him. He was a Bingo, you see. He belonged to Dacca itself and East Pakistan had begun kicking up one hell of a row to get separated from West Pakistan. We called him a 'Bingo' and a 'traitor' and Sheikh Mujibur Rehman's ADC.[3] I went a step further and called him the 'Marshland minion'. I told him he would be the minion of old Mujib and since all his land was marshland—hence the title!

But Tajassur kept quiet about these things. He was quite a kid and kids can't get serious about politics and suchlike grown-up things. So came the D-Day and we passed out. Tajassur had got many badges of rank, cap and stuff even from juniors. I thought it a shame to accept things from juniors and said so. He smiled sheepishly and told me that presents could not be denied. I told him he would bring shame to the army by being so unprincipled.

'I have my own principles, Safeer,' he replied gravely.

'And what damned lousy Bingo principles may those be, sweetie?' I taunted. I was getting angry.

'Look, Safeer. They are not reasoned out. I just do what makes me happy and what makes people happy. And "Bingo" has nothing to do with it.'

'Happy!' I cried. 'That's a fatheaded thing to say and I will let you know it is. The sergeant would excuse us drill to make us happy. The soldiers should not kill the rebel Mukti Bahinis to make them happy. And girls should get laid in order to please grinning morons. Happy—oh now you know that's ungentlemanly and unofficer-like.'

'I am not much of an officer,' he rejoined.

'So much the worse for the army,' I replied.

Just then our bearer came in and Tajassur started telling him what to do with his shoes once he left. The bearer goggled like a fish and seemed to relish the idea of laying his vile paws on those good shoes, coats and shirts.

I went into the infantry and so did Tajassur. We got our regiments in the main dining hall of the battalion mess. Whenever someone was assigned to Headquarters Eastern Command, a sibilant half-deriding sound came from the cadets. The adjutant was terribly annoyed and threatened us with restrictions but the sound still didn't stop entirely.

'Sher Nawaz Khan,' called the adjutant, '36 Cavalry, Kharian Cantonment.'

We all clapped. Sher got red in the face and sat down.

'Mohammad Adil Siddiqui, Daedaulus's Horse. Report to Multan Cantonment.'

This time the clapping was thunderous. Daedalus's was a much-coveted armoured regiment with aristocratic traditions.

'Ali Ahmed,' continued the adjutant, 20 Baluch, Quetta.' Applause greeted him too.

'Safeer Ahmed—15 Punjab, report to HQ Eastern Command.'

I sat down amidst a low hissing and the fellow on my right laughed mirthlessly. Then some people clapped. The adjutant went red in the face. 'What's wrong with you buggers? Are you all yellow? I'll kick the whole lot out of here if I hear that damned hissing.' Then he went on with the names.

Some people congratulated me on getting the infantry. It was my choice.

'Tajassur Ullah,' said the adjutant with a smile. The applause was thunderous as he stood up shyly. He was blushing, the sissy. 'For the course favourite the GHQ[4] decrees—report to HQ Eastern Command, 15 Punjab.'

The hall went wild. There was loud hissing mixed with clapping. The adjutant looked down and fumbled with the papers. I thought everyone made a fool of himself because Tajassur was treated like a baby, not like a grown-up man. I would have been ashamed to be in his shoes. But he sat down cheerfully and thanked the people around him with a bright smile.

We got only three days to report to the stations of duty. On the plane I met some of my course mates. The rank of second lieutenant was new on our shoulders. It was fun to wear it. Very few people have the honour of being Class-I officers of the government at the age of nineteen or twenty. We were among such lucky ones and I felt proud of myself and happy.

When we reached the unit there was an atmosphere of tension and hurry. The adjutant was a certain Captain Maqsood Hussain. He told me to look sharp in my battle dress and to be fifteen minutes early for all parades. Tajassur also reported late that evening and Captain Maqsood ragged him a great deal for grinning like an ape. He seemed to be a strict adjutant. In the evening we went to the mess on bikes.

An old bearer served us soft drinks and we sat listening to the conversation. Then the Commanding Officer (CO) came and everyone stood up. He was a middle-aged man with a balding head, bushy eyebrows and a very serious grim face.

'Let me introduce Second Lieutenant Safeer to you, sir,' said Captain Maqsood presenting me first since I was senior by number to Tajassur.

'How do you do,' said the CO. 'What was your passing out number?'

'Fifth, sir,' I replied.

'Good. The Punjab Regiment likes bright youngsters. Good.'

Then Tajassur was presented. The clown smiled even at the commandant though the colonel was as serious as a church as he took his paw in his big hand.

'And what is your passing out number?'

'Twentieth, sir,' he replied.

'Well, well. Work hard in the regiment. Your professional life begins here,' said the CO. I could see that I had made a good first impression.

The CO talked to the senior officers and we kept listening. Nobody addressed us again. Then, supper was announced and we moved to the table. The CO began talking about history.

'I admire the courage of John Nicholson and Sir Hugh Rose in 1857,' he said.

'Yes, sir, the battle account is inspiring,' said Major Dost Muhammad, the Second-in-Command.

'Sir, the Vietcong too are brave,' said Major Azhar Khan, one of the Company Commanders.

'Yes, yes, that is wonderful,' replied the CO. 'Though they are short-statured people. They don't seem to be a martial race.'

'I think there are no martial races,' Tajassur's voice startled me. Everyone turned to look at him. The adjutant was scowling darkly. Everyone seemed to have been struck by a bolt from the blue.

'People are forced to fight when they are exploited and transgressed against, and bravery is good only if it is used in a just cause. If it is used to oppress, it is evil.'

There was pin-drop silence in the room. The CO looked as if he would have a fit. His face was red with anger. He did not reply. Then the silence reigned in an ominous way and the meal came to an end. The CO left for his room and the adjutant took us aside. He struck a cigarette and slowly turned to Tajassur.

'How dare you,' he hissed between clenched teeth, 'talk so insolently to the CO?'

'But I merely expressed my opinion, sir,' said Tajassur with genuine surprise.

'But damn your idiotic opinion, you bloody tit of a second lieutenant! Don't you dare utter a squeak when your seniors are talking! OK? Do I make myself clear?'

'Yes, sir.'

The adjutant kept glaring at us. We kept standing at attention. Tajassur looked down.

'Seven days orderly officer duty for you, Tajassur. You will check the guard and report to me thrice every night.'

'Yes, sir,' said Tajassur in a muffled voice.

Captain Maqsood turned and stalked off. His boots crunched the loose shingles. Tajassur stood completely humiliated. They had petted him and spoiled him at PMA. I had always told him that the army was no place for suave young juniors who didn't know how to respect seniors. Now he was crying.

O God! I couldn't believe it. He had tears in his eyes. 'Don't be a sissy, Tajassur!' I said to him. It was most exasperating to see him disgracing our course like that. A most effeminate thing to do! He didn't reply. When I reached the room I found him asleep.

Soon enough Tajassur was in everyone's bad books. He got late for parades. He was too chummy with the other ranks and addressed the non-commissioned officers as if they were officers. He had, strangely, no respect for the seniors. He contradicted them and thrust his opinion as if he knew more than all those who had put in so much service. Everyone told me that PMA was not training even the regular courses well. Even I was given long lectures when he did something wrong. As I had expected, Tajassur was a very poor specimen of an officer.

Then one day the CO called a conference and apprised us of the enemy situation. The Mukti Bahini—i.e., rebel Bingo troops—had started playing havoc with our supply line. Since January Sheikh Mujeeb had become even more absurdly adamant about his 'six points'. I never knew what the damned six points were but anything coming from a loony like Mujeeb must have been crap. Tajassur kept sitting like a stooge throughout the conference. That evening we were supposed to crack down on a village where the bastards were in hiding. I was in the room when Tajassur came in. He wasn't smiling. In fact he had become glum. 'Hey, Safeer. Ready?' he said amiably.

'Yeah. What about you?'

'OK.'

He sat down and started playing with my watch. It annoyed me. Goodness, wasn't he grown up enough to stop fooling with other people's things? It made a man sick to have such a childish room-mate.

'Stop playing with it,' I said.

'What does it matter,' he replied. 'What does anything matter?'

'What matters now, partner, is that we better roast your Bingo friends alive,' I said wearily.

'Why?'

'Why? What the hell do you mean why? Because they are Pakistan's enemies. Because they want to divide our country. Because they are Indian agents and anti-Pakistan. That's what we are being paid for. The CO orders us, and we go. That is loyalty.'

'But where is your conscience?'

'My conscience tells me to rid Pakistan of its enemies.'

'Listen Safeer,' he said sitting on my bed. 'This is propaganda. Pakistan was not created to be a slave colony. Bengal was treated as a colony by the CSP[5] officers. The army officers made fun of our men and beat them. Everyone took our wealth...' As usual his voice became choked with gushy tears. He clenched his hand. 'And now that we have risen against this exploitation, this tyranny, they are telling the army to shoot our people. The army has entered villages before and shot our innocent people. They've raped our girls. It's monstrous and unjust. Can't you feel it, Safeer?' He caught my hands and his lips twitched and trembled.

'Can't you see that this lovely lush green land is under hobnailed boots? Can't you hear the foul orders of hate-filled fat men in Islamabad who are sending poor innocent boys to kill people they have never even met before? Come on, Safeer, where is your conscience...?' he trailed off.

I shook him off. He was mad. I had never seen him so passionate. I was a little scared of him. These Bengalis were a treacherous race.

Batmen[6] had been known to have murdered their officers. This vile race knew no loyalty, nor even unit spirit. Nothing noble appealed to their conscience.

'Go to sleep. Go to sleep. Don't talk like that or you'll be caught, you fool,' I muttered.

In the evening the news shook everyone. Second Lieutenant Tajassur had become a deserter. They straightaway called his absence desertion because his pistol was also missing and it was well known that Bingos took to their heels to join the enemy treacherously. I was surprised. He was too much of a sissy, I thought, to have dared to run away. It is risky after all.

We did roast the traitors in that village. First the troops surrounded it and then the machine guns blazed away. The vermin came out and the crack-shots took them on ever so happily. It must have taught them a lesson not to hide the traitors anymore. They took prisoners too who were handed over to the Intelligence Units. These Intelligence chaps knew how to get the truth out of stubborn Bingos for sure.

Days passed and I became a responsible subaltern. In March I did so well that I got recommended for the Commander-in-Chief's commendation letter. The GOC,[7] Eastern Command, shook hands with me. In the unit the CO called me 'hot-rod Commando' and was very proud of me. Major Ali Ahmed was an expert in bringing in Bingos as a net brings in fish. We would shoot them slowly one by one. It improved my target practice a good deal. The bastards cried for pity and whimpered like dogs. I think this is a race of slaves. They look up at a person as if he were a god and then they are so treacherous that they stab you in the back. We used to kill them whenever we got news that our brethren had been killed anywhere. It didn't compensate for our losses, but it made one take out one's anger at someone. Some officers delighted in torturing the Bingos to extract information from them. In the beginning, I thought it was excessive but soon enough I found out that these stubborn people didn't talk as long as you treated them humanely. Besides, everything is fair once your national integrity is at stake.

One day we were ordered to clear a village of the Muktis. I was in charge of a platoon and we moved off on jeeps at first light. It was very early dawn when we struck. The scene was rather like some Second World War movie, except that brown-skinned people ran out like chickens with the heads cut off. The Bingos are such cowards in front of soldiers, I thought, as I turned the machine guns on the main exit. The rush of the women stopped as many rolled in blood and confusion. Then hell broke loose. Our jeeps were hit by bullets and they swooshed and whistled past my ears. I heard the Company Commander yell the order to retreat. I jumped into a tree. But I managed to rush off behind another jeep and got bogged down into their blasted flooded paddy fields. Frightful shapes advanced towards me and I was hauled out of the jeep. The pistol was yanked out of my hands and I was given a blow on the head which made everything go dark in front of me.

When I regained consciousness I was in a little dark room. There was a window but, blast their treacherous brains, they had barred it with steel bars. I went around it once. Twice. This didn't happen. Officers of the Pakistan Army couldn't be caught like this by the Bingos. As I sat down trying to think some way out of it all, the door opened and a small mean-looking Bingo beckoned me to follow him. I did and was brought to a room in which a number of ragged ill-clothed men were sitting on cots. One of them was in uniform and he was sitting on a chair.

'Lieutenant Safeer of the 15th Punjab,' he said in English, 'I am Major Saif-ur-Rehman of the Bangladesh Army,' he continued, getting up to shake my hand. I was stunned. There was no bloody Bangladesh and no damned Bangladesh Army, I was about to burst out. But then I remembered where I was and kept my mouth shut.

'Yes,' I said.

'Yes, sir, Lieutenant,' replied the Major smiling impishly. I wanted to bash his ugly black Bingo mug in. But I had to be tactful.

'Yes, sir,' I said.

'That's better,' he replied.

The other Bingos shouted. Their faces were angry. They looked like animals. I had never seen men like that. Their animal faces scared me. This was not like war against a civilised army. These apes knew no Geneva Convention nor did they know what an officer was. But this Major was more of a fellow officer. At least he knew these things.

He must have been in the Academy.

'You will be tried,' said the Major.

'What for, sir?' I asked him.

'For killing innocent civilians. For butchering exactly twenty-two women, nineteen children and seven men of Bangladesh.'

'I did my duty.'

'Which code of morals asks you to kill people at the orders of an unscrupulous government?'

At this the people raised a shout. They seemed to understand what was going on. I found out why this was so. An interpreter kept up a constant chatter conveying what was going on to the avid audience. My heart sank. It was terrible. Those people were mad. 'I am defending my country against Indian insurgents and rebels. When the people hide them we have to take action. That's all,' I replied.

'And why do they hide them?' the Major's eyes were hard and glittering. 'Have you ever tried to get out of your propaganda and use your mind and eyes? They hide them because they love them. Because they are their own people. Because they hate you. That's why they kill you when you stray out of your little fortresses. But one day all your fortresses will vanish and we will be free—then you will be pushed out into the Bay of Bengal and the lotus will be out of your reach. You are colonists, like the French in Algeria and the Belgians in the Congo. Had you been as sensible as the British you would have withdrawn gracefully. But no! You'll get innocent youths fresh from PMA and open-mouthed recruits butchered first before your generals see any sense. You will have to be pushed out. You won't go.'

The room jeered at me. Their voices rose to a hysterical crescendo and the walls reverberated. Their voices had a ravenous hunger in it and the hope of life seemed to fuse in me. The bodies were brown and lean and naked, yet they were not in a cage where I could shoot them. They were not being kicked or raped. They were not pleading. There was a maniacal confidence in their eyes. They were not slaves, it seemed. And looking around, I felt my feet go cold. My throat was parched and I felt very weak. My heart was beating like mad.

'You will be shot in the morning,' said the Major. I was taken back to my room. Its walls closed upon me and seemed to move physically. The light showed a star in the sky and I looked at it. The thought came and struck me like a blow in boxing—I wouldn't see it again. I wouldn't feel the wind on my face again. How wonderful was the mess with the waiter bringing Coca-Cola for you. How lovely the feel of the beer as it makes one light-headed and heavy-lidded. And never would I feel that rising intoxication. Nor even would the black sky have silver stars again. I turned around and the hard damp ground resisted me. The soft skin of the girls was no more.

I remembered the evenings of PMA when we sat on the terrace of the cafeteria and looked at the green valley. Tajassur often treated me. He was so lively and soft-spoken. And tomorrow I would be dead. What was the use of it all? I would die and Bengal would live on. I don't know how many would die and then something would happen. But who was in the right? ...And was there a right at all? I didn't know anything. I didn't want to think. It was agony to be alive.

I didn't know what time it was when I heard a knock. I was going to abuse the man so much that he would run away. It was bursting in me like a tidal wave. All the dirty words of Urdu, Punjabi and English were coming to my lips. I hated these Bengali bastards. I hated them all. I hated the army. I hated...

'Safeer, Safeer,' came a soft low voice.

'Yes,' I replied. It was a familiar voice. My ears strained for its melody. There was hope in its music. I liked that voice at that moment. It was Tajassur. I put my arms around his neck and almost stifled him. He was trembling. I too was trembling. I kissed him on the cheeks.

'Come with me,' he said in a low voice.

We stole out like shadows. The Bengali soldiers saluted him. He wore a captain's rank and the same uniform that I had seen on the Major. There was a jeep outside and in it we sped away from that loathsome house. We didn't talk. He took me to a house where a woman with soft eyes like Tajassur's gave me food. A girl brought me rice and cooked fish. It was excellent and I enjoyed it.

'This is my family, Safeer,' said Tajassur. 'You'll have to stay here till I can send you back to where you belong.'

'But Tajassur, why don't you send me soon? Right now in fact!'

'It's impossible,' he smiled. 'This area is now under the joint command of the Indian and the Bangladesh Army. The Pakistan Army is surrendering.'

'No!'

'Yes, Safeer,' he said and his voice was gentle and tired. 'The war is coming to an end.'

I lived there for three days and that soft-spoken family wafted me to states of mind I had never known before. A languorous peace filled me up as I drank milk and ate my rice. Tajassur's sister, Amina, had a charming languor in her eyes which made me eat my rice ever so softly. There was no hurry, no protocol and no friction. They had soft, cute, childlike smiles. They spoke a bit of Urdu and Amina knew a little English too. There was a warmth in their house which made me melt. It was lovely.

So when Tajassur came to take me to Dacca, I was sad at the parting. His mother put a talisman around my neck and his sister gave me chocolates, money and a lovely smile! He took me out tenderly to a jeep. And I was about to get in when the deafening burst of a machine-gun rocked us violently out of it. We stretched out on the ground and I saw Pakistani Commandos enter the house. Tajassur leapt like lightning but before he could shoot, he was bayoneted. I saw the bayonet go into his stomach and with a cry he fell back and the blood ran all over his belly and legs. The commandos were in the house. I got up forgetting caution. 'Hey wait!...wait I am Lieutenant Safeer of 15 Punjab!' I shouted like a madman.

'Thank God you are safe,' said an officer, embracing me. 'We'll have to get away to Dacca. They have surrendered.'

I heard the meaningless words. What was surrender? It was all meaningless. There were commando soldiers. And inside the house were Amina and Tajassur's mother. And Tajassur lay dead in a puddle of blood and his guts had come out and sprawled on his thighs like snakes. And he looked so boyish and lovely and young.

'What are they doing, sir, your soldiers?' I cried, shaking the Captain.

'Let's go in and see,' he said calmly, loading his sten-gun again.

We went in. The world broke into mad patterns. Amina was naked, raped—dead? Stabbed! And Tajassur's mother was wild. She tore her hair. She flung things around. She was frantic. I couldn't meet her eyes. I couldn't stand her grief. She was living the agony of death. Her husband had died much earlier. I took the Captain's sten-gun and shot her—to end her agony with pity in my heart. She looked at me once as if unable to believe the depth of human ingratitude. Then she fell down dead. I emptied the sten-gun on the ground. On the mud of free Bangladesh.

'Bloody Bingos,' said the Captain of the SSG.[8]

'Let's go, sir,' I said. I wanted to cry.

And we sat in the jeep and went away. Nothing mattered anymore. Tajassur and his mother were no longer alive to accuse me. Bangladesh was free and the Pakistan Army had surrendered.

Notes

1. Company sergeant major.
2. Flexible single master operations.
3. Aide-de-camp.
4. General Headquarters, Pakistan Army.
5. Civil Services of Pakistan.
6. A military officer's orderly or personal servant.
7. General officer commanding-in-chief.
8. Special Service Group.

16 The Woman with the Matted Locks*

JHUMUR PANDAY

The train left the station after a few whistles. The woman with the matted locks was looking all the while at the train. As it started to leave, she continued to gaze at it with attention. When she turned away, her eyes met Samir Das. Samir was a mechanic who repaired gas stoves.

What are you doing here?

I come to watch the train.

Oh yes. Carrying a mountain on your head…

The *Charak* procession with Shiva and Durga was winding its way down the road. Someone was singing while another collected money from the passersby. Shiva was painted silver and Durga was wearing yellow. They sported wigs of matted locks and began a dance in front of the paan shop. The woman too stopped to watch the gods dance and then started to walk away. When she walked, it was like a moving mountain: a mountain of many peaks, gorges, with a crest on top. She carried a huge sack on her head filled with household items: plates, glasses, a bowl. A wok and other cooking utensils were stuffed on two bags hanging from her shoulders and elbows. In one hand she carried half a jerrycan of kerosene oil. The woman had to carry all her things about with her as she couldn't leave them in her small room in the slum.

Right on her path was a *radhachura* tree, laden with yellow flowers. A crow sat on a flower-decked branch, pecking at something. When she noticed the crow eating, the woman felt hungry too. She hadn't had a chance to eat in the morning. The water had started to flow in the tap but she couldn't get even a jerrycan of it. When

*Originally published in Bangla as 'Jotawali' in the literary magazine *Parichay* edited by Abhra Ghosh (Kolkata, 2016).

she returned to her small room, she saw that the water she had stored in an earthen pot and covered with half a coconut shell had been stolen. A shaft of anger ran through her. Nowadays, the woman with the matted hair got angry quickly. She swore under her breadth: *Kon moron jaat amar paani loiya morshorey! Mor, mor!* The lowly stricken folk who stole my water, you will die thirsty! Die! Die! She was shaking so much with anger that she had to sit down. Some neighbourhood children, some clothed, some stark naked, were shouting: *Jotawali, Jotawali, pagli, pagli!* Look at that madwoman with the matted locks!

'All your families are mad too!' she shouted back. She'd picked up a splinter of wood to throw at the tormenting children, but they ran away and the stick went and hit the mangy dog, the one that had littered behind her room. The pups had been a mixed lot, some brown, some black and white and they were always hungry. Then the Naga boy came and took them away; he relished dog meat. Good in a way. The woman had no means to feed herself; how could she have fed those pups?

The dog whimpered in pain when the splinter hit her. The woman felt a quick pity: when she cooked a bit of rice she would feed the dog. A few yards from her room lay the river: the Barak river. She could have collected some water—there was enough! But the water was murky, opaque. And she was unable to walk down to the river because of the muddy banks. She would have to break the lumps of clay to walk and when she tried to pull her feet up, they sank in further. Earlier she would cross the mud banks easily to reach the river, to wash clothes or to bathe. But during the last floods, while running to reach the school building, she had broken her foot. She had been laid up at the Medical College for two months. From then on, her right foot did not work too well. She limped a bit and she couldn't wear her slippers. She had to walk barefoot, summer or winter. During winter she went down to the river often, treading on the sand. In the cold months sand lay everywhere and the water became clear: like a mountain spring. She had seen a mountain spring once at Patichora where she had gone to visit her sister. Her sister had since then disappeared in the Jotinga river floods. Good in a way. Her husband had gone to Cherrapunji to work in the coalmines; there was no news of him for three or four months. They had a son, who also left to work in Chennai or Bangalore. There was no news of him either. The sister's hut had fallen in the last storm along with a huge mango tree. At last, her sister too had floated away, perhaps to her husband or her son, no one knew where! Gopal, her sister's neighbour, who came to sell vegetables at the market at Sadarghat, had told her all that. The woman had wept for two days. During the Bangladesh war in 1971, they had come over. It was not called Bangladesh then; they knew it to be East Pakistan. Four brothers and two sisters had crossed the border with their paternal uncle and aunt. Their parents, along with two other sisters and a brother had remained behind. They were all ill, so they could not travel. Earlier, the woman would get news of them, but that had soon stopped. She came to know of her father's death two years after he died. An old neighbour had come through the smuggling route and had told her of his death. That man would come often but not anymore. Who knew where the rest of her family was! Only the sister in Patichora had been there for her, but she too was gone.

The woman sat under the *radhachura* tree, legs splayed out in front. She had put down the mound of things she was carrying. The crow flew off. Other birds were cawing loudly and flying about. She could hear them clearly, although people said she was going deaf! She noticed the body of a crow lying further away. Maybe it was dead and all the other birds were crying after it. Humans were so different. A few days ago she had seen a beggar hit by a car: he was groaning in pain, lying on the road, but people just stood around and nobody helped him up. They stood there watching him writhing in pain and moaning loudly. The woman muttered to herself: Death to you all! *Mor! Mor!* Die! Die!

She rummaged through her bundles and found a *biri* and matches. She had a few matchsticks left; it was time to buy a new box. In the slum where she lived, many women smoked in their rooms but she had no such qualms. Why should she be ashamed of anything? When her man had died of dysentery, so many men used her, who came to her room in the dead of night. Even one she had called 'Uncle.' She too had her hunger. But when a young one, young even to be her son, came to her room, she had wept. She was not known as *Jotawali* then, the woman with the matted locks. Her name was Binata: Binata Rani. She had once been attractive, not like the stick that she was now. One day, the other women of the slum had beaten her up and thrown her out of her room along with her things. They shouted: *Bayir ho!* Get out! You lead our men astray, you prostitute! Oh all these pure women! No one who had visited Binata to enjoy her body had ever paid her a rupee, so how could she be a prostitute? That day, Subal's wife and Samir had gathered up her things to bring them back to the room. Her son had disappeared some time ago and people said he had been kidnapped by a *tantric* for human sacrifice. Someone else said that he had seen the boy begging in Guwahati station and he was lame. But she believed that her son would return to her one day. That was why she came to the station every day to watch the trains come and go: in case she caught sight of her boy!

Subal was in his rickshaw, singing and driving along. She could hear a snatch of his song, a song of longing, under a leaden sky:

> *Gurguraiya megh dake,*
> *Gogon hoilo kala*
> *Koi roila pranbondhu re…*

She could hear the thunder roll. It would rain any moment. The cars, autos and rickshaws were rushing around to avoid the impending shower. Their horns blared. She took one last drag on her *biri* and threw it away. Her stomach was growling with hunger. The crows were still milling about the dead bird, cawing loudly. The woman with the matted hair lifted up her earthly possessions onto her head. The thunder growled.

She sat looking at the river. Dusk was long gone. Some people were gathered on the far bank, maybe to cross the river. The sky was filled with stars, along with a bright moon. Maybe there was a meeting with the moon at the centre and all the light blue clouds milling around? She had been told the names of the stars and the clouds that gathered around each other: they seemed to be meeting. That was what the old woman had taught her. Before she had got married, her uncle had got her a job as a maid in Bimalbabu's house. She had worked like a slave, not getting a moment's rest. Like a disc she was perpetually on the move, fetching and carrying and even at night she had no rest. When Bimalbabu came home late, she had to get up to open the door for him. One day she had slept through the knocking and Bimalbabu's wife had beaten her badly. She had left that very night, but her uncle sent her back. What shall we eat if you don't work? And then the expenses of your wedding...they had said.

So Binata Rani had to go back. The only person in that household who was kind to her was the old woman, Bimalbabu's mother. Binata would oil her hair and the old woman would tell her all kinds of stories. She would do puja in a white sari and she often gave Binata things to eat. At night, the old woman would gaze at the sky and teach her the names of the stars: the Milky Way, and the meeting on the moon where all the clouds and stars gathered to have a *sabha*.

The woman with the matted hair looked around her room. The last storm had blown away the roof. Samir had put a tarpaulin sheet in its place. In 1971, she had crossed over to this side with Samir's parents: only his mother had managed to cross; the father had disappeared on the way. The Pakistani Army had killed Samir's grandfather in their village. The woman remembered the soldiers, the tanks, the desperate wailing of the wounded and the dying. When they arrived on the other side, they had taken shelter in a school building. At that time, as the war raged on, Indira Gandhi had become a household name. Samir's sister and his mother died of cholera. She too fell ill, but somehow she had survived. The woman let out a long sigh. Samir had used a few bamboo poles to hold down the tarpaulin, but another strong gust of wind would blow it away. The room was four feet by six; there was hardly any dry space if the water came in. Even her mud oven got wet as did all of her things.

The woman with the matted hair once had a daughter. She had sent the girl to work as a maid in a house at Ambikapatti and would often visit her. One day however the girl's employer said that she had gone with the daughter-in-law to visit her parents. Then the daughter-in-law returned, but her daughter did not. It had taken her three months to find out the address where the daughter-in-law's parents lived; it was in Guwahati. Later she also came to know that the girl had been taken there to look after a disabled son of the family. When she pestered the employer, they said the girl had run away. Someone in her neighbourhood had said that perhaps the girl had been sold to a brothel! Samir had urged her to inform the police or contact some women's organisation, but she did not have the courage to do so. Her son too had gone away and then her husband had died...

Shyam the groom will soon arrive
So hurry and adorn the grove
Stitch it with colours bright
And the joy of your friend...

She heard the wedding songs and remembered that it was the wedding day of a neighbour's son. Women and girls were singing as they went to collect water for the *adhibaash*. No one invited her anymore after her hair grew long and matted, and she too didn't feel like going. Only the hunger in her belly told her she was still alive.

The woman looked up at the sky: a flock of ducks was sailing away. The moon was up, shedding a magic light. Was it a waning moon? She had learnt about waning and waxing moons from Bimalbabu's old mother who would recite verses from *Khona's Bochon*. The women were walking back with filled water pots, singing.

Had gone to fetch water, *sakhi*
Saw a black cuckoo there, my friend...

She had been married once. They were living at the Silkuri camp after they crossed over in 1971. She had bathed in turmeric-scented water and her aunt had carried a bamboo tray filled with betel leaves and sung a wedding song.

> Journey on, o Binodini Rai
> Your destination is Vrindavan
> Carry the tray with betel nuts and camphor
> Your destination is Krishna

She was cold. She wrapped one end of her worn out synthetic sari to try and ward off the cold. In the Silkuri camp, she remembered the dark-skinned young man who had once plucked some lotus for her from the camp pond. She could still smell the fragrance of the flowers. Where was he now, that young man? Would he recognise her now with her long, matted hair? When she sat alone, all kinds of memories assailed her. She had gotten married to a man who played the *khol* in a *kirtan* party. He used to dress up as the goddess Kali during *Charak*. Although she was his second wife, he loved her in his own way.

It looked like rain. The moon had vanished behind the clouds. She went in and fished out a small kerosene lamp. She had hidden it in a small box: otherwise it would have been stolen by now. She had collected some dry sticks to cook. Most days she begged at the vegetable market and people gave her a few things that were a little rotten. That day she had managed a couple of potatoes, an aubergine and a few green chillies. She lit her mud oven and started to cook rice in a small aluminum bowl. She then added the vegetables to the boiling rice. She would eat all of it with a pinch of mustard oil and green chillies: as soon as the thought came to her head her hunger grew sharper. But did she have any oil? No oil and kerosene could be had by begging! She rummaged in a jute bag and took out a small glass bottle. When she held it up to the lamp, she saw a few drops of oil at the bottom. That would be enough. She could still hear the wedding songs.

> Shyam the dark-skinned one
> Will soon arrive
> So hurry and adorn the grove…

Binata Rani had once taken part in so many wedding rituals; her uncle had bought her wedding things: a small tin trunk painted with flowers, a red-sequined sari, a pair of conch bangles, a perfumed soap, a box of vermillion, and a small mirror. The tin trunk was now discoloured and dented, but she carried it around on her head with care. She nurtured those memories deep within her breast. She had saved the sari for many years, but when she had nothing left to wear, she had taken it out. People had laughed at her: *Binata Ranir ishtyle barse*! Look at the stylish Binata Rani, they had mocked. She used to work as a part-time maid in three homes and could make ends meet. But once her hair started to matt she had worn her sari end over her head; but Kanu Ghosh's wife saw it one day and threw her out. So did the others. No one wanted to employ her: it was a sin to make a person with matted locks do menial work as only the gods sported such hair. When she could not tolerate her hunger anymore, she had begun to beg. Samir Das had advised her to sit with a few incense sticks and a candle: people would come to pay obeisance and give her money. But something had stopped the woman from doing that.

She could hear the thunder roll. Earlier she would hang a small lock on the door when she went out begging, but one day someone just broke it open as well as the rickety door. After that things were stolen all the time: vegetables, her bathing mug, a bowl, her clothes, even her stack of firewood. Therefore she now carried all her earthly possessions on her head when she went out. It was not foolproof though. She had been resting with her bundles near her head and had dozed off when someone came and stole the small bundle that had all her savings: five hundred rupees in small change. She had wept and cursed all humanity that day. Die, die! When her hair matted up, people called her *Jotawali*. And when she began to walk around with her bundles and things, they added the word *pagli*, the madwoman. She began to hum under her breadth:

Amar Krishna kuthau pai go sakhi
Kun deshe te jai…

Which country do I go to, my friend
Where do I find my Krishna…

The woman felt cold as she hummed her song. She took out a blanket that she had bought with the money she had received during the last elections. One political party was distributing two hundred rupees each, while another gave three hundred. Everyone voted for the latter. But the woman with the matted hair had not been able to vote. How could she go carrying her entire household on her head? She heard the thunder roll and went up to the empty doorway. She saw the dog sitting there and thought: I will feed you some rice...

She didn't know why she felt like singing and laughing aloud. Ha-ha-ha-ha...he-he... she laughed to herself. That war in '71: they had crossed the border, leaving behind their land. She had watched helplessly as the Pakistani soldiers had abducted Subal's sister and had left her half dead in the rice fields after three days. The girl had been so beautiful, the woman remembered with a pang. So many had died then. So many cried and beat their breasts as they crossed over. She remembered everything.

The woman with the matted locks was dreaming. She could smell incense and see a candle burning. She was sitting with her legs folded as people came to pray to her: all her neighbours, so many famous men and women. As did the police and the politicians; even the man whose security had beaten her when she had stopped to watch his cavalcade pass. The rice that she had cooked with vegetables had turned to ambrosia: everyone was eating it; even her lost children were there in that crowd. Her two brothers who had disappeared while crossing the border were also there. *De...De...* they all cried in unison. Give us some, they implored her. She could see the dark-skinned boy coming towards her, his arms full of lotus flowers. The Barak river ran with a gentle sound: the river that took the name Kushiyara and reached her ancestral village on the other side of the border. The woman with the matted locks stretched out her arms to embrace the ever flowing proud waters.

Translated from the Bangla by **Debjani Sengupta**

17 The Beginning of the End*

RAIHANA HASAN

After the ban on political activities was lifted on 1 January 1970, there were several incidents of public meetings and processions of one political party being disrupted by the followers of a rival party, resulting in injuries and death. Invariably such instances were followed by vociferous demands for strong government action but when action was taken, there was an outcry for the release of the people who had been responsible for the disturbance in the first place.

The tea district was spared the worst of this turmoil except for a spot of labour trouble in Shamshernagar, where that redoubtable disciplinarian, Mukhtar Raja, now presided. With characteristic highhandedness, he called in the police and there was some firing. The *bastee-wallas*, the labour force and babus simmered with resentment but Mukhtar ignored their sullen looks and carried on as usual.

The Fairfaxes were retiring and there was a huge crowd at their farewell party, sentimental speeches reducing Elizabeth to tears and causing Donald Fairfax to respond as though he had a constriction in his throat. Everyone went to see them off at Bhanugach so that the tiny platform was a seething mass of planters and their tearful wives. Donald Fairfax was the last of the old generation and his going was like the closing of a chapter in the history of tea.

To stave off the evil day when we would have to send our children to boarding schools, the wives of the Patrakhola planters

---

*Originally published in *Sips from a Broken Teacup: Sketches from Life on an Assamese Tea Plantation* (Karachi: Ushba Publishing International, 2011). This extract from the novel, pp. 178–191, is reproduced here with the kind permission of the author.

started a small school in the little cottage once occupied by Jamshed. I happily enrolled both my sons, now five and four, and began spending half the day teaching at the school. Soon we were able to invite an 'inspection team' from other plantations to take a look. Its members watched the school in action, stayed on for lunch and tea, and began sending their children all the way from Manu, so that we soon had fourteen students, divided into four classes. The wife of Kabir, the new Bengali assistant, came every day from Madabpore to teach Bengali and the Patrakhola wives handled the other subjects.

The head office informed us that the American Political Attaché in Islamabad and the Vice-Consul General Dhaka would be visiting Patrakhola in mid-July and would be staying with us. ('Why on earth would they visit Patrakhola?' I demanded of Ashhad. 'It's not as though this was a known tourist spot or anything.') They arrived in a gorgeous, all-weather vehicle, all shiny with chrome and bristling with gadgets, bearing a gift of two bottles of whisky. The planters' reputation seemed to have reached the ears of even the foreign diplomatic circles in Islamabad. I could imagine the two of them being briefed by their public relations people, 'They drink like fish there. Better take along some whisky to oil the wheels.' They must have been nonplussed to find their host and hostess cold sober.

They stayed a day and a night but disappeared for most of the day, refusing all offers of a guide or even our company. Where they went and why and what they did when they got there we never found out. They turned up again at twilight and we took them along to a *milad* and dinner at Chatlapore where Asif Khan was now manager. I have no idea what they made of the *milad* but I thought it would do no harm to give them a glimpse of Pakistani culture and they seemed to enjoy the planters' company and their uproarious behaviour at the dinner, guffawing at their jokes and appearing to match them drink for drink. Next morning, they were up at *gunti* time and disappeared again in their car, and when they re-appeared for lunch, looked tired and a little grim. They left soon afterwards.

Their visit was followed by a gaggle of Army generals who came ostensibly for *shikar,* made a tremendous noise, bagged an enviable number of pheasants and drank up the whisky brought by the Americans.

With October came the month of fasting. On 24 October, a noisy but minor cyclone swept across the offshore islands to the mainland, causing some damage to life and property in the southern districts of the province. This was only the prelude. The major event was yet to come.

Over the last hundred years or so, the area that was now East Pakistan had been ravaged by more than forty cyclones of varying intensity. After the devastation wrought by the 1965 cyclone, the government had promised to build embankments and establish a flood control system. A radar station was set up at Cox's Bazaar in the extreme south to spot cyclones and issue warnings, but little was done about flood control and it fell upon the people in the rural areas themselves to make embankments of packed mud, none of them more than twenty feet high, certainly not high enough to withstand the monster that was slowly heading their way from the sea off the Andaman Islands.

On the night of 12 November[1] a fifty-foot wall of water crushed homes, people and animals on the offshore islands and roared towards the coast, irresistibly propelled by a ferocious wind. Exploding on the mainland, wave and wind together wrought a fifty-mile swathe of destruction. When the wave ultimately receded, it swept thousands of people, animals, wrecked homes and vegetation into the Bay of Bengal. Communications, such as they were, were all destroyed and it was two days before the rest of the province discovered the extent of the disaster. The tea district was miles from the catastrophe but even so we had felt the force of the gale shaking our bungalows as we huddled under our blankets.

The final estimates ranged from 300,000 to a million dead, the damage to property and livestock incalculable. The newspapers were full of heart-rending stories of parents watching their babies being swept away, of mothers having to decide which child to hold and which to surrender to the waters, of entire families and whole islands annihilated. The pictures were enough to turn the food to ashes in our mouths: bloated animal corpses; lifeless naked children caught in branches, twisted bodies of men and women spread-eagled over ravaged shores.

The cyclone was a calamity in more ways than one. It destroyed an entire generation on the coast and it exacerbated East Pakistan's anger at the Government's neglect. And in some way, the anger and grief was directed against all those who had links to West Pakistan.

It heralded the beginning of the end.

The general elections had been held and the results, declared at the end of the year, made for a conundrum. Sheikh Mujibur Rahman's Awami League had a clear win in East Pakistan, Zulfikar Ali Bhutto's Pakistan People's Party in the West Wing. The Awami League was the overall winner with almost fifty-two percent of the total votes cast. The verdict was unmistakable, the message uncompromising, the implications catastrophic. A crisis was at hand.

And there was to be yet another disaster to mark the end of that terrible year, 1970. On New Years' Eve, the PIA[2] plane from Dhaka to Shamshernagar crashed on landing. We were to have been on that plane, on our return from vacation in India, but had taken an earlier flight and were safe in Patrakhola when a messenger brought us the news. The planters rushed to the site to help and by the time Ashhad and I arrived on the scene, the corpses had been discreetly removed, but the plane was still smouldering. Blackened, twisted bits of metal and scorched clothing littered the runway. The nauseating smell of burnt flesh mingled with the overpowering stench of burning fuel.

The Sub-Divisional Officer in Sylhet and Colonel Sikandar, the Martial Law Administrator, happened to be present at the airport and together, they pulled out several passengers from the burning aircraft. The planters took charge of the twenty-nine survivors. The young woman in our charge was Mohsin Maqbool's bride of one month. Mohsin, who had replaced Jamshed in PCI's headquarters, had been bringing her to meet the planter community at the Manu New Year's Ball. Mohsin had pushed her out but had perished himself.

We took the survivors to Shamshernagar. Mukhtar Raja and his wife, with the help of his assistants and the Doctor Babu, had turned the *Burra* Bungalow into a makeshift hospital. Here the survivors rested, were given hot drinks and treated for burns and injuries, until a relief plane eventually ferried them back to Dhaka.

Omens

Patrakhola: January to March 25, 1971

> 'If you are cold, tea will warm you; if you are depressed it will cheer you; if you are excited it will calm you.'
>
> —William Gladstone (1809–1898)

The plain white envelope arrived at breakfast time, along with the rest of the *dak*. Assuming it was an invitation card, I left it to the last and went on with rest of the post. Ashhad lit his after-breakfast cigarette and immersed himself in *The Morning News*, as usual delivered a day late.

At length, when I slit open the white envelope, a little yellow booklet fell out. It was a Bengali primer, cheaply and badly printed. I looked in the envelope again and found a note, hand-written in big block letters:

'IF YOU WANT TO LIVE IN THIS COUNTRY,
IT IS HIGH TIME YOU LEARNT THE LANGUAGE.'

There was no signature.

I showed the note and the booklet to Ashhad and together we examined them. There was no clue to the sender's identity. The postmark on the envelope was blurred and told us nothing.

'Strange,' I said. 'Why would anyone go to such trouble?'

Ashhad had gone back to his newspaper. 'Some sort of joke?' he hazarded.

'I don't find it funny,' I said. 'I wonder who's behind it.'

'Couldn't be anyone in Doloi. Almost everyone is talking about the progress you've made in learning the language.'

'I wonder if it's Tony? He's always had this chip on his shoulder about West Pakistanis not bothering to learn Bengali.'

'Could be anyone. There's a lot of post-election hysteria building up. Mujib is making dire predictions about attempts to thwart his coming to power. The hard-core Awami Leaguers must be getting a mite fretful.'

We would have forgotten all about this incident had we not discovered that all the non-Bengalis in the district had received the booklets. This discovery caused misgivings and formed the subject of speculation, but as the days went by, we put it out of our minds. Few of us recognized that this was the first alarm bell that warned of what was in store.

Who could worry about politics when the tea gardens were at their loveliest? That January of '71 was particularly glorious in Patrakhola. The sun-warmed days, all blue and gold, were made to bask in, and the crisp cold that set in at dusk made fire-lit evenings a delight. I surrendered my senses to the loveliness of the season and the delights of Nizam's cooking. I was, at this time, three months pregnant and perpetually hungry.

Breakfast was laid under the shade of the gigantic old bottle brush tree on the front lawn, where the fragile blooms came floating down to spread a filmy overlay of pink and scarlet on the grass. Beyond lay the swimming pool, screened by a trellis covered with bougainvillea, now in full bloom, forming a vivid scarlet backdrop. The garden was a blaze of colour, with row upon row of red canna lilies, mauve and white cosmos, purple antirrhinums and pink and white phlox. The children's school was closed for the holidays and I had plenty of leisure. After Ashhad had left for work, I would read, write or sew, whilst the sun caressed my skin and the hum of bees filled me with contentment. The boys ran wild all day in the grounds and grew sturdy, brown and rosy-cheeked. At eleven, the Ayah brought their milk and I was served an elegant tray of coffee and confections dreamed up by Nizam. The hours until lunch were interspersed with more rounds of snacks: fresh-cut coconut, diced pineapple, ginger biscuits. How I stuffed myself!

Behind our bedroom wing was a sheltered square of ground in which bougainvillea bushes had been allowed to grow unpruned, the stems had intertwined to become like gnarled tree-trunks and their branches had formed a canopy of pink, white and crimson: an arbour just big enough to accommodate a table for four. Here, in the dappled shade, an al fresco lunch would be served, which was one of the highlights of the day, because Ashhad was home, there was time enough to linger over the meal, and the children could play nearby.

The boys and I stayed out-of-doors until the warmth had gone out of the sunlight, when we moved to the drawing room. Here, by the fireplace, we took tea and supper on a trolley. Whenever we were free of social commitments, the evening would be spent reading, playing Scrabble, or just watching our sons tumbling about on the carpet. It was a peaceful, leisurely, gracious time, very like that winter when I first came to tea, except that we now lived on a somewhat grander scale and had the children.

One chilly evening, Ashhad and I sat at our tea in the firelight. He looked preoccupied, so I kept up an inconsequential chatter to distract him. When he spoke, his voice was gruff. 'The telegram came this morning.' He fished an envelope out of his shirt pocket and thrust it at me.

The telegram from Gorakhpur had taken the better part of a week to reach us. Frustration exacerbated grief. Even if the Company sanctioned a few days' leave, we wouldn't get another visa so soon. And then going to India was put entirely out of the bounds of possibility. On 30 January, two young Kashmiri Muslims hijacked an Indian Airlines Fokker aircraft to Lahore, to draw world attention to the plight of Indian-occupied Kashmir. The Pakistani press and the public took the fugitives to heart and had a field day. Zulfikar Ali Bhutto visited Lahore Airport and welcomed the hijackers in a fiery speech. India made protesting noises, the hijackers burned the aircraft to ashes amidst great jubilation and Indira Gandhi retaliated by banning Pakistani aircraft from over-flying India. We wondered whether India had stage-managed the whole hijacking incident to achieve this very objective but few could understand to what purpose.

That was the second alarm bell.

The papers were full of Sheikh Mujibur Rahman's speeches. His Six-Point Formula provided rich material for discussion and argument in Readers' Columns and radio programmes. The newspaper headlines one day would scream: 'Constitution Based on 6-Points will be Framed!' and on the next: 'Awami League Alone Competent to Form Central Government.' On and on raged the arguments in the press, for and against, whilst the planters' lives ran along the familiar groove of their winter routine: clearing wooded slopes for fresh planting, tidying old sections; caring for the *charabaris*; all the myriad preparations for the busy time come spring. Sleek and shiny, the tea bushes lay dormant, resting after their feverish growth during the monsoons. In the *charabaris*, the round green seeds fattened and grew hard. The plantation was once again as dry as a bone and fire drills were practised regularly to guard against conflagrations.

Preparations were also afoot in the country for the transfer of power to the newly elected leaders. The President visited Dhaka and described Mujibur Rahman as the future Prime Minister. Excitement at the implications of this statement had reached fever pitch. Drawing rooms, campuses, and market places buzzed with debate and argument. Even the normally apolitical planters were drawn into the discussions and the conversation now turned from the cussedness of the *teela* babu to speculations on this development.

At dusk, a small group sat in the shelter of the club porch. The men were cooling off after their games and glasses of *meethapani* and cups of tea were being handed round. Saeed, the lone Sindhi planter and an avid Bhutto supporter, was despondent. So was Tariq Bajwa, the genial Punjabi artist.

'Life won't be worth living, *yaar*,' Tariq muttered morosely. 'Imagine being ruled by that *goonda*.'

'The Bingos will over-run every nook and cranny,' grumbled Saeed. 'The whole country will become one vast Dhaka or

Chittagong; the smell of *maachh* everywhere and *Bangla bhasha* coming out of our ears.'

The prospect increased Tariq's gloom. 'This isn't what we voted for! Why should we put up with it?'

'Democracy, my friend, democracy,' Ashhad put in mildly.

A silence fell as Aziz came up to join the circle, but the conversation was far from over. Aziz was full of the same topic. 'Yahya has proved to be an honest man, after all,' he exulted as he flung himself into a chair and wiped the sweat off the back of his neck with his towel. 'Mujib the next Prime Minister! You wait and see, *Bhabhi*,' he added, turning to me, 'the quality of life under Mujib will improve beyond all recognition.'

'For whom?' asked Tariq acidly.

'The Bengalis, naturally!' Saeed ejaculated, with a whoop of uncontrollable laughter.

Aziz bristled. 'And why not? Haven't they been exploited long enough? How long d'you think a minority should be permitted to keep the majority downtrodden?'

As this argument was a frequent factor in Mujib's speeches, Aziz's audience grew restive and he changed tack. 'And not only the Bengalis,' he continued, 'Also the Sindhis, the Baluchis, the Pathans, the Mohajirs. Didn't you read the statement the *Banga Bondhu*[3] made in Dhaka? "There is no difference between the suffering humanity of Bengal and of other provinces." Equal opportunities for all...'

Saeed was grinning wickedly. 'But surely more equal for some, eh Aziz my old *roshogullah*?'

'And what d'you mean by that?' Aziz asked, frowning.

'Oh come now, my dear *Banga Bondhu*,' retorted Saeed, 'Who's going to get the plum jobs? People like me? Don't tell me! It's going to be Bengalis, Bengalis and Bengalis. Isn't that what makes Mujib's power so attractive?'

'Ah,' said Aziz. 'Now that the boot is on the other leg, it pinches does it? Makes your *meethapani* turn to piss in your mouth? Why shouldn't Bengalis prosper?'

'Surely not at the cost of others.' The new voice was mild. It belonged to Ghulam, one of the newer Bengali assistants, who had been attracted to the discussion and had joined the circle. 'The trend of domination by one race must end. Let it not be said that Bengali rule only perpetuated the evils of the past.'

Ashhad put a stop to the argument. 'It's getting on,' he said, glancing at his watch. 'Time to go home and dress for the evening.'

'That got a little unpleasant,' I remarked as we drove home.

'It's likely to get worse by the time we're done with the transfer of power,' Ashhad said gloomily. 'Passionate people, these Bengalis; they get all worked up.'

That was the third alarm bell.

But who was listening?

Notes

1. The 1970 Bhola cyclone was a devastating tropical cyclone that struck East Pakistan and the Indian state of West Bengal. It remains the deadliest tropical cyclone ever recorded and one of the deadliest natural disasters.

2. Pakistan International Airlines.

3. 'Friend of Bengal,' a popular moniker and title given to Sheikh Mujibur Rahman by his followers.

18 Breaking Links*

RAZIA FASIH AHMAD

Zari and Shams work in the tourism department in West Pakistan. Shams is from East Pakistan, Zari is from West.

Shams tells the grievances of the people of East Pakistan

Zari came from the kitchen and said in her sweet voice, 'Khushal, don't get so upset. Why don't you discuss something with Shams? He'll be more than happy to tell you the grievances of the people of East Pakistan.'

Shams said, 'We think that people from West Pakistan do not try to understand our culture and our customs. Instead, you people ridicule us because we lead simple lives. We were, and still are, far advanced in education. People have now started saying that just as India has not willingly accepted the existence of Pakistan, the West Pakistanis haven't accepted the majority of Bengalis in Pakistan. Why didn't they declare Bangla as the second national language along with Urdu? Other provinces have their names, for example, Punjab, Sind, Frontier, and Baluchistan. Our province has no name, and if we try to give it a name, they interpret it as if we are creating a separate state. I know there is as much poverty here as in the East wing. When visitors come to West Pakistan, they are given tours of the neat and clean suburbs of Karachi and Islamabad, and

---

*These extracts, divided by sub-headings, have been selected by the author from her Urdu novel *Sadiyon ki Zanjeer* (1986), translated into English by Razia Fasih Ahmad herself as *Breaking Links* (Pakistan: Oxford University Press, 2007). They have been published here with edits with her kind permission.

of the big factories in Lahore and Faisalabad. They get the wrong impression: that West Pakistan is rich and prospering, while East Pakistan is getting poorer.'

'Why do you consider the expansion of Dhaka as your right, and the construction of Islamabad as an injustice to you?' Khushal asked.

'Most people think that we don't need a new capital and that Islamabad is being built with earnings from our jute. They also think that our floods and cyclones are not your problem, or a concern to immigrants, because they don't live in the coastal regions which are hit by cyclones.'

'Do you think that the Bangla Nationalist Movement is going to be a real danger?' Khushal asked.

'If certain things are not taken care of, yes,' said Shams.

Zari sincerely wanted to start a new life

'Do you think, Shams, they will accept me as one of their own?' Zari asked doubtfully.

'Certainly, they will. You have a husband from East Pakistan, came to his part of the world and speak his language. What else would they want?'

'Shamshu!' Zari said coaxingly, 'would any of your relations come to receive us at the Dhaka airport?'

'My half-brother Ronjhu might come. He studies at the Dhaka University.'

Zari parted the window curtains. She saw the moon shining down below like a gold disk. She did not hear the last part of Shams's sentence, and wonderingly lifted her head to look up—there was a moon there, too!

She was amazed. 'Why do I see two moons?' she almost screamed.'Am I seeing double?'

Shams laughed. 'No, because this is Bangladesh: the magical region, the land of ponds and rivers! What you first saw was not the moon but its reflection in the water.'

'How beautiful!' Zari said. 'It is just as shiny and real as the one in the sky.'

At the airport, a small boy handed Shams a note. Zari could only see that it was in Bangla script.

Shams said to Zari, 'Please wait here. I will be back in a minute.'

A boy in his twenties advanced towards him and said, 'Shams-ul Bhai, *As-salaam-Alaikum*!

'You're a grown man now, Ronjhu,' Shams said pleasantly in Bangla. He felt proud to be able to speak perfect Bangla after so many years.

'A person grows with time, doesn't he?' said Ronjhu, his white teeth flashing. The mysterious lustre in his eyes proudly intensified. 'Come, let's have tea.'

'Your sister-in-law is waiting for us downstairs,' Shams said.

'Oh!' the piquancy of his tone suddenly vanished, 'So now she is my sister-in-law?' said Ronjhu. 'I am sorry but I cannot welcome her. You don't know…many things have changed here recently. Let me give you a hint,' he added with sarcasm, 'Working in the department of the National Integration Council is no longer a matter of pride; it is a disgrace!'

'Why?'

'The very concept of national integration is history. I know you've been kept in the dark about many things.'

'Whatever the situation, I want to make it clear: if you do not want to have any relationship with your sister-in-law, you will have none with me.'

'As you wish. Goodbye then,' said Ronjhu, and left.

National Day in East Pakistan

Under the leadership of Noor Alam Siddique, they were celebrating National Day in East Pakistan on March 3, and had a large public meeting at the Paltan Maidan.

They sang the national anthem of Bangladesh for the first time. Everybody present repeated the words of the anthem: *My golden land, I love you.*

The public got a view of the national flag of Bangladesh, a purple sun above the green earth, with the map of Bangladesh in between.

Sheikh Mujib declared, 'As long as power is not transferred to the people's representatives, no taxes will be paid.' The newspapers gave front-page coverage to Sheikh Mujib's instructions. 'I hereby order that all government, as well as non-government institutions, will work from 2:30 to 4:30 pm to facilitate disbursement of salaries during the strike hours. The banks shall function during these hours. All transactions will be done through the two banks of East Bengal. We will not let a paisa go to West Pakistan. The letters and telegrams to foreign countries shall be sent via Manila and London.'

Between November 1968 and November 1971, much water had flown down the rivers Indus, the old Ganges, the Ravi, and the Thames. Uprooted from their homes, many people fled to West Pakistan or England, leaving behind all their money, property and belongings.

The night of 25th March

The Pakistan Army stationed at the library was shelling the students' hostels in Dhaka University. Iqbal Hall and Jagannath Hall were falling apart. The rusted water pipe dislodged from the wall, water from the overhead tank gushed forth to the ground. Some of the boys living on the second floor ran towards the stairs. Others chose to swing down to the ground from the branches of trees outside their rooms. People ran helter-skelter into the dark. Dense clouds of smoke rose from every direction and blackened the moonlit night. The lucky ones were able to run into the nearby fields and find shelter. Those whom death caught lay on their beds, on the floor, on the thresholds, across windows and on the smouldering verandahs.

Some of them might have launched an unsuccessful counter-attack. A message received at the Martial Law Headquarters said, 'We are facing stiff resistance.' Two hours later, the army gained total control of the area.

After that, the army targeted East Pakistan rifles in the Peel Khana and the police headquarters in Roger Bagh. In the office of *The People*, copies of the daily's 23 March issue, with the Bangladesh map spread across several columns with the caption: 'The martyrs' blood has given birth to a new flag today' were now burning incessantly.

In the end, the Pakistan government made an announcement: Everything is normal in East Pakistan. The people who went to India have come back, and schools, colleges, offices, banks, and factories were all functioning normally as of old.

Despair

Coming home from the hospital, Zari was thinking that this was the most turbulent time for her child to be born. The doctor had told her she should expect her baby any day.

As she entered her living room, she saw a framed picture hanging on the wall, a young man, with long hair and an overgrown beard. He had dark glasses over his eyes and a scarf around his neck. He looked like a runaway convict trying to hide his real identity.

Zari had never seen this man before. 'Who is this?' she asked Shams.

'Oh, he is my brother, Ronjhu.'

Zari looked at the photograph again. 'Where did you get this picture?'

'He sent it to me.'

'You told me that if he didn't accept me as your wife, you wouldn't have anything to do with him. Then why did he send you this picture?'

'What's the harm?' After all, he is my brother.'

'Shams, don't talk to me like that.'

'Please don't ask me embarrassing questions. Ronjhu wants to save us because this time, people from the Mukti Bahini are doing a house-to-house search looking for weapons and people against Bangladesh. Ronjhu's name is a guarantee for our safety. You better be prepared to declare this man your husband's brother and that you are proud of him.'

'I don't understand.'

'Because you don't know what is really happening. You insist on listening only to Radio Pakistan and live under an illusion.'

'Why don't you tell me the truth?'

'If you have the courage to hear the truth, I can tell you.'

'Tell me.'

'The Pakistan Army is losing the war. Each passing moment is bringing them closer to doom. The Indian Army is advancing with a three-pronged attack on Dhaka. There are only fifteen hundred soldiers in this city, and they cannot defend the city.'

'No...!' Zari put a hand over her mouth, trying to suppress her scream. She wanted to cry on Shams' shoulder, but she kept looking at him without blinking, as if asking: Why are you saying all this so calmly? What happened to your claims of integration? You too have changed, Shams. She turned her face away.

Shams felt extremely sorry for Zari. He should have prepared her earlier for this calamity. It was already hard for her to move about and do the household chores. What a great shock he had given her in this condition!

He went closer to her. 'Don't get upset, my love,' he whispered. 'We cannot control what's happening, but you and I will always be together... Always.' He gently removed her hands from her face.

Zari looked up at him. 'Shams, I can see it in your face: you look victorious... And now I am truly disillusioned.'

'That's not true, Zari. Let's hope for the best.'

He went towards the door.

'Are you going out?' Zari asked.

'Yes.'

'Where?'

Shams was silent for a moment, then said, 'I'll tell you when I come back. In the meantime, you can chat with your uncle.' With these words he quickly left, closing the door behind him.

Zari started crying. 'Tell me, Chachaji, what is happening? Who is telling the truth? The newspapers and radio tell you one thing, and the people here say another.'

Omar approached her and put his hand on her shoulder. 'Conditions aren't good, my dear. Hope is giving way to despair.'

'But how did it happen?' Zari asked.

'The Pakistan government was hiding things from the public,' Omar said. 'They were hoping that conditions might change. Not only the public, but the soldiers, intellectuals, politicians and military officers, even the commander of the Eastern Command was in the dark. They were hoping that help was about to arrive from friends, meaning China and the United States. When that hope too was gone, they kept it a secret to gain more time for the representatives of Pakistan to seek a ceasefire mandate from the United Nations.'

The Indian attack

On 14 December 1971, there was a sudden blast. The Indian Air Force attacked the Government House in Dhaka and hit the left portion of the building. The Governor, along with his ministers and secretaries, ran out towards the trenches. The debris of the roof fell over the big fish tank and the flower vase, smashing them to pieces. The fish, the flowers and the little buds fell all over the debris.

The Secretary to the Governor, covered with dust and smoke, ran about looking for the Governor. His shoes crushed the beautiful buds and the writhing goldfish as he walked over them. Seeing the others rush out, the Secretary also ran towards the Governor's bunker.

There was another air raid and everyone ran out towards the shelters. The entire building emptied out in minutes. Only the telephones kept ringing ceaselessly in some of the offices, like the cries of anguished hearts which no one heard.

'Should I move my family to the Intercontinental Hotel today or tomorrow?' the Governor asked the United Nations' representative, John Kelly.

Gavin Young, correspondent of the *Sunday Observer*, London, leaned forward to listen to their conversation.

'Right now, sir...!' said John Kelly, as another air attack cut him mid-sentence. Another heap of mortar and dust fell from the Governor House.

The Governor took out a piece of paper from his briefcase and a pen from his pocket. He wrote his resignation and of his council of ministers. He handed them to Mr. Kelly to send to the President of Pakistan. Then he went to the adjoining bathroom of the bunker, performed his ablutions, covered his head with a handkerchief and stood silently in a corner of the bunker to offer his prayers.

Gavin Young looked out through the door of the bunker. After the third attack, the debris of the Governor House was still slowly falling to the ground. The trenches were crowded with civilians who worked in Governor House. Those who could not find a place in the trenches had found shelter under the trees. Between two attacks, some had courageously come out of the trenches. They ran to a declared neutral zone, the Intercontinental Hotel. Almost all the foreign correspondents were staying at this hotel.

Towards evening, when the air raids stopped, all those who had held high positions in the Governor House, made the most important decisions, gathered at the Intercontinental Hotel, looking depressed, crestfallen and wretched. They entered the hotel building sluggishly, with heads bowed like somnambulists. The cameras clicked as usual. Those people were used to posing for the cameras; but this time, coated with soot and dust, their hair disheveled, the fear of death writ large on their faces, this exposure was a torment. They did not move from the range of the cameras only because they did not have the energy left to do so.

After the Fall of Dhaka

Zari was in Hotel Intercontinental. The explosions of the aerial attacks interrupted her restless sleep. Once, during a short interval between bouts of sleep, Zari heard John telling the doctor, 'General Manekshaw has given his last ultimatum. The grace time for surrender is from five this evening to nine tomorrow morning. There won't be any bombardment from their side during this period, and if they do not surrender thereafter, he has threatened to destroy all the cantonments and military camps of the Pakistan Army.'

Zari found it hard to discern if she had really heard those words or they were part of her hallucinations.

In the morning, at first she heard an air raid siren. Then the telephone started ringing.

Without telling his name, someone said to her, 'The Pakistan Army is going to surrender today. Come to the Jasmine Room. All the guests will be given instructions about staying at the hotel.'

'To hell with you!' Zari wanted to say. But she knew it was not right to be mad at her caller.

'The doctor has advised me to take complete rest,' Zari said. 'I'd be obliged if you could give me instructions on telephone.'

'Okay. I'll be brief,' the caller said. 'This hotel will continue to be a neutral zone, but no one will be granted political asylum. Everyone will have to leave either as a prisoner of the Indian government or under custody of the Bangladeshi government. The mob may target this hotel. Please don't go out of the hotel at any time. You will be safer inside the building. You can get a form from the Red Cross office in the hotel to inform your family about your welfare.'

Zari remained in her room. When she came to know that the lecture in the Jasmine Room was over, she went down to meet John Kelly. Fortunately, she found him alone in one of the offices.

'If you can't protect those who have sought refuge here,' Zari said, 'and you are going to hand them over as prisoners to one party or another, I wouldn't like to stay on here. I'll try to save myself. I don't want to be arrested as long as possible.'

'I will advise you to stay,' he said. 'Local people and the Mukti Bahini are after non-Bengalis. It might be dangerous, very dangerous to go and live outside anywhere. There are lots of people like you here.'

'Why should I be arrested?'

'Try to understand. It will be very hard for you to live in a filthy refugee camp, and there is also a grave risk there.'

'Mr. Kelly, either promise to get me out safely from here or just leave me alone.'

'Try to understand my position. How can I take anyone out from the hotel? It's just impossible!'

'I don't think I can expect help from helpless people! Anyway, thanks for your advice.'

'Listen, my dear, you are still weak. I assure you this hotel is the safest place. I beg you to return to your room and take rest. I'm very busy. The draft of surrender might be prepared in this hotel, and I wish to be there to ensure that nobody's rights are violated.'

'Okay. I'll go to my room.'

'So far, there's news of General Arora, Air Marshall Diwan, and Vice-Admiral Krishnan coming for the surrender,' she heard somebody say.

Zari went to her room directly. She could see the crowd gathering around the Dhaka Radio Station and could hear them shouting '*Joi Bangla!*' with great euphoria. It was from this radio station that she had broadcast talks of national integration.

Removing the Pakistani flag from the building, one Bangladeshi supporter had torn it to pieces. Holding the shreds between thumb and finger, he set fire to it and scattered the ashes in the air. Within minutes Zari saw a Bangladeshi flag hoisted in its place.

Have all these people been hypnotised, she wondered. How can plain and simple men, who once led humble and innocent lives, kill their companions and neighbours and rape their daughters? How can people see their husbands and wives, with whom they had shared their beds, slaughtered before their very eyes? They have certainly been brainwashed, she decided.

The Maulana

The Maulana from East Pakistan had never seen such cruelties as those that now singed and scorched his soul. People told him, '*Dada*, my wife's stomach was ripped open, in the eighth month of her pregnancy. Calling the baby a serpent, they killed him first and then also the innocent mother,' one person told him.

Another said, '*Chacha*, 23,000 residents, the entire population of Shantahar, was eliminated. Those who ran to seek shelter at the railway station and hid themselves there didn't get drinking water for weeks.'

Yet another said, 'I know for certain that in Sylhet the man who drives non-Bengalis to the slaughterhouse gets a reward of hundred rupees.' Yet another wailed, 'Maulana, by God, my grandsons were butchered piece by piece before my eyes and flags and maps of Bangladesh were engraved on their bodies with bayonets.'

Mass murders, mass rapes, and mass graves—how could they be validated? The inner voices in the Maulana's heart made his life unbearable.

The angry young Bengalis were threatening the Maulana, 'You are a Bengali. Why do you take their side? They are informers. They are our enemies.'

Some called him an agent of the Pakistan Army. One man from the crowd ran to kill him but another, who knew the Maulana, stopped the man, saying, 'He is an old man. Leave him alone. How many women and children can he save after all?'

Zari and Ronjhu

Switching on his bed-lamp, Shams was trying to read the newspaper, which was once called the '*Pakistan Observer*,' then became '*The Observer*' on 18 December 1971, and finally changed its name to '*Bangladesh Observer*' from 23 December 1971.

Zari was not there beside Shams, but all her things were in their place. Shams was deeply sad and lonelier than he had ever been before.

The doorbell rang, and Shams found Ronjhu at the door.

Ronjhu confessed that he had arranged to send Zari out of Bangladesh. He said, 'I did it because your life and hers were in danger. I told Zari your husband no longer wants to live with you.'

'I don't think your intentions were so honourable. You just did not want her here,' Shams said sarcastically.

'We have to make sacrifices for our freedom, brother. This is what happens in a revolution. People die and get separated.'

'I'll never forgive you for what you have done to me.'

'I saved your life,' Ronjhu said angrily. He handed Shams an envelope, saying, 'This is from your wife…Goodbye.' And he walked out of the room, banging the door shut.

Shams opened the envelope and started reading. It was neither a letter nor a message. Perhaps a questionnaire from all women to all men of all times:

> *What do you men want from us women? At times, you want us to be like water that takes the shape of the vessel. At times, you wish us to turn into steel, but at the same time be soft like silk, to be squeezed in your hand. You want us to say 'yes' to your demands, be a slave to your commands, change with you when you change your ideology, live at your pleasure, and die at your mercy.*

Shams read the letter many times over with tears in his eyes. He could imagine how disappointed Zari must be in him. Their son died the day of the Indian attack. Shams was not at the hospital that day.

I want to live with her—always. She does not know how torn and wretched I feel without her. Whatever the cost, I am going to get her back.

19 Noor*

SORAYYA KHAN

If Nanijaan hadn't already suspected that Noor was listening to her conversations with Sajida, she would certainly have believed just this when she came across Noor's painting. At first, Nanijaan's attention was absorbed by Ali's handwriting, a neat, exaggerated slant distinct from anyone else's in the family. She was intent on memorizing the spelling of the river so that she might look it up in an atlas to discover where in Bengal a river like that might be. But when she studied the image, the river divided by a rough pencil mark, pink and gray on either side, and the black, wet banks of the river, she heard Sajida's description, hands tied together, as if Sajida were standing right next to her.

In the drawing room, supervising the servant retrieve the old atlas from one of the highest shelves of the bookcase, Nanijaan couldn't remember the last time she'd used the book. Peering through her reading glasses, using a magnifying glass to help decipher the tiny print, she found the river. It was nothing but a thin scribble in the pale green of the map.

It was strange, after so many years, to come across a detail of Ali's war. For a long time after Ali came home, the only reminder of the war was in Lahore which Nanijaan visited once or twice. There, she recalled, she saw a large red and white banner hung taut across Mall Road. In bold white print, the banner read BRING OUR POWS HOME. The first time she saw the banner, she told

---

*Excerpted, by permission of the author and publishers, from the novel *Noor* by Sorayya Khan (USA: University of North Carolina Wilmington, 2006).

her friend sitting next to her in a taxi that had Ali been a POW, she would have died. When two and a half years passed before the POWs came home, Nanijaan thought she'd been right. Parents were not meant to endure certain things, among them a child's death or a child languishing in prison a thousand miles away.

As if she were putting many years behind her, Nanijaan closed the heavy atlas in her hands with a thud. It came to her. Indeed, she had questions. They could not be answered by books, intricate maps or anything else she might read. Something entirely different was demanded. She would have to stand in front of her youngest son, her favourite of all, and find the words. What did Ali do in East Pakistan? What did he see? What did this boy find so far away?

She'd seen a river like that once. On the drive to Peshawar, stopping at the astonishing juncture where the Indus and Kabul rivers meet, observing the unlikely blue of one river combine with the silty gray of the other, two distinct streams converged. For all the clarity, it was impossible to pinpoint exactly where the two streams became one murky river.

Later that night, neither able to sleep, Nanijaan and Ali stumbled into each other in the storeroom in their independent search for sugar to replenish the kitchen supply. Recalling his once sturdy frame and observing the one made more fragile with time and the dim light in the pantry, Nanijaan met Ali's gaze. At that moment, with Sajida's details still ringing in her ears, she was overwhelmed with urgency. She took a step closer to Ali and it tumbled out.

'You killed someone?'

She said it directly. She didn't falter. It came out right the first time, without pauses or stammers or anything that might have cushioned it. Ali liked it that way. Big and whole, in the open, so he could very nearly touch it. And it wasn't, as Ali had feared all along, Sajida who asked the question.

'What did you think I was doing?' he asked, his hands in the air waving the empty sugar bowl.

'Who?'

'Who?' Ali answered incredulously. 'Is that what you think war is? Excuse me, before I shoot you, what's your name? So I can tell my mother when she asks?'

'You killed someone and don't know who?'

'No. I didn't kill some one.'

'More than one?'

'You need a number? More than one and less than a hundred? What did you bloody think I was going to do when I told you I was going there? Did you think it would be a party?' Ali hadn't known he could speak to his mother this way. But her questions emboldened him and he fell into the unfamiliar tone as if he were accustomed to this form of disrespect.

'You knew what you would do?'

'I didn't. But you did. You said war was an animal gone mad.'

'That's what I said? I was right?'

'You're the one who let me go. Maybe you're the one who should stand trial.'

'No one is on trial here, Ali. I just want to know.'

'But, why? You've never wanted to know anything else. About Sajida, for example.'

'That's not true! I asked you where she came from...'

'You asked me once.'

'Listen,' Nanijaan said, mustering up her strength, speaking deliberately and emphatically. 'Your deeds are yours. I did my part. I taught you the best I could. What you have done is yours to bear. When you stand in front of God...'

'God does not divine what I have seen.'

'And what have you seen? Yourself killing? Beating? What else, Ali?'

'War is war, after all,'

'Why did you do it?'

'We're not so different. I was running for my life. Just like you.'

'What?'

'You killed papa. What did you say to him that day when he fell over and died?'

The question shocked Nanijaan. Her hands trembled and her legs felt as if they would give from under her. She took a few steps outside the storeroom into the kitchen and sat on a lone chair.

'But I didn't say anything to him,' she answered quietly. 'He spoke to me!'

'What did he say?'

'He wished I were dead.'

'And then he died? This was his exclamation point? You expect me to believe that? And you were glad...'

'I was glad that he couldn't beat me anymore,' Nanijaan said, touching her face where Ali's father had once punched her before slamming her against the display cabinet, knocking knick-knacks from their places.

'I didn't do anything to them that they didn't do to us first,' Ali offered.

'They didn't kill you,' Nanijaan said, raising her voice. 'You're standing right here.'

'That was luck. They meant to.'

'There is no such thing as luck in war.'

'That's all there is!'

'By God's grace, you survived.'

'God was nowhere to be found, Mamma.' When Ali said this, he remembered with certainty that he'd called his mother Mamma before Nanijaan became her name.

'Don't pretend to be so high and mighty. You are common, like the rest of us. God sees you as He does everyone else.'

'We were fighting for our lives. Not for you. Or this country. For ourselves. We were out there in the fucking swamps, fighting stingers, Indians and Bengalis alike; it was just that we couldn't see them...'

Nanijaan stood. She walked through the swinging door into the dining room and Ali followed her. Stopping, she turned to him and asked, 'How could it be that you could kill someone and not see them?'

Ali thought of saying. That's why we could, you see? But he knew better than to give his mother any answer at all, much less to lie. Some he hadn't seen, others he had.

'I didn't mean to,' he said, instead, nodding. And this was the closest Ali came to offering his mother an explanation for what he'd done.

'To see or to kill?' Nanijaan angrily retorted before she reached for a *tasbee*, one of the sandalwood prayer beads strung in a necklace and stored in a deep bowl on the fake fireplace mantel, and left the room.

She'd asked to set the record straight. In her own mind. He was her son; she had a right to know. It had taken years, how many had it been?, to realize she'd lacked the courage to ask earlier. All these years, she'd spent being grateful for Ali's life. She was still grateful. But when she and Sajida spoke, sharing what they thought they knew, an urgency set in. Until then, she hadn't wanted to know, and still didn't want to know, because she'd been afraid of the answer. It was as simple as that. But in a strange way, she reasoned, she deserved credit for this. At least she had known enough to be afraid. She hadn't asked earlier, she suddenly thought, because it would have been like asking him when he'd been a child, who finished the last cookie in the cookie tin?, knowing full well it was he. What was the point? Nanijaan caught herself. She wasn't as big a person as she'd hoped.

How many years did she have left, anyway? Life was running out, as it always did once you pass a certain age, and she'd passed that age a long time ago. She felt a new responsibility to have answers, and when she was ready, to take them with her when she went. So she'd be equipped in case she was asked, so she could pray for him if it was required, so she could be his closure, if that's what he needed. She could no longer tie his shoe for him, but this she could surely do for him.

Out of all her boys, Ali was the one who'd stayed home. Or, rather, had come back home. Lived his life, with his child, with her. After their conversation, though Nanijaan would think of him differently: out of reach. He was no longer her youngest son, he was Ali. She looked at him when they sat at the table together, when she poured him his tea, and when she instructed the *dhobi* to stop starching Ali's shirt collars so sloppily, and thought: This is Ali, he fought in a war, and he killed someone. It was in moments like those, rather than in the conversation they'd had or the long months he'd been in East Pakistan, that Ali was separated from her. Her other sons, oceans, land, great distances between them, it was understandable. But this boy, in one night, with words—she hadn't seen it herself—flung himself further from her than any airplane could take her.

Her head spun with questions, but she would not ask any of them. What does it feel like, to kill someone? Where do you put that knowledge during the day? At night? Ah, sometimes, when it rains, you still can't sleep for remembering! What does it feel like, to know you are the reason for someone else's grief? You've thought of that, right? The mother? The father? The child, one, two, three, perhaps, left behind?

The next day, entering the bedroom with freshly ironed clothes while Noor emerged from the bathroom partly undressed, her bra strap falling from her shoulder, her black hair as yet uncombed covering her growing breasts, Nanijaan was almost delirious with fear. Killing is what you did, right? She imagined saying to him. Nothing else?

Nanijaan tormented herself with these questions and more. The noise overtook her head like a train rushing through a village. The rumbling became the backdrop of her days. She loved and laughed and played despite it, but it was only when she slept that the rumblings did too. Quietly, in a momentary pause, she rested and rested some more.

POETRY

Alokeranjan Dasgupta
Naushad Noori
Moushumi Bhowmik
Faiz Ahmad Faiz
Jharna Rahman
Afzal Ahmad Syed
Minar Monsur
Zehra Nigah
Bimal Guha
Naseer Turabi
Jan Nisar Akhtar

Overleaf photograph: Moyna Mazumdar

20 Beyond Question*

ALOKERANJAN DASGUPTA

Calling out to this one or that, I still raise
Needless queries.
They continue to stare at me,
Gently indifferent.
Though, before departing,
They draw on my forehead
A victory sign of sympathy.

I realise that they have not
Rejected me totally. That is why
I question someone else perhaps,
'Is this day February 21st too?'

When he does not give any answer
I direct the question to someone else,
'Has the full moon of winter
Appeared in spring?'

He raises his eyebrows
On hearing my appealing enquiry,
At times addressed to the sky,
At times addressed to a sown love,
'Is this day February 21st too?'

Translated from the Bangla by **Subhoranjan Dasgupta**

---

*Originally published in Bangla as 'Proshnateet' in *Nowalkishore Eseche Buker Toley* (Bangladesh: Yukta Publishers, 2013).

21 Mohenjodaro*

NAUSHAD NOORI[1]

It could have been a storm
Or a river
Or a vanquisher
Or a plunderer
That buried an entire civilisation
Under a mound of dirt
Languages and dialects
Under a mound of dirt
Today, the historians call it
The Mound of the Dead

Perhaps an epidemic broke out
Or a calamity fell upon it

O people of my city
Hold on to your *Geeta* and *Puthi*[2]
Your folk tales and fables
Your songs and ballads
Your letters of the alphabet
Your languages and dialects
Inscribe them on copper and iron
And on leaves, stones, skin and papyrus
That same epidemic has broken out again
That same calamity has befallen

Translated from the Urdu by **Rakhshanda Jalil**

---

*Originally published in Urdu as 'Mohenjodaro' in *Afkaar* (Reflections) from Karachi. It is translated for this volume with kind permission of Naushad Noori's son, Mohammad Haikal Hashmi.

Notes

1. Naushad Noori was one of the most remarkable Urdu poets from Bangladesh who was also an ardent supporter of the Bangla language movement and the creation of a new country based on linguistic and cultural affinity rather than religion and jingoistic hyper-nationalism. Written in 1952, this poem seems so prescient, pointing towards the portents of disaster waiting to unfurl.

2. The earliest forms of literature in medieval times in Bangla were found in *puthi* or palm leaf manuscripts, beautifully decorated and bound by two wooden slats. The *Mangal Kavya*s that may be taken as the most ancient form of modern Bangla were found in such form. The *puthi* would also refer to other religious texts and many early examples of Buddhist narratives also used the same way of transmission. The Asiatic Society in Kolkata has a wonderful collection of *puthi*.

22 Joshor Road*

MOUSHUMI BHOWMIK

I

Hundreds of eyes watch the sky
Hundreds and hundreds of people wait –
The pavements of Joshor Road are lined
With bamboo shelters, mud and filthy water.

And tainted with that filth stand crowds,
Crammed together, watching the sky;
Where hangs the throne of a dead god:
Tell me now, who will answer their prayers?

They are homeless; sleep eludes them,
Since war ripped open their land,
In their heads fly bomber squadrons
O when will this black night end?

Unnumbered faces tell '71's sadness.
The story uncoils along Joshor Road.
So many dead faces; on feet close to death,
East Bengal trudges towards Kolkata.

II

History follows the highway of time
And the people march on Joshor Road
September, sorrow of '71,
Oxcarts and mud, and slippery roads.

---

* A song originally written in Bangla, this English translation was first published under the same title in the booklet accompanying the album *Weaver of Words/Ekhono Golpo Lekho* by Tareque Masud, Catherine Masud and Moushumi Bhowmik (Dhaka, 1999). It is reproduced here by kind permission of Moushumi Bhowmik.

Myriads of people die begging for food
Myriads are washed away by woe,
Floating and rootless, so many wander
Countless mothers are close to despair.

In the refugee shelters the famished children
Have bellies swelling with emptiness,
Such small children, with huge, hungry eyes,
Who can the friendless mother turn to?

September, sorrow of '71
Filled with a slow procession of faces.
War comes, and death, but dreams still live,
Of golden fields, and bliss left behind.

III

To whom can I tell the woes of starvation?
To whom say, 'O help us, help us live'?
To whom cry out, 'Make death desist
And give back what it stole from life'?

You are close to tears, O people,
Your wounds almost obscure your skin.
On mother's laps sit starving babies –
What kind of Life in Death is this?

You are small, O multitudes,
Living in the great shadow of death.
The bullets shredded all you had,
Leaving you diminished, with fugitive dreams.

September, sorrow of '71
Homes broken like eggshells by the storm.
Here are the survivors, lining Joshor Road,
Why have so many died without cause?

Translated from the Bangla by **Rimi B. Chatterjee**

23 Upon Returning from Dhaka*

FAIZ AHMAD FAIZ

We who have remained strangers after so many hospitalities
After how many meetings will we become acquaintances

When shall we espy the stainless verdure of spring
After how many rains will the stains of blood be washed away

The moments of love's painful ending were heartless indeed
After the kind nights the mornings were very unkind indeed

My heart ached but my broken heart gave me no respite
After all the prayers to make some complaints and reproaches

All that I had gone to say to them at risk of life, Faiz
After all the talks and meetings that remained unsaid

Translated from the Urdu by **Rakhshanda Jalil**

*Originally published in Urdu as 'Dhaka Se Wapsi Par' in *Nuskha Hai Wafa*, this was written in 1974, after Faiz's return from Dhaka and his first visit to Bangladesh since the creation of the new country. It is translated for this volume and published here by kind permission of the Faiz Foundation Pakistan.

24 The Hero of Our Nation*

JHARNA RAHMAN

So long as you lived in each of your footsteps
The grassland crackled thickly
In sounds that slowly reverberated
Across fifty-six thousand square miles...
So long as you lived breathing pure air for each breath
The forest in the south leaped up swiftly
Skylarks flew through the skies to be at the centre of your
Besieged eyeballs that fixedly stared casting motionless shadows...
So long as you lived, the turbulent waves of the Bay of Bengal
Roared upon your tongue. Hundreds of millions of
Pregnant shells reared the pearl-seeds of your love.
So long as you lived, your voice soared from the north-east
To the south-west within a roaring typhoon.
So long as you lived, the moon lost its shape inside the darkness
Taking the anguish of your dreaming eyes.
So long as you lived, fiery arrows pierced the horizon through
Your raised fists like spearheads.
So long as you lived, the greatest souls moved ceaselessly
In silent procession through your heart.

When the killer bullets pierced the precious map of your chest
Your fallen body lay in twisted metallic shapes on the stairs
Your blood marks stained the pierced holes on the walls
Pieces of your radiant brain spilled on the ceiling
Your spectacles spread like star dust upon that untimely hour
When you fell asleep forever.

---

*Originally published in Bangla as 'Maanchitrer Pranpurush' in *Niler Bhetor Thheke Lal* (Dhaka, 2007).

Your body was kept under the bosom of your mother
Your photograph was kept hidden behind stony walls
Your spectacles and blood-stained cloths were kept inside a museum
Only your bloodstream flowed, unfailing, down the stairs
Finding its way to the Bangladesh flag.

Translated from the Bangla by **Kamrul Hassan**

25 We Should Forget*

AFZAL AHMAD SYED

We should forget that brick
Under which we had kept the key to our home
The home that shattered in a dream

We should forget that kiss
That is stuck in our throat
Like a fishbone and refuses to come out

We should forget that yellow colour
That was distinct from the sunflower
When we were recounting our afternoon

We should forget that man
Who spreads sheets of iron
Upon his hunger

We should forget that girl
Who fills Time
In her medicine bottles

We should forget that debris
Whose name is Heart
From which no one can be pulled out alive

---

*Originally published in Urdu as 'Humey Bhool Jaana Chahiye', while it contains no explicit reference to the creation of Bangladesh, like much of Afzal Ahmad Syed's poetry, circles back to his years in East Pakistan. Despite his sympathy for the Bangla-speaking people and their right to a country of their own, he suffered terribly in the last years of his stay which included being labelled an 'internal sympathiser', causing him to flee the new country and make his home in Karachi.

And there are some words that we should completely forget
Such as
Humanity

Translated from the Urdu by **Rakhshanda Jalil**

26 What Answer Can I Give, Poetry?*

MINAR MONSUR

Your doubts about my health, my being alive
Will all be cleared one day.
Thoughts about the consequences of my strange life,
Chanting slogans in demonstrations, carrying illegal arms
That cause you insomnia, anxiety and letters wet with tears
Will all unknowingly turn normal one day.
I know your numerous letters and thousand questions
Will all suddenly be answered.
Your hands will throw away all the blooms of waiting, all the silver burnings;
You will wipe your wet eyes, the last sign of sleeplessness.
And you will then seek out your own address
And find your own destination effortlessly.

As for me—which of these paths shall I take? And where shall I stand?
Living an uncertain life every moment,
Before me an eroding mess of society.
The plotting spider weaves a snare,
A thousand questing arrows pierce me,
Turn my memories bloody.
How can I resist this? Tell me, how can I answer?
If Salam and Barkat send letters
In blood-smeared envelopes from the streets of 1952,
If they anxiously ask: Where have you kept those gold-bright alphabets

---

*Originally published in Bangla as 'Kobita Ki Jobab Debo' in *Ei Auboruddho Manchittre* (Dhaka, 1983).

That we gave you, alphabets printed in our blood?
Tell me, what shall I say?

If a bullet-ridden Monu Mia from the roaring sea of 1966
Asks in anger: I gave you a flag coloured with my fresh blood,
Where have you kept that crimson flag of equality?
Tell me, how shall I answer him?
If the freedom fighters of 1971, their lion roars all-encompassing,
Send an ultimatum in their dazzling envelope of skulls,
All our love, dear Freedom
Daubed with youthful warmth, our Constitution—
Written in our sisters' honour and brothers' blood—we put in your safe hands
Where is that love, where are those sacred beliefs?
Where have you preserved them?
What will be my answer then?

If the masses of 1975—not men, women and children but Courage incarnate—
Climb down swift and silent in the dead of night
From the ornate frames hanging on the walls,
Knock at our doors and shout, tearing the quiet of the midnight radio:
We had a dream that touched the horizon!
We had a desolate people full of dreams!
Where are those bright horizon-reaching dreams?
How are they, our wretched dreaming people?
What will be my answer then?
How will I tell them about this impotence, these sins, these
Self-annihilating games of war that we play?

Translated from the Bangla by **Mainul Hasan Chowdhury**

27 Send Mercies Upon Us, O Prophet Ji*

ZEHRA NIGAH

There was a home, and an open ground
A few fields and farmlands
She was not alone in her home
The pot was bubbling on the hearth
The dough was kneaded and ready

There was a baby in a hammock, too
And a parrot in a cage
And the Quran in a niche
The Quran in which she had complete faith
She would coo to her baby
She would puff into her stove
She would teach her parrot
My dear Mr Parrot, say:
'Send mercies upon us, O Prophetji
Send mercies upon us, O Prophetji
I beseech you in the name of your kin
I beseech you in the name of your kin!'

Suddenly, one day it so happened
Someone kicked the door open

*Originally published in Urdu as 'Bhejo Nabi ji Rehmatein' in *Warq*, Zehra Nigah's second collection of poetry, the poem is about the rape and molestation of women in East Pakistan by the West Pakistan armed forces who pillaged and plundered innocent civilians, entering homes and brutalising people, especially women. Interestingly, the poem carries no specific reference either to the act of rape or the context and geographical location. Zehra Nigah has alluded to this in several conversations and interviews, and thus the poem's context has been revealed.

And an animal-like human
Waving its claw-like hands
Came into the room
And kept coming all the way in
Darkening everything in its shadow

The veil was ripped off her head
The face of the Quran was covered
The roti burnt on the pan
The pot on the fire boiled over
The baby fell from the hammock
The parrot cried out in agony:
'Send mercies upon us, O Prophetji
Send mercies upon us, O Prophetji
I beseech you in the name of your kin
I beseech you in the name of your kin!'

But no one came.

Translated from the Urdu by **Rakhshanda Jalil**

28 The Poetry of 1971*

BIMAL GUHA

Today, with magic prayers I place these poems on the soft grass
Today, they have the charmed strength to stand up,
To look back
Poems have become the marksmen who go to war,
Who cross mountains and gorges in one breath and
Track enemies who will be pierced in their eyes and breast
And vanquished with death bullets.

Today, with magic prayers I place these poems on the soft grass
Today, they have learnt to be the mines hidden in the green blades
That suddenly explode and
Behead the Al Badr Pak soldiers who looted women.
Poetry has taken root on 7th March in Mujib's thunderous voice
To chants of liberty
Today, poetry is the handgun of the *muktijoddha*
With one stroke of the trigger, bullets bloom
To smear the enemy's breast with blood.

Today, with magic prayers I place these poems on the soft grass
They are now lively, self-determined bullets
That travel in all directions through the ether,
Through the secret radio *Freedom Bangla,*
Through voices that thunder and roar
In the homes of Bengalis, in the war camps,
Today, poetry has waged a war of freedom.

Translated from the Bangla by **Debjani Sengupta**

---

*Originally published in Bangla as 'Ekattorer Kobita' in *Pratibadi Shwobder Michil* (Dhaka, 2000).

29 He was a Fellow-Traveller But He and I were Never Compatible*

NASEER TURABI

He was a fellow-traveller but he and I were never compatible
It was always sun and shade between us, never a severance

Not my own sorrow, nor the suffering of others or your regret
Never have I so squandered the night of separation and longing

The journey of love and friendship so unfolded
With the travellers heart-broken but not exhausted

There were animosities, neglects and griefs aplenty
The one who separated had all these but no disloyalty

At the time of separation his eyes carried my ghazal
That too a ghazal I had not yet recited to anyone

Who was it that the sinking day was calling out to
I heard its call but paid no heed to its plea for justice

There was a time when there was great unanimity between us
And now this stage as though there was never any friendship

The path of poetry is strange indeed, see, O 'Naseer'
We have finally reached there where we had no access

Translated from the Urdu by **Rakhshanda Jalil**

---

*Originally written in Urdu as 'Woh Hum-safar Thha Magar Uss Se Hum-navaii Na Thhii', this ghazal was the definitive lament for Bangladesh long before it was used as the title track for a well-received Pakistani television drama series and gained immense popularity as sung by Qurratulain Baloch. Turabi was in his office when he heard the news of the Fall of Dhaka on 16 December 1971 and wrote this ghazal with tears streaming down his face, as he has said in an online interview.

30 The Bangla Victory*

JAN NISAR AKHTAR

Whenever there's cruelty in any corner of the world
We have raised our voices saying: Stop this bloodshed
Stop this incantation of your dirty politics
Stop this oppression, this cruelty, this madness

Dear Bangla: We could not watch you being erased
The blood of camaraderie woke up in every vein
The blood of honour woke up in the fire of duty

You that are the birthplace of Tagore and Nazrul
Our allegiance was with you yesterday and is with you today
We have learnt the custom of love from your songs
Your poems have taught us the lessons of rebellion

How could we have remained indifferent to you?
Our borders are joined with yours
Like arms lovingly intertwined

We clasped to our chest and our bosom
All your trampled and crushed peoples
We rose up for you out of love
We paid no heed to the storms of fires

We shared your sorrows, we shared your pain
We fulfilled every vow of friendship with you
Not mere words, we offered you our blood
Humanity! We have enhanced your honour
Shown how to bear solidarity with the oppressed
We have shown the world a new path

---

*Originally published in Urdu as 'Fateh Bangla' in *Hindustan Hamara* (1974).

We have fought shoulder to shoulder with you
We have seen the steadfast courage of your dreams
Whenever your hands have been lit up in dark nights
We have seen burning gunpowder and palaces
Wherever the blood of your young men has fallen
We have seen lotuses bloom from that soil

Every inch of your land shall bear witness one day
Soldiers from both countries shed blood together
And why make a difference between blood and blood
Man is always one and his blood is the same

The story of your liberation that was begun yesterday
It isn't just that you are the completion of that tale
For all the caravans that have set out in search of freedom
You shall be the new milestone in their path

Dear Bangla! We salute your youthful springs
We salute the gurgling banks of river Padma
We salute your pathways filled with happiness

But now we must leave your borders
With our blessings to your buds and blooms
We must bid you adieu
You are beautiful and so are your fragrant tresses
Your eyebrows are beautiful and so are your eyes

Dear Bangla! You have to become yet more beautiful
Countless stars shall embellish your hair in the years ahead
Many, many springs shall come to dance in your garden
Who knows whether your fragrance will reach us or not
Who knows whether you will remember us or not!

Translated from the Urdu by **Rakhshanda Jalil**

Glossary

Abbu	father
Apa	sister; polite address for a woman
arre	expression of surprise, joy or wonder
adhibaash	dawn rituals on the day of marriage
bagaan	garden
Bangla, Banga	Bengali, of the province of Bengal
Banga Bandhu	'Friend of Bengal,' a popular moniker and title given to Sheikh Mujibur Rahman by his followers
bari	home
bastee/basti	village, hamlet, settlement
batasha	homemade sweet usually made of jaggery and looks like a thick yellow coin; those made of sugar are white
bhaat	boiled rice
bhabhi	sister-in-law; brother's wife; a polite, affectionate address for a friend's wife
Bingo	slang for Bengalis
bindiya/bindi	a dot or embellishment on a woman's forehead
beedi/bidi/biri	local Indian cigarette made of tobacco hand-rolled in a tendu leaf
bok	egret
boka	stupid person
bondhu	friend
boti/bonti	a long, curved blade fixed upright to a wooden platform held down by foot; both hands are used to hold the object to be cut and move it against the blade
birangana	in independent Bangladesh, a term for women who were sexually abused and violated by the Pakistani Army
bratakatha	stories about the miraculous activities of gods and goddesses often recited during worship rituals
burra	big

charabaris	tea gardens
chara	fodder, seeds
Charak	a folk festival to honour Lord Shiva
charas	marijuana
chhatro	student
chhoto	younger; small
chela	a disciple or follower
dak	post, mail
dhoti	a piece of unstitched cloth worn by men on the lower part of the body
didi	elder sister
Doljatra	Holi, a festival to celebrate the arrival of spring
ektara	literally, 'one-string', a one-stringed instrument used in folk and traditional music across Bangladesh, Pakistan and India
ferishta	angel
ghat	a wide set of steps descending to a river, especially a river used for bathing and/or as a means of transport
goonda	thug
gunti time	Anglicised tea-garden version of the Urdu word *gintee*, which means counting; in the context of 'The Beginning of the End', a counting of heads to check who is present
Haldi ceremony	application of turmeric on a bride-to-be as part of wedding rituals
Hai Jamalo	a popular Sindhi song
jawan	soldier
jhalmuri	a popular snack of puffed rice (*muri*) mixed with raw onions, green chilly, mustard oil and other condiments
jhola	a cloth bag carried on the shoulders
Kaka	paternal uncle, father's younger brother; a term of kinship and polite address used widely in Bengal, along with *Kakima* (wife of *Kaka*)
Kalima/kalma	six texts to memorise to teach and learn the fundamentals of Islam
khayer-jarda	chewing tobacco

kirtan	devotional songs often accompanied by the *khol*, a double-sided drum made either of wood or terracotta
log/lok	people
lungi	garment worn by men on the lower part of the body, often by poorer classes
maachh	fish
Magrib	Islamic prayer time
mama	maternal uncle; mother's brother
mami/maima	maternal aunt; wife of *mama*
meethapani	literally 'sweet water', meaning lemonade or any cold sweet drink.
milad	a gathering to celebrate the birth of the prophet Muhammad (PBUH), with songs interspersed with prose passages about his life and message
Mukti Bahini/ Mukti Fauj	the group of guerrilla fighters who resisted the Pakistani Army during the Bangladesh Liberation War of 1971
muktijoddha	soldiers of the *Mukti Bahini* or *Mukti Fauj*
nashta	tiffin; snack
panjabi	a loose shirt (with or without collar) worn by men
pranam	an act of obeisance by touching the feet of elders or by folding the palms together in greeting
Rashpurnima	the period of full moon in the month of Kartik when Hindus celebrate Krishna's *Raslila* or the lord's dance of divine love with Radha. It also symbolises Shiva's victory over the three demons: Vidyunmali, Tarakaksha and Viryavana.
razakar	term given to those who supported the Pakistani Army during the Bangladesh Liberation War
roshogulla	Bengali sweetmeat of cottage cheese
saala	term of abuse
sabzi bari	vegetable patch, garden
sabha	a gathering
Santal/Santhal	Adivasi people who live in parts of West Bengal, Bihar, Chhattisgarh, and Bangladesh
sauve-qui-peut	literally, 'save himself who can' in French, it is a state of panic, disorder or complete rout where every man is for himself

sehri	a pre-dawn meal eaten before the first of the five daily prayers for a Muslim
shaheed	martyr
shankha	bangle made of white conch shell that married Bengali Hindu women are traditionally supposed to wear; *shankhari* are the craftsmen who make these bangles.
shikar	hunt; hunting as a sport
sindoor	vermillion, traditionally applied in the parting of the hair by a married Hindu woman
Sonar Bangla	Golden Bengal
tanpura/tambura	a large four-stringed lute used in Indian classical music as a drone accompaniment
thaan	borderless white dhoti
thakuma	grandmother; father's mother
thakurdalan	part of the courtyard where the family deity is placed and worshipped
yaar	friend, fellow, mate
zohr	Islamic prayer time

Bibliography

Ahmad, Feroze. 1992. 'The Language Question in Sindh'. In *Regional Imbalances and the Regional Question in Pakistan* ed. Akbar S. Zaidi. Lahore: Vanguard Books.

Ahmad, Rafiuddin. 1981. *The Bengali Muslims 1871-1906: A Quest for Identity*. Delhi: Oxford University Press.

Ahmad, Razia Fasih. 2007. *Breaking Links*. Pakistan: Oxford University Press.

Ahmed, Salahuddin et al. eds. 2009. *Ekattorer Chithi*. Dhaka: Prothoma Prokashon.

Ahsan, Syed Ali. 1951. 'Purbo Pakistaner Bangla Sahityer Dhara'. *Mahe Nau* 3(5): 49–54, August.

Akhtar, Jamna Das. 1971. *The Saga of Bangla Desh*. Delhi: Oriental Publishers.

Akhtar, Sanjida. 2002. *Bangla Choto Golpey Deshbibhag, 1947-1970,* 71–86. Dhaka: Bangla Academy.

Akhtar, Shaheen. 2011. *The Search*, trans. Ella Dutta. New Delhi: Zubaan.

______. 2018. *Beloved Rongomala, A Novel,* trans. Shabnam Nadiya. Dhaka: Bengal Lights Books.

Akhtar, S. et al. eds. 2001. *Narir Ekattor O Juddhoporoborti Koththo Kahini* (Oral History Accounts of Women's Experiences During 1971 and After the War). Dhaka: Ain-O-Shalish-Kendro.

Al Azad, Alauddin. 1978. *Portrait Number Twenty Three*, trans. Kabir Chowdhury. Dhaka: Bangla Academy.

Ali, Colonel Nadir. 2007. 'Aik Fauji Ki Yadasht'. Interview with BBC Urdu.

______. 2011. 'A Khaki Dissident on 1971'. *Viewpoint*. 'Liberation War – Historicising a Personal Narrative', talk given at BRAC University, Dhaka, March.

Ali, Tariq. 1983. *Can Pakistan Survive? The Death of a State*. London: Penguin Books UK.

Armitstead, Claire. 2016. 'Tahmima Anam: "I Have a Complicated Relationship with Bangladesh"'. *The Guardian*, 13 May. Available at https://www.theguardian.com/books/2016/may/13/tahmima-anam-i-have-complicated-relationship-with-bangladesh-interview (accessed 15 March 2021).

Ayoob, Mohammed. 1972. *The Liberation War*. New Delhi: S. Chand.

Azim, Firdous. 2018. 'The Forgotten Women of 1971: Bangladesh's Failure to Remember Rape Victims of 1971'. In *Unveiling Desire: Fallen Women in Literature, Culture, and Films of the East*, eds. Devaleena Das and Colette Marrow. New Brunswick, Camden: Rutgers University Press.

Aziz, Qutubuddin. 1974. *Blood and Tears*. Karachi: United Press of Pakistan.

Banerjee, Sumanta ed. 1987. *Thema Book of Naxalite Poetry*. Calcutta: Thema.

Bass, Gary J. 2014. *The Blood Telegram: India's Secret War in East Pakistan*. New Delhi: Random House.

Berlatsky, Noah. 2012. *East Pakistan: Genocide and Persecution*. Greenhaven Press.

Bhutto, Zulfikar Ali. 1971. *The Great Tragedy*. Karachi: Pakistan People's Party Publication.

Bhutto, Zulfikar Ali, Mujibur Rahman (Sheikh), Agha Mohammad Yahya Khan et al. 1978. *The Bangla Desh Papers: The Recorded Statements and Speeches of Z. A. Bhutto, Mujeeb-ur-Rahman, Gen. Yahya Khan, and Other Politicians of United Pakistan, 1969-1971*. Lahore: Vanguard Books.

Bose, Neilesh. 2014. 'Purba Pakistan Zindabad: Bengali Visions of Pakistan, 1940–1947'. *Modern Asian Studies* 48(1): 7, January.

Bose, Sharmila. 2011. *Dead Reckoning: Memories of the 1971 Bangladesh War*. Gurgaon: Hachette.

Brass, Paul. 1991. *Ethnicity and Nationalism*. New Delhi and London: Sage Publications.

Chaudhuri, Maria. 2014. *Beloved Strangers: A Memoir*. New York: Bloomsbury.

Chaudhury, Anis. 2010. *The Perfect Model and Other Stories*, trans. Kaiser Haq. Dhaka: Writers.ink.

Chowdhury, Rukhsana Rahim. (n.d.). 'A Search for the "Self": Trials and Tribulations of Urdu Writers in Bangladesh'. BRAC University, Dhaka. Available at https://www.academia.edu/27724254/A_Search_for_the_Self_Trials_and_Tribulations_of_Urdu_Writers_in_Bangladesh (accessed 24 November 2021).

Datta, Pradip Kumar. 1999. *Carving Blocs: Communal Ideology in Early Twentieth Century Bengal*. New Delhi: Oxford University Press.

Deen, Hanifa. 1998. *Broken Bangles*. New Delhi: Penguin Books.

Dhar, Maloy Krishna. 2009. *Train to India: Memories of Another Bengal.* New Delhi: Penguin India.

Elias, Akhtaruzzaman. 1997. *Sanskritir Bhanga Setu,* introduction by Sibaji Bandopadhyay. Kolkata: Naya Udyog.

Forrester, Duncan B. 1996. 'The Madras Anti-Hindi Imposition Agitation, 1965: Political Protest and its Effects on Language Policy in India'. *Pacific Affairs* 39(1/2): 19–36. University of British Columbia.

Gangopadhyay, Uttara. 2017. 'Come to Kolkata to See How the Traditional, Aristocratic Houses Celebrate Maa Durga's Visit to Her Paternal Home'. *Outlook Traveller,* 21 September. Available at https://www.outlookindia.com/outlooktraveller/explore/story/61216/top-10-bonedi-bari-durga-puja (accessed 30 March 2021).

Ghani, Jafar. 2013. 'Of Bangladesh and Balochistan'. *Pakistan Today,* 15 October. https://www.pakistantoday.com.pk/2013/10/15/of-bangladesh-and-balochistan/ (accessed 12 June 2020; link discontinued).

Ghosh, Vishwajyoti (curated). 2013. *This Side, That Side: Restorying Partition, Graphic Narratives from Pakistan, India, Bangladesh.* Delhi: Yoda Press.

Government of Pakistan (Official Spokesman). 1971. *The Present Crisis in East Pakistan.* 5 May, Karachi.

Guha-Thakurta, Tapati. 2015. *In the Name of the Goddess: Durga Pujas of Contemporary Kolkata.* Delhi: Primus Books.

Gupta, Anirudha. 1971. 'Forms of Struggle'. In *Bangladesh: A Struggle for Nationhood,* ed. Mohammed Ayoob. Delhi: Vikas.

Hai, Hasnat Abdul. 2008. *Sultan,* trans. Kabir Chowdhury. Dhaka: The University Press Limited.

Harrison, Selig S. 1981. *In Afghanistan's Shadow: Baluch Nationalism and Soviet Temptations.* New York and Washington: Carnegie Endowment for International Peace.

Haque, Mahmudul. 2012. *Black Ice,* trans. Mahmud Rahman. New Delhi: HarperCollins India.

Hoque, Abeer Y. 2016. *Olive Witch: A Memoir.* Noida, UP: Fourth Estate.

Hoque, Anisul. 2018. *The Ballad of Ayesha,* trans. Inam Ahmed. New Delhi: Harper Perennial.

Hossain, Mir Mosharraf. 2016. *An Ocean of Sorrow,* trans. Fakrul Alam. Dhaka: Bangla Academy.

Hossain, Selina. 1983. *Plumed Peacock,* trans. Kabir Chowdhury. Dhaka: Chaturanga.

______. 1987. *The Shark, the River and the Grenades,* trans. Abedin Quader. Dhaka: Bangla Academy.

______. 2016. *River of My Blood,* trans. Jackie Kabir. Kolkata: Rupa Publications.

Husain, Syed Shahid. 2010. *What was Once East Pakistan.* Karachi: Oxford University Press.

Hunter, W. W. 1871[1974]. *The Indian Musalmans: Are They Bound in Conscience to Rebel Against the Queen?* Lahore: Premier Book House.

Islam, Shamsul. 2015. *Muslims Against Partition: Revisiting the Legacy of Allah Bakhsh and Other Patriotic Muslims.* New Delhi: Pharos.

Jacob, Lt. Gen. J. F. R. 2011. *Surrender at Dacca: Birth of a Nation.* Delhi: Manohar Publishers & Distributors.

Karachi Pakistan Publications. 1971. *Government Action in East Pakistan.*

______. 1971. *Terror in East Pakistan.*

Khan, Engr Imtiaz Alam. 2019. 'History: The Fall of Dhaka from Bihari Eyes'. *Dawn,* 15 December. Available at https://www.dawn.com/news/1522385 (accessed 24 November 2021).

Khan, Mosarrap H. 2015. 'Faiz Ahmed Faiz and the Bangladesh Liberation War (1971)'. *Café Dissensus,* 15 May. Available at https://cafedissensus.com/2015/05/15/faiz-ahmed-faiz-and-the-bangladesh-liberation-war-1971/ (accessed 24 November 2021).

Khan, Naveeda. 2010. *Beyond Crisis: Re-evaluating Pakistan.* New Delhi: Routledge.

Kifait Ali, Mian. 1971. *Pakistan vs Bangladesh: An Exposition of Pakistan's Case.* Lahore.

Lahiri, Anjali. 1999. *Smriti O Katha.* Dhaka: Ain O Salish Kendra (ASK).

Mookherjee, Nayanika. 2015. *The Spectral Wound: Sexual Violence, Public Memories, and the Bangladesh War of 1971.* Durham: Duke University Press.

______. 2019. '1971: Pakistan's Past and Knowing What Not to Narrate'. *Comparative Studies of South Asia, Africa and the Middle East* 39: 212–222.

Moon, Penderel. 1998. *Divide and Quit.* New Delhi: Oxford University Press.

Moraes, Dom. 1971. *The Tempest Within: An Account of East Pakistan.* New York: Barnes & Noble.

Mudditt, Jessica. 2010. 'Breaking the Silence of the Camps – Urdu Speakers in Bangladesh'. *The Independent*, June. Available at https://jessicamudditt.com/2010/07/24/breaking-the-silence-of-the-camps-urdu-speakers-in-bangladesh/ (accessed 24 November 2021).

Nasrin, Taslima. 1998. *Meyebela: My Bengali Girlhood*, trans. Gopa Majumdar. South Royalton: Steerforth Press.

______. 2018. *Split: A Life*, trans. Maharghya Chakraborty. New Delhi: Penguin Random House India.

Niazi, A. A. K. 1998. *The Betrayal of East Pakistan*. Karachi: Oxford University Press.

Rahman, Tariq. 2000. 'Language and Ethnicity in Pakistan'. In *Contemporary Issues in Pakistan Studies*, ed. Saeed Shafqat. Lahore: Azad Enterprises.

______. 2007. *Language and Politics in Pakistan*. New Delhi: Orient Longman Pvt. Ltd.

Rashid, Azra. 2018. *Gender, Nationalism and Genocide in Bangladesh*. London: Routledge.

Ray, Manas. 2002. 'Growing Up Refugee'. *History Workshop Journal* 53: 169–170.

Rehman, Hamoodur. 2001. 'Extracts from Declassified Portion of Commission Report'. *Dawn*, 2 February.

Saikia, Yasmin. 2011. *Women, War and the Making of Bangladesh: Remembering 1971*. Duke University Press.

______. 2016. 'Perpetrators' Humanity: War, Violence, and Memory After 1971'. *ReOrient* 2(1): 73–90, Autumn.

Salik, Siddiq. 1977. *Witness to Surrender*. Karachi: Oxford University Press.

Salim, Ahmad ed. 2012. *We Owe an Apology to Bangladesh*, 114. Shahitya Prakash.

Sengupta, Debjani. 2016. *The Partition of Bengal: Fragile Borders and New Identities*. Delhi: Cambridge University Press.

Shafqat, Saeed ed. 1995. *Contemporary Issues in Pakistan Studies*. Lahore: Azad Enterprises.

Sircar, Jawhar. 2021. 'In a Calcutta Gripped With Naxal Violence and Police Brutality, People Lost Sons, Brothers and Friends'. *The Wire*, 11 March. Available at https://thewire.in/history/calcutta-naxal-violence-police-brutality-1971 (accessed 23 March 2021).

Tripathi, Salil. 2014. *The Colonel Who Would Not Repent: The Bangladesh War and its Unquiet Legacy*. Delhi: Aleph Book Company.

Uddin, Sufia M. 2006. *Constructing Bangladesh: Religion, Ethnicity and Language in an Islamic Nation*. New Delhi: Vistaar Publications.

Williams, L. F. Rushbrook. 1972. *The East Pakistan Tragedy*. London: Tom Stacey Ltd.

Zaheer, Hasan. 1994. *The Separation of East Pakistan: The Rise and Realization of Bengali Muslim Nationalism*. Karachi: Oxford University Press.

Zaidi, Akbar S. ed. 1992. *Regional Imbalances and the Regional Question in Pakistan*. Lahore: Vanguard Books.

Zakaria, Anam. 2019. *1971: A People's History from Bangladesh, Pakistan and India*. Penguin Books.

Zaman, Niaz. 2000. *A Divided Legacy: The Partition in Selected Novels of India, Pakistan, Bangladesh*. Oxford: Oxford University Press.

Notes on Contributors

Ali Ahmad is an academic and translator, from Bangla and English, based in Dhaka, Bangladesh.

Razia Fasih Ahmad is an Urdu and English fiction writer who has published eight novels, two novelettes, five collections of short stories, two travelogues as well as humorous essays in English. She received the Adamji prize for her novel *Abla Pa*, the Ahmad Nadeem Qasimi Award for her novel on the Bronte Sisters, the Sair-e-Pakistan Award for her travelogue, and a Lifetime Achievement Award. She has also written plays for the radio and television, and stories for the BBC, London.

Wasi Ahmed is a Bangla fiction writer known for his distinctive short stories that deal with complex social and personal realities. He has published nine collections of short stories and six novels, winning several literary awards, including the Bangla Academy Award in 2019. His short story collections include *Shinga Bajabe Israfil* and *Shoitto Probaho*, and *Eka Doka* and *Tolkuthurir Gaan* are novels.

Jan Nisar Akhtar (1914–1976), an Urdu poet who began his career as a writer of soft, sentimental, romantic *ghazals* and *nazms*, changed his style under the spell of the Progressives. His early *nazm* 'Girls' College ki Lari' made him popular. He later penned rousing poems like 'Khana Badosh', 'Bagola', 'Jahan Main Hoon', and 'Yeh Ho Kar Rahega'. 'Khamosh Awaz' (The Silent Voice), written on his wife's death, is considered his finest. *Zer-e-Lab* is a poignant collection of letters exchanged between him and his wife.

Shaheen Akhtar is a Bangladeshi writer who has published five collections of short stories, and is the editor of the volume *Zenana Mehfil: Selected Writings of Bengali Muslim Women Writers 1904-1938*. She won the *Prothom Alo* Best Book Award (2004) and the 3rd Asian Literary Award (2020) for her novel *Talaash* (translated into English and Korean); the Akhtaruzzaman Elias Kothashahitya Award (2015) for her novel *Moyur Shinghashon*, and the Bangla Academy Award (2015); and the Jemcon Literary Award (2019) for her novel *Ashukhi Din* on the Bengal Partition.

Meher Ali is a doctoral student in the Department of History, Princeton University. She works on modern South Asia, focusing on questions of mass politics, social movements, and urban political culture. She received her MA degree from the University of Chicago, and was awarded the Fulbright and AIIS fellowships to study in Kolkata and Lucknow.

Rasheed Amjad is an Urdu fiction writer, critic and intellectual; born in 1940 in Srinagar, Kashmir, he migrated to Pakistan after independence and lives in Rawalpindi, Pakistan. The editor of Urdu literary magazines *Daryaft* and *Takhilqui Adab*, he has received awards from both Pakistan and India, including the Pride of Performance Award in Pakistan. His published works include: *Bezaar Aadmi ke Bete, Tamanna Betaab, Kaghaz ki Faseel, Sehpehr ki Khizan, Patjhar Mein Khudkalami, Bhagay Hain Biaban Mujhsay,* and his autobiography *Aashiqi Sabr Talab* (2015), among others.

Masood Ashar, or Masood Ahmad Khan, is an Urdu short story writer, journalist and translator. Born in 1931 in Rampur, he came to Pakistan in 1951. Former editor of the Urdu national paper, *Daily Imroze*, he has published four collections of short stories, including *IntikKhab Masood Ashar*, and presently works as editor at Mashal, a publishing NGO.

Trishna Basak is a Bangla poet and writer, and a translator who also works from Maithili, Hindi and Malayalam. Her novels include *Barighor, Agniboloy* and *Chorer Manush*; *Ukoon, Chayajapon* and *Atmaramer Natun Khancha* are some of her short story collections. She received the West Bengal Bangla Academy's Somen Chanda Memorial Prize in 2018, and lives and works in Kolkata.

Chittoprasad Bhattacharya (1915–1978), a self-taught artist from Bengal who believed that true art cannot be apolitical, became famous for his works documenting the aftermath of colonialism and the anguish and suffering of the 1943 Bengal famine. He worked mainly with ink and printmaking, and through his works helped draw the world's attention to India's battle for independence; but Chittoprasad never received the attention due to him in his lifetime.

Moushumi Bhowmik is a Bangla singer, music researcher and songwriter considered to be a significant artiste of the 1990s. Her critically acclaimed music albums are *Tumio Chil Hao* (1994), *Ekhono Golpo Lekho* (1999), and *Songs from 26H* (2017). Bhowmik created *The Travelling Archive* based on field recordings of Bangla songs sung in various geographical locations.

Alvira Burney is a student of psychology at university in the United Kingdom, enjoys music, poetry, reading and travelling, and speaks fluent

Spanish. One of her poems was published in a poetry anthology titled *Dilliwali*.

Tabinda J. Burney is a doctor working for the NHS, and lives in the United Kingdom. She is the author of the cookbook *How to Feed Your Child (and Enjoy It!)*, and has an avid interest in gardening, baking and travelling.

Rimi B. Chatterjee, a Kolkata-based writer, teaches English literature at Jadavpur University. Her novels *Black Light* (2010) and *The City of Love* (2007) were published to critical acclaim. Her book *Empires of the Mind: A History of the Oxford University Press in India During the Raj* (2006) won the SHARP DeLong Prize in 2007. A translator between Bangla and English, she has translated several works of Abanindranath Tagore and Mahasweta Devi.

Afsan Chowdhury is a journalist, writer, war researcher and activist. A professor at BRAC University, Bangladesh, he has authored and co-authored several books, made radio series and video documentaries on Bangladesh's War of Liberation, and received the Bangla Academy Award (2018) for his contribution to literature on the War.

Mainul Hasan Chowdhury is a professor of English, University of Chittagong, Bangladesh. He has translated Harold Pinter's play *The Caretaker* into Bangla, and Chowdhury Jahurul Haque's Bangla play *Kolpito Kolpona* into English. He has published extensively on drama and trauma theory in national and international journals.

Alokeranjan Dasgupta (1933–2020) taught comparative literature at Jadavpur University, Kolkata, and at the University of Heidelberg, Germany. A noted poet, he has over twenty volumes of poetry, and was a distinguished translator from German and French. His essays have been collected in *The Shadow of a Kite and Other Essays* (2004). His critically acclaimed poems can be found in *Alo Aro Alo* (2009) and *Ekhon Nobhonil Amar Tohobil* (2014).

Subhoranjan Dasgupta is a professor of human sciences at the Institute of Development Studies, Kolkata. He is the co-editor, with Jasodhara Bagchi, of two volumes of writings on the Partition in the East titled *The Trauma and the Triumph: Gender and Partition in Eastern India*. He lives in Kolkata and devotes himself to reading, writing and translating from Bangla.

Kalyani Dutta is a writer and translator. She co-authored, with Meena Bhargava, *Women, Education and Politics: The Women's Movement and*

Delhi's Indraprastha College (2005). A recipient of the Katha Translation Award, her translation of Rokeya Sakhawat Hossain's *Freedom Fables: Satires and Political Writings* (2019) was nominated for the Crossword Translation prize; and her translation of Abanindranath Tagore's *Rajkahini* was published to critical acclaim in 2005.

Akhtarruzzaman Elias (1943–1997), a powerful writer of Bangla, was born in Gaibandha district, undivided Bengal, and taught at Jagannath College and Dhaka College. His novels *Chileykothar Sepai* (1986) and *Khoabnama* (1996) are acclaimed. His short story collections are *Onyo Ghare Onyo Swar, Khoyari, Dudhbhate Utpat, Jal Swapno, Swapner Jal* and *Dojokher Om*. He received the Bangla Academy Literary Award (1983), the Ananda Puraskar (1996) for *Khoabnama*, and the *Ekushey Padak* (1999) posthumously for his contribution to Bangladesh's literature, among others.

Faiz Ahmad Faiz (1911–1984), an Urdu poet who wrote prolifically and compellingly on events that shaped the subcontinent, he also wrote newspaper editorials and gave interviews on subjects that reveal an astonishing range of concerns and a highly political mind. In an oeuvre spanning seven collections of poetry, Faiz carried Marx's message of egalitarianism, social change and empathy for the poor to a younger generation of Urdu readers.

Bimal Guha, a poet from Bangladesh, has published twenty-two volumes of poetry, of which *Protibadi Shobder Michil* (2000) is notable; these include nine written for young adults and children. He has also authored two travelogues. He received the Bangladesh Parishad Literary Award for poetry in 1979.

Kaiser Haq, an English language poet, essayist and translator, taught at Dhaka University. His poetry collections include *Pariah and Other Poems* (2013) and *The Triumph of the Snake Goddess* (2015). He received the Bangla Academy Award in 2014, and lives and works in Dhaka.

Khalid Hasan was the press secretary during prime minister Zulfiqar Ali Bhutto's tenure, has worked as editor of OPEC News Agency in Vienna, a reporter for *Pakistan Times* in Lahore, and as managing editor for *South* in London. His published works include *A Mug's Game* (1968), *The Crocodiles are Here to Swim* (1970), and *Zulfiqar Ali Bhutto: Speeches and Writings* (1973).

Raihana Hasan is a freelance editor, translator, columnist and writer based in Karachi. She served in various capacities at Pakistan

International Airlines, retiring from there as general manager. Her published translations include *Sunshine and Shadows: The Autobiography of Dr. Fatima Shah* (1999), Sayyid Hamid's *Muslim Malaise and the Road to Resurgence* (2005), and Mirza Farhatullah Baig's *The Last Lamp of Delhi* (2008). Her novel *Sips from a Broken Teacup* (2011) is her fifth book.

Salima Hashmi, daughter of the Urdu poet Faiz Ahmad Faiz, is an artist, art historian and writer. Dean of the School of Visual Arts and Design at Beaconhouse National University, Lahore, her published works include *Unveiling the Visible: Lives and Works of Women Artists of Pakistan* (2003), and *Memory, Metaphor, Mutations: Contemporary Art of India and Pakistan* (2006), with Yashodhara Dalmia. A committed pacifist, she works towards Indo-Pakistani reconciliation by developing artistic projects that go beyond the two countries' borders.

Kamrul Hassan is an academic and translator based in Dhaka, Bangladesh.

Selina Hossain is a major Bangladeshi writer who has published thirty-seven novels, and thirteen short story collections including *Manushti* (1993), *Ekaler Pantaburi* (2008) and *Mrityur Nilpadma* (2015). Her novels *Hangor Nadi Grenade* (1976), *Japita Jiban* (1981), *Poka Makorer Ghor Boshoti* (1996), *Gayatri Shondhya* (1996) and *Purno Chhobir Mognota* (2008) have won her critical and popular acclaim. She is the recipient of the Bangla Academy Award (1980), the *Ekushey Padak* (2009), and the SAARC Literary Award (2015). She lives in Dhaka.

Intizar Husain (1925–2016), an iconic contemporary writer of Urdu, was born in Dibai, Bulandshahr, and migrated to Pakistan in 1947. His novels include *Chaand Gahan* (1952), *Din Aur Daastaan* (1959), *Basti* (1979), *Tazkira* (1987), *Aagey Samandar Hai* (1995), and *Naya Ghar* (2005). One of the finest novels on Partition, *Basti* received global praise. His other writings include *Hindustan Se Aakhri Khat, Shehr-e-Afsos, Janam Kahanian* and *Wo Jo Kho Gaye*. A finalist of the 2013 Man Booker Prize list, much of his fiction has been translated.

Rakhshanda Jalil is a Delhi-based writer, critic, literary historian, and translator from Urdu and Hindi. A prolific author, her recent works include *But You Don't Look Like a Muslim* (2019), *Shahryar: A Life in Poetry* (2018), *The Great War: Indian Writings on the First World War* (2018), *Liking Progress, Loving Change: A Literary History of the Progressive Writers' Movement in Urdu* (2014), *A Rebel and Her Cause: The Life and Work of Rashid Jahan* (2014), *Release and Other Stories* (2011); and her translation of Intizar Husain's novel *Aagey Samandar Hai* as *The Sea Lies Ahead* (2015), which won the German Embassy-Karachi Litfest Pakistan Peace Prize.

Shehreen Ataur Khan is Assistant Professor at Jagannath University, Bangladesh. Her research areas of interest are gender studies and ecology. She is also a translator.

Sorayya Khan is the author of *Noor, Five Queen's Road,* and *City of Spies,* which won the Best International Fiction Book Award, Sharjah International Book Fair, 2015. She was awarded a Fulbright Grant to conduct research in Pakistan and Bangladesh, a Malahat Review Novella Prize, and a Constance Saltonstall Artist Grant. Her work has appeared in several anthologies and publications including *Guernica, Longreads, The Kenyon Review, North American Review,* and *Journal of Narrative Politics.*

Minar Monsur is a prominent poet, essayist and researcher. In 1983, his first book of poems, *Ei Abaruddha Manchitrey* was confiscated by the then ruling military junta. He is currently serving as the Director of The National Book Centre, Ministry of Cultural Affairs, Bangladesh.

Shabnam Nadiya is a writer and translator based in California. Her translations include Moinul Ahsan Saber's *Mercenary* (2018), Shaheen Akhtar's *Beloved Rongomala* (2018), and Leesa Gazi's *Hellfire* (2020). A graduate of the Iowa Writers' Workshop, she was awarded the Schulze Fellowship (2013), the Steinbeck Fellowship (2019), a PEN/Heim Translation Grant (2020); and the *Himal Southasian* Short Story Competition (2019), for her translation of 'Milk' by Mashiul Alam.

Sameena Nazeer, an entomologist by profession, has a diploma in theatre arts and script writing from National Academy of Performing Arts, Karachi. She has written plays, short films, TV serials and web series, and produced, directed and acted in theatrical productions. Her book *Kallo* is a collection of six short stories and two plays. She is presently writing a novel set in Africa, where she has lived and worked for fifteen years.

Zehra Nigah is a poet who began to recite her poetry at *mushairas* from a young age. Born in Hyderabad, India, she migrated to Pakistan in 1947. She has published four collections of poetry: *Shaam ka Pehla Tara, Warq, Firaq,* and *Gul Chandni.* Treading the fine line between feminism and feminine poetry in a career spanning six decades, she has held her own in the male-dominated *mushaira* circuit through the sheer grace and substance of her poetry.

Naushad Noori is a poet who joined the Progressive Writers' Association, but who attracted infamy in 1952 for standing up for the Bangla language. He made a name for himself as an Urdu poet, but was vocal against the imposition of Urdu as a national language. Some of his iconic poems include 'Bhikari' and 'Lahu Mein Sharabor Raat', written especially on the liberation of Bangladesh.

Jhumur Panday is a writer and poet who lives and works in Silchar, Assam. Her published works include the short-story collections *Jol Khaben Bonodurga* and *Sukh Gacher Golpo*, a volume of poems *Kichu Bolar Chhilo*, the novels *Alexanderpurer Kathakata* and *Gang-gatha*, and a book of stories for children *Pisti O Sei Swapnopakhi Surela*.

Jharna Rahman, a retired professor of Bangla, is a poet, lyricist and singer. Her collections of poetry include *Noshto Jyotsna Noshto Roudro*, *Neeler Bhetor Theke Laal*, and *Joloj Ponktimala*. *Jolpori o Nooher Nouka* is a collection of short stories, and *Briddha o Rajkumari* is a play. She is the editor of *Troimasik Agrasar Bikrampur*, a magazine of history and heritage.

Papree Rahman is a writer based in Dhaka. Her published works include the well-received short-story collections *Mridu Manusher Motion Picture* and *Mamuli Jibaner Joltorongo*, and the novels *Pora Nodir Swapnopuran*, *Boyon* and *Palatia*.

Tariq Rahman is a Fulbright scholar and writer based in Lahore. His numerous books include *Names: A Study of Personal Names, Identity and Power in Pakistan* (2015), and *Interpretations of Jihad in South Asia: An Intellectual History* (2018), which won the Habib Metropolitan Bank Award for best non-fiction; and *Work and Other Short Stories* (1991). Joining the army as an officer in 1971, he resigned his commission in 1978 as a conscientious objector to the military action in East Pakistan—in recognition of which, the Government of Bangladesh conferred upon him a civil award.

Manas Ray retired as a professor from the Centre for Studies in Social Sciences, Kolkata. He is the author of numerous essays and monographs, including the critically acclaimed *Growing Up Refugee* (2002). He is the editor of *Crises of Liberal Deliberation: Facets of Indian Democracy* (2021), and *State of Democracy in India: Essays on Life and Politics in Contemporary Times* (2021).

Debjani Sengupta, a Partition scholar, writer and translator, teaches English literature at Indraprastha College for Women, New Delhi. She has authored *The Partition of Bengal: Fragile Borders and New Identities* (2016), and edited *Mapmaking: Partition Stories from Two Bengals* (rpt. 2011). She has co-edited, with Tarun K. Saint and Rakhshanda Jalil, *Looking Back: The Partition of India, 70 Years On* (2017); and co-edited, with Rakhshanda Jalil, *Women's Writings from India, Pakistan and Bangladesh: The Worlds of Bangla and Urdu* (2019). Her translations from Bangla include works by Taslima Nasreen, Selina Hossain, Tilottama Majumdar and Suchitra Bhattacharya.

Haider Shahbaz is the translator of the novel *Hassan's State of Affairs* by Mirza Athar Baig (2019), and Khalida Hussain's short story 'The Sea', which won the Jawad Memorial Prize for Translation (2020). He is currently pursuing a PhD in Comparative Literature at University of California, Los Angeles.

Agha Sohail (1933–2009) was an Urdu writer born in Lucknow, Uttar Pradesh. A professor at Forman Christian College, Lahore, Pakistan, he authored several collections of short stories and novels, which include *Ghubaar-e Koocha-e Jaana* (1968), *Til Barabar Aasman* (1986), *Shahr-e Na-Pursaan* (1983), *Kahani Ahd-e Zawal Ki* (1991), and *Khaak ke Parde* (2004), as well as works of literary criticism such as *Dabistan-e Lucknow ke Dastani Adab ka Irtiqa* (1988).

Afzal Ahmad Syed, an Urdu poet born in 1946 in Ghazipur, India, and has lived in Karachi since 1976. His *nazm* collections include *Chheeni Hui Tareekh* (1984), *Do Zubaanon Mein Saza-e Maut* (1990), and *Rococo aur Doosri Duniyain* (2000). He has translated many poets, playwrights and novelists, including Mir Taqi Mir, Gabriel García Márquez and Jean Genet, and been widely published in Urdu periodicals such as *Shabkhoon*, *Aaj*, and *Dunyazad*. He teaches at Habib University, Karachi.

Naseer Turabi (1945–2021), a Pakistani poet and broadcaster, penned the lyrics for the theme song 'Dil Ka Jo Mol Chukatay Honge' for the television series *Mol*, and for *Zindagi Gulzar Hai*. He also wrote the lyrics of 'Dil Aitebaar' for *Khwab Saraye*, and for *Yaqeen ka Safar*. His first collection of poetry, *Aks-e-Faryadi*, was published in 2000. Turabi was a member of the Pakistan Writers' Guild.